A Life of
Anne Brontë

Edward Chitham

Date Due	

T 19903

Copyright © Edward Chitham 1991

The right of Edward Chitham to be identified as author of this work has
been asserted in accordance with the Copyright, Designs and Patents Act
1988

First published 1991
Reprinted 1991
First published in paperback 1993

Blackwell Publishers
108 Cowley Road
Oxford, OX4 1JF
UK

238 Main Street
Cambridge, Massachusetts 02142
USA

A CIP catalogue record for this book is available from the British Library.

Library of Congress Cataloging in Publication Data
Chitham, Edward.
A life of Anne Brontë / Edward Chitham.
p.   cm.
Includes bibliographical references.
ISBN 0–631–18944–0 (pbk.)
1. Brontë, Anne, 1820–1849—Biography.   2. Novelist, English—19th
century—Biography.   I. Title.
PR4163.C4 1991
823'.8—dc20   89–18571
[B]   CIP

Typeset in 11 on 12 pt Bembo
by Graphicraft Typesetter Ltd, Hong Kong
Printed in Great Britain by T.J. Press Ltd, Padstow, Cornwall

This book is printed on acid-free paper.

Contents

Illustrations

(between pages 120–121)

Plates 1, 2, 4, 5, 6, 7, 9, 10 are from the Brontë Society collection at the Brontë Parsonage Museum, as is the picture, untitled, but sometimes called 'Sunrise over Sea', on which the jacket is based. Plate 13 is from a private collection; on loan to the Brontë Parsonage Museum (C 107). Plate 15 is reproduced by permission of the Royal Commission on the Historical Monuments of England. Plate 11 is from a collection at Scarborough borough library. Grateful thanks are extended to the owners of all these illustrations. Plates 3, 8 and 12 are from photographs by the author, and plate 14 is drawn by the author on the basis of various nineteenth-century maps mentioned in the text. Plate 16 is based on an old newspaper photograph.

Acknowledgements

I should like to express my gratitude to the many people and institutions without which I could not have completed this study: Durham University Library; Leeds City Library; Bradford City Library; North Yorks County Archives; The British Library; Birmingham University Library and Birmingham Reference Library.

J. Goodchild of Wakefield Library helped to locate information on Crofton Hall and Kirby Hall; Ms Janet Burhouse of Huddersfield guided me to material on Roe Head and Lascelles Hall; Mr John Nussey's permission to use information from his articles on Blake Hall is much appreciated; C. Roy Hudleston's investigations in Cumbria Record Office provided the basis of the section on the background to William Weightman; at a late stage of the preparation of the book I was most fortunate to be put in touch with Helier Hibbs of Ouseburn, who provided unstinting help on the Thorp Green background.

A conversation and many letters exchanged with Joanna Hutton directed my attention to aspects of Anne's work, especially her pictures; at Haworth Dr Juliet Barker and Sally Johnson searched for references and illustrations. I have owed a great deal over the years to conversations with Tom Winnifrith. Members of my family measured, drew and redrew versions of the 'gun group' portrait with and without topknots, while Rachel brought Anne's song-book to life and discussed her copying technique.

Previous Brontë scholars always put new biographers in their debt. Once again I should like to acknowledge the pioneering efforts of Winifred Gerin, who took Anne's reputation in hand and removed the 'nun-veil' in which Charlotte had clothed her.

Edward Chitham
Harborne

Because the road is rough and long,
Shall we despise the skylark's song?

No! while we journey on our way
We'll notice every lovely thing
And ever as they pass away
To memory and hope we'll cling.

Anne Brontë, 'Views of Life'

To Eleanor, John and Rachel

Introduction

'All true histories contain instruction,' writes Anne Brontë at the beginning of *Agnes Grey*. She then begins a work of fiction. Any biographer will wish to present his or her work as 'true history', though the art of biography has something in common with portraiture, in that subjective elements inevitably invade the process however carefully the artist sifts and reconsiders. It is especially necessary in writing about one of the Brontës to explain the bases of the work, since the story of the Brontë family has proved so interesting to so wide a range of readers, both academic and lay. I therefore try, in this Introduction, to remind readers of the stages through which Brontë biography has gone, and to explain the principles on which I have been working during the many years since I began to be interested in the writing and life of Anne Brontë.

An extensive literature has grown up concerning Brontë lives and Brontë work. Much of this, at any rate up to the second half of the twentieth century, consisted of glosses on the first published biography, Elizabeth Gaskell's *The Life of Charlotte Brontë*, written after Charlotte's death with the encouragement of her father and the co-operation of Charlotte's friend, Ellen Nussey. Readers of this work (whether or not they had read the Brontë novels or poetry) found their lives were intrinsically interesting. For a generation Mrs Gaskell's *Life* was almost alone in the field, and Charlotte was the member of the Brontë family whose work was highly regarded. Emily's novel was thought a curiosity, and Anne's work, though it continued in print, found fewer readers. The next development came in the 1890s, and was largely due to the efforts of Clement Shorter and T. J. Wise, who, with others, set up the Brontë Society and collected the manuscripts of the Brontë family's unpublished work, issuing it piecemeal, often in limited editions. Many of the manuscripts, which they had bought quite cheaply from Charlotte's husband, who had remarried and was living in Ireland, were bound and sold expensively on both sides of the Atlantic. There is some evidence to suggest that the manner in which these manuscripts were treated bordered on the fraudulent.[1]

An examination of the *Brontë Society Transactions*, as well as much of the large quantity of Brontëana published every decade since the 1890s, will show that the family stimulates more than literary interest. While *Jane Eyre*, *Wuthering Heights* and some of Emily's poems are masterpieces with a wide audience outside the literary establishment, it is clear from the tone of many of the contributions to the *Transactions* and scores of the biographical articles and volumes produced during the last century that the lives of the Brontë continue to elicit as much profound interest as their books. While some of this interest is traceable to Mrs Gaskell's biography, it seems that an almost mythic quality in the lives and situation of these four siblings attracts and fascinates a public which has not read Mrs Gaskell and is familiar with little of the Brontës' work beyond the story-lines of *Jane Eyre* and *Wuthering Heights*, even these being sometimes absorbed through film or stage versions. This interest is not completely unliterary; one of its bases is a perception of the unusual strength of the fictional Jane, Rochester, Cathy and Heathcliff, whose power is recognised as being created by the literary skill and energy of two exceptional sisters. Such an interest in the lives of artists is entirely legitimate, though twentieth-century attitudes in literature departments of schools, colleges and universities have not generally encouraged it, or found ways in which it may be included as a recognized part of the literary curriculum.

Research on the Brontës, then, begins with a biographical as well as a literary aspect. In the early years of the twentieth century Brontë biography was dominated by the work of Shorter and Wise, under whose aegis most of the biographical as well as the literary material emerged. These endeavours culminated in the *Shakespeare Head Brontë*, typically issued in a limited edition, which contained texts of all the published novels and poetry. Planned on a grand scale, it included volumes of biographical material and attempted to print

Charlotte's letters as well as juvenilia and unpublished work by Charlotte and Branwell. Some of this was reproduced in facsimile, apparently because the editors did not feel able to provide accurate transcriptions of the large quantity of manuscripts written in ' Brontë small script', a form of writing the four had adopted as children, and originally intended to imitate the print of contemporary journals. The Shakespeare Head Press edition has proved a valuable quarry for texts and biographical material, but the scholarship of the last twenty years has resulted in major modifications to both text and biography.

Meanwhile, during the later part of the twentieth century there has been no slackening in the interest of the public or of students in the works and lives of the Brontës. The biographical material was widely explored by Miss Winifred Gerin, who published biographies of Anne (1959), Branwell (1961), Charlotte (1967) and Emily (1971). She was also associated with the writing of her husband, John Locke, and W. T. Dixon's *A Man of Sorrow* (1965), a life of Patrick Brontë, the father of the family. A popular re-examination of Mrs Gaskell's biography entitled *The Brontë Story* was published by Margaret Lane in 1953. It may fairly be said that all these works took Mrs Gaskell's as their basis, using her text or the text of the Shakespeare Head Press letters as their primary source. Miss Gerin added much interesting peripheral material, but we need to remember that her volume on Anne was the first she wrote, and she may not have discovered at that time how frail was the reliance which could be placed on published texts of the letters or the editions of poems and novels of the whole family, which had often been affected by the cavalier attitude of Wise and Shorter to textual authenticity. Miss Gerin was the first writer to try to reinstate Anne's reputation, but she took too simplistic a view of the autobiographical elements in *Agnes Grey*, on which she based a good deal of her new life of Anne.

There was clearly a great need for a sceptical look at the sources of our knowledge of the Brontës, both biographical and literary, and an attempt to discover a more sophisticated way of looking at the relationship between the lives of the four Brontës and their writings. Tom Winnifrith's *The Brontës and their Background: Romance and Reality* (1973) began this reappraisal. He had started by questioning the major primary source of evidence on the lives of the Brontës, Charlotte's letters as printed in the *Shakespeare Head* edition, from which most of the quotations in existing biographies had been taken. He found major discrepancies between the texts of samples of letters in the Needham collection of copies and the printed texts, and his suspicions were deepened when he examined available manuscript letters. He was also concerned at the chaotic way in which the manuscripts discovered by Wise and Shorter in the 1890s had been scattered among libraries in Britain and America, sometimes after publication of editions based on faulty transcripts, and intended to supply the wants of book collectors rather than academics. In this way many Brontë texts were effectively buried, while a plausible but inaccurate record of their contents had become available in academic libraries and served to divert scholars from an attempt to construct new texts from manuscript sources.

However, the Clarendon Press had become interested in producing a new version of the Brontë novels, and under the general editorship of Ian Jack, such editors as Herbert Rosengarten, Margaret Smith and Hilda Marsden undertook a completely new examination of the texts and transmission of all the fiction works of the three Brontë sisters. G. D. Hargreaves, working from a bibliographical basis, drew attention to the defective tradition of texts of *The Tenant of Wildfell Hall* (which I shall hereafter abbreviate to *Wildfell Hall*) and showed that these very prevalent texts had emasculated the book Anne Brontë had originally written, which he was able to restore in his Penguin edition of 1979.[2] In the same year I published *The Poems of Anne Brontë*, which attempted a new edition based entirely on manuscript sources. This volume included an introduction in which I tried to modify Winifred Gerin's approach to the relationship between Anne Brontë's life, as it was known through external sources, her poems, and the two novels, especially *Agnes Grey*, which Miss Gerin had seen as virtually an autobiographical document. The present volume is a continuation of this revaluation, and takes into account the consideration I have given to the literary and personal relation between Emily and Anne, including both the presuppositions they shared and those where they came to differ strongly.

I have suggested above that a life of Anne Brontë will need to satisfy the demands of readers who find biography of intrinsic interest as well as those who wish to study the complex interrelation between life and works. In the remainder of this Introduction I propose to examine and evaluate the sources available for the construction of a life of Anne Brontë, and explain my principles in the use of such material and in the writing of the book. Although this may appear unduly tedious, the production of Brontë biographies in the past has been the excuse for imaginative flights in which the distinctions between proved fact, rational conjecture and wild fancy have not been observed. A reviewer of *A Life of Emily Brontë*, remarking on my observation that speculative elements in the book would be indicated as such, commented that all biography was to some extent speculative. For this reason there was an objection to frequent use of such qualifying words as 'seems' 'perhaps' and 'probably'. Other reviewers saw that to assert as a known fact something which could reasonably be inferred but was not documented would be illegitimate, and they praised the work for not overstating its case. I need to make it clear, then, that I intend to include in this biography all material which may relate to Anne Brontë's life, but that this will sometimes involve discussion which cannot be conclusive, and where the only honest indication I can give the reader is that we do not fully know the facts, though subsequent research may still turn up more concrete evidence.

There are few documents directly relating to the life of Anne Brontë which could rank with the kind of primary sources usually studied by biographers. We have five of her letters, though we know she wrote hundreds.[3] She may have kept a journal or diary, but if so, it has not survived. Two of her 'journal papers' or diary papers have been printed, but the manuscripts have been lost. There are also two similar papers written jointly with Emily, in which Anne takes a subordinate part.[4] None of her juvenilia has survived: her earliest known poem dates from 1836, when Anne was sixteen, though all the Brontës wrote from a very young age. Ellen Nussey left us some contemporary descriptions of Anne, some of which material is incorporated in Mrs Gaskell's *Life of Charlotte Brontë*. Charlotte herself is the filter through which Anne is presented in Mrs Gaskell's *Life*, and for various reasons Charlotte was not able to see Anne objectively. Other reminiscences are sketchy in the extreme; a phrase here from her pupils, an unclear tradition from Blake Hall, and so on.

In this situation, we have to look elsewhere for ways to

build up a picture of Anne Brontë and her life. There are broadly two areas where we may look, and both have their dangers. The first is Anne's own writing, so extensively used by Winifred Gerin, but so fraught with difficulties and opportunities for misunderstanding. One of our reasons for seeking a biography of any author is to help to illuminate that author's works; but if the major source for that biography *is* the corpus of those works, how can we avoid a vicious circle in which we read autobiography into the literature and then use our observations to show how the fiction grew form the life? Such a proceeding is common with Charlotte and Emily Brontë, so that one develops great skill in sensing places where the fictional life of Jane Eyre and the real life of Charlotte Brontë have been merged, and close investigation sometimes yields scraps of evidence to justify one's hunches. The reader of this book, however, is entitled to a more thorough explanation of methodology, and this will be attempted in due course.

The second neglected source runs the opposite risk. As well as searching the writings of Anne Brontë for clues to her biography, we may look for all sorts of objective records which were created very near to Anne topographically or chronologically, though they do not mention her at all. In studying Emily's poems, for example, I found weather records, which had been kept without any reference to Emily's life whatever, turned out to be illuminating in understanding her poetry. From these meteorological data we could tell whether, and in what degree, she was describing in dated poems weather she was actually experiencing at that moment. Similarly, very careful combing of the district round Law Hill where Emily taught produced some landcape or built features of the environment which tallied with items mentioned in *Wuthering Heights*.[5] Emily's work was not 'pure fancy', however one might define it; she did in fact take her own precise contemporary surroundings as the basis for her fiction. Once one had seen that this was the case, it was possible to look for more examples within Emily Brontë's work, without falling into the trap of discovering a real-life source for every imaginary event described in the fiction or poetry. In *Brontë Facts and Brontë Problems* I was able to suggest how certain poems developed from the moment of observation and inspiration to their finished form.[6] In the case of Anne Brontë, it is essential to examine with the greatest care the topography of the places where she lived and worked, and the chronology of events. From a very careful study of these factors an idea of her background may be constructed, which can be compared with the fiction. Only by this method can we avoid the circular arguments which earlier biographers sometimes used. External evidence about Anne's surroundings and about the personalities she encountered can never be irrelevant, and may often be the only unbiased evidence we have access to. In the following paragraphs I wish to explain how these two very divergent types of evidence have been used in this book.

The arguments I am about to use recapitulate to a considerable extent the principles set out in *The Poems of Anne Brontë* (Macmillan, 1979), and *Brontë Facts and Brontë Problems* (Macmillan, 1983), and they have been used to some extent in *The Brontës' Irish Background* (Macmillan, 1986) and *A Life of Emily Brontë* (Blackwell, 1987). Readers familiar with the points I made in those works may wish to avoid the following section, but unless these principles are understood it may be hard to appreciate the aims of this biography, and caution may be mistaken for evasiveness, while matters associated with the ambient topography or chronology could appear distant from the concerns of a reader of Anne Brontë's novels and poetry. Nor will this biography be a bloodless one; it is part of the biographer's task to bring his subject to life, to explain her attitudes, feelings and thoughts. In the case of Anne Brontë, a rounded picture can be given despite the unpromising nature of the sources, though it has to be given judiciously, without overstating the case or making assumptions. The fresh reader also needs to be aware of the existence of a number of biographical *cruces* in Brontë studies, which it is the business of Brontë scholars to address. These include the question of precisely what were the personal relations between Branwell Brontë and Mrs Robinson, his and Anne's employer, during 1843–5; what was the nature of 'Gondal', the imaginary world of Emily's and Anne's sagas; what was the literary relation between *Jane Eyre*, *Wuthering Heights* and *Wildfell Hall*; and what were the attitudes of the three sisters towards each others' work? The answers to these questions cannot be settled, but it is incumbent upon a serious researcher to examine the contexts for all these matters among many others and to formulate rational theories.

I shall first examine the matter of the relation between the real life of Anne Brontë and the purportedly autobiographical elements of the poems and *Agnes Grey*, beginning with the latter. Winifred Gerin writes throughout as though the implication of the quotation with which I began this introduction were to be taken as literal fact: 'All true histories contain instruction' seems to imply that the story of Agnes Grey is factually that of her creator. Though it is not my purpose here to attack the very readable pioneering book Miss Gerin produced, it must be said at once that this equation is followed simplistically throughout, and no evidence is produced to show how far the fictional Agnes represents the life, opinions or attitudes of Anne Brontë. As a result, events in the story are reproduced as though they were events in Anne's own life, and we are asked to accept as demonstrable facts what the biographer is silently inferring from the fictional account. There is always some kind of relation between an author's fiction and his or her life, but the nature of this relation varies enormously, and the biographer cannot evade the task of showing how far fact relates to fiction in any given case.

Let us take the first four paragraphs of *Agnes Grey* and see how far Anne's account of Agnes tallies with her own life. The first paragraph places the work in a tradition – that of Swift and Defoe – in which verisimilitude is thought crucial, and a confiding author 'buttonholes' his audience in such a way as to secure their trust. Anne writes of Agnes's 'own obscurity', 'the lapse of years' and 'a few fictitious names'.

There are no real names in *Agnes Grey*, even the towns being referred to by misleading initials. For example, a town clearly identifiable as Scarborough is called 'A'. None of the characters is given a name that coincides with those of real people whom Anne Brontë is known to have met, though the names are plausible, realistic names, some of which are common in Yorkshire. The events of *Agnes Grey* to some extent correspond, as we shall see, with events in Anne life between 1839 and about 1843; the phrase 'the lapse of years', therefore, is somewhat exaggerated.

The second paragraph begins, 'My father was a clergyman of the north of England', an assertion true of Anne Brontë as well as Agnes Grey; but, unlike Mr Brontë, he lives partly on the income of a 'snug little property'. There is a social distinction between Agnes's mother and her father, which mirrors, but slightly exaggerates, that between Patrick and Maria Brontë. Agnes was one of six children, as was Anne Brontë, but of Agnes's family only two survived childhood, while four of the Brontës did so. Agnes's family 'combined to spoil me', that is they cosseted her and treated her in a patronizing way. Some of Charlotte's letters reveal a similar attitude towards Anne.[7] As a result Agnes becomes 'helpless and dependent'; as the youngest of the six Brontës, Anne was in a position to feel both of these emotions, and we may well judge that here *Agnes Grey* is accurately reflecting her author.

In these opening paragraphs we see Anne Brontë's method unfolding. She uses fictional but convincing names for people, glosses over the precise identification of places by name, since she wishes to employ topographical accuracy, blends some of the facts of her own life with invention, and implies chronological distance. But the heroine's similarities to Anne are also apparent; she is a young girl, a clergyman's daughter, who is the youngest of the family and therefore responds to her position in the family in a manner typical of the youngest. Anne is being modest in her fictional aims to reflect what she may well have considered her modest capability. Her heroine coincides in sex, age, class and family background with herself. She will also undertake a profession of which Anne knows a great deal. Our author is writing of areas of experience with which she is well acquainted, and this will enable her to give a powerful air of conviction to the narrative.

As the story progresses, Agnes, like her creator, leaves her home for two periods of employment as a governess. The parallels between the fictional Agnes and Anne Brontë will require to be analysed event by event, and this cannot be attempted in this introduction. One that might be mentioned is the correspondence between the children of the first family Agnes encounters, the Bloomfields, with what we know from external sources of Anne's first pupils at Blake Hall. The identification is almost total. However, this kind of correspondence is not carried over into the description of the children of the second family, which consists initially of two boys and two girls, whereas at Thorp Green there were three girls and one boy. *Agnes Grey's* experiences coincide with Anne Brontë's only in part. It will not be legitimate to infer details of personalities, places and events in Anne's life from a reading of *Agnes Grey*. However, what does emerge, and has already been seen in the first pages, is a general consistency between the attitudes of Agnes and her creator.

Turning to Anne Brontë's poetry, we need to examine the assumptions she brings to poetic composition, which of course she shares to some extent with other members of the family. Evidence for the close co-operation that took place from their childhood until about 1846 between Emily and Anne is abundant. I have already mentioned the shared diary papers, one of which, that from 1837, shows a thumbnail sketch of the two girls sitting at a table and working together on the Gondal saga. In those days, as will be seen later, Emily both protected and dominated Anne. Both girls developed two genres of poetry, the 'Gondal' work, which was concerned with an imaginary environment in some ways similar to Yorkshire, but in others very different, and a group of personal poems based on situations encountered in actual life. The identification of these two genres, and the classification of the poems into one or other group, with a few poems left as transitional, was one of my purposes in *The Poems of Anne Brontë*, and it is not possible to argue the case in full here.[8] That some of Emily's and some of Anne's poems have a personal content, with little or no difference felt between the 'I' of the poem and the poet herself, can be shown adequately. This does not absolve us from handling this autobiographical material carefully, but it does mean that we have another source for understanding the personal feelings and thoughts of Emily and Anne Brontë, provided these poems are used cautiously, with every attempt made to compare their information with external data.

What kind of artefact is a poem? 'Agnes Grey' answers that she sees a poem as a kind of 'pillar of witness'. The passage, in chapter 17 of the novel, is worth studying:

When we are harassed by sorrows or anxieties, or long oppressed by any powerful feelings which we must keep to ourselves, for which we can obtain and seek no sympathy from any living creature, and yet which we cannot, or will not wholly crush, we often naturally seek relief in poetry – and often find it, too – whether in the effusions of others, which seem to harmonize with our existing case, or in our own attempts to give utterance to those thoughts and feelings in strains less musical, perchance, but more appropriate, and therefore more penetrating and sympathetic, and, for the time, more soothing, or more powerful to rouse and unburden the oppressed and swollen heart. Before this time, at Wellwood House and here, when suffering from homesick melancholy, I had sought relief twice or thrice at this secret source of consolation; and now I flew to it again, with greater avidity than ever, because I seemed to need it more. I still preserve those relics of past sufferings and experience, like pillars of witness set up in travelling through the vale of life, to mark particular occurrences.

The gist of Agnes Grey's argument here is that poems are made when the poet is alone and 'harassed by sorrows or anxieties' for which there is no external sympathy. At such times, she reads or writes verse, and sometimes preserves the results of her labour. This account coincides precisely with processes that are observable in Anne Brontë, for example, in the making of her last poem, entitled by Charlotte 'Last Lines' and written in two sections during the early months of 1849, when Anne had been told she was likely to die. The circumstances of this composition will be dealt with in its chronological place, but for this period of Anne's life we have an unusually large amount of external evidence in the form of Charlotte's letters to Ellen Nussey, W. S. Williams and others, with which to compare the manuscript of the poem which is at Haworth.[9] We are therefore in a good position to judge for this poem how far Anne Brontë's practice accords with that she predicates of Agnes Grey. The two accounts converge remarkably, so that it seems as if the Agnes Grey passage, written in 1845–6, is accurately representing the attitude of Anne Brontë in 1849. For Anne, one kind of poem is personal, 'occasional' poetry, based on one kind of Thomas Moore's poems, which he in turn is modelling on what he understood to be the attitude of the Latin poets (and of course, many others) to the function and purpose of one type of poem. As I have already stated, another kind of poem, the verse fiction, was also written by Anne, as well as Emily, but the two types are distinguishable.

Given that Anne's poems, as clearly exemplified in 'Last lines', include a group which springs direct from immediate experience, and that identification of these poems is possible, there should be no difficulty about a judicious use of this material in constructing Anne Brontë's biography. Though we cannot use them naively, we are certainly entitled to delve into the poems and try to understand their significance as personal documents, since that is what Agnes Grey, speaking here (though not always) for Anne Brontë, says they are. Statements by poets in their poems have to be taken very cautiously, but my analysis of the way in which Emily Brontë's Law Hill poems relate to her experience there adds weight to the interpretation I now wish to give to a fairly extensive group of Anne's poems.[10] For this biography cautious reliance on these poems will be essential, since Anne's letters are too few to enable us to obtain an understanding of her subjective character from them, though they do support, despite their small number, the attitude, beliefs and principles I wish to attribute to Anne.

If there is a danger that a reading of Anne's non-Gondal poems may lead us to assume too readily that we can understand her attitudes and feelings, and we need to adopt a cautious attitude when considering them, our other proposed source of understanding Anne Brontë's life may seem too factual and unconnected with her personality. I have spent a good deal of time researching the locations where she worked from contemporary sources. For example, much new evidence on the Thorp Green district has emerged from such documents as George Whitehead's diary, covering exactly the time when Anne was living at Thorp Green and attending the church at Little Ouseburn. I have been able to identify the subject of one of her drawings as Little Ouseburn church and thus link her firmly with the locality. Anne Brontë, like her brother and sisters, had an observant eye and it is not credible to think that she lived at Thorp Green for five years without taking stock of her surroundings, the house itself, the River Ouse, the church and the surrounding fields, or the people she encountered day by day. A puzzle which I could not solve in *The Poems of Anne Brontë* was finally clarified when I discovered that 'The Long Plantation', a poem written on 30 December 1842, was given as the name of a wood on the Kirby Hall estate on the first large-scale Ordnance survey map. This discovery once again helped to situate Anne's poems in a precise, real, locality. Her observant eye describes the wind in the trees of a real copse. It is entirely relevant to describe in detail what we can discover from external sources about the area in which Anne Brontë lived, and from which she drew her fictional inspiration. The reader has a right to be put in a position to visualize Anne's milieu with her eyes, though this has to be done very carefully. In *A Life of Emily Brontë* I used conditional verbs such as 'would see' 'would hear' to describe her perceptions of which there is no record, but which we can infer with total certainty from an examination of external sources. I shall use the same method with Anne.

Recent research by John Nussey and others has painted a detailed and accurate picture of Blake Hall in the time of the Inghams, which interestingly tallies closely with Agnes Grey's description of 'Wellwood House'. I have personally given much attention to Scarborough during the 1840s, an investigation which was successfully begun by Winifred Gerin. It is of prime importance to know everything we can about the Robinson family with whom Anne spent five years of mixed emotion, all their connections being of concern to her when she wrote the many counselling letters which Charlotte mentions, but which unfortunately are all lost. The precise circumstances of Branwell's disgrace have been a matter of controversy among Brontë scholars for many years, and more can now be added to that discussion. It is legitimate to ask where Anne found her material for *Wildfell Hall*. The many concerns which led her to write this book will be discussed in their due place, but it needs to be emphasized at this point that her former pupils, whom she regarded as her responsibility, and whom Charlotte was less than happy to receive when they made a personally demeaning pilgrimage to Haworth in late 1848, were writing frequently to her from Derbyshire, and there is a clear inference that they discussed the society into which they were being introduced by their mother, who was seeking to procure marriages for them, at the very time Anne was writing about the procurement of a young girl's marriage in *Wildfell Hall*, and showing its disastrous results. Derbyshire, as part of the Robinson and Gisborne milieu, must be part of our investigation.

My aim is to produce a live portrait of Anne Brontë, and in the absence of almost all personal records other than her poems, every avenue must be scoured for data to help build up our portrait. But the need for authenticity is so great that I shall not assume anything that cannot be supported by evidence. This will necessitate many footnotes and some pedantic expression. Speculation is inevitable, but will always be shown as such and will be supported by citation. It is to be hoped that the reader will tolerate conditionals and a number of qualifying adverbs, though they do unfortunately blunt the clarity of style I should like to aim for. Direct quotations from the works of Anne Brontë and her sisters will be necessary at times, although I have tried to keep them short.

At a time when the importance and influence of women writers *as women* is being much stressed, I have tried to give full weight to this aspect of Anne Brontë's work, though we need also to keep in mind the kind of equality she herself sees between the sexes, as expressed in the 1848 Preface to *Wildfell Hall*.[11] An extremely fair and detailed exploration of this whole matter is contained in Elizabeth Langland's *Anne Brontë*: *The Other One* (Macmillan, 1989), and I acknowledge a debt to this work.

It should be explained for readers of earlier works on the Brontës, and of earlier biographies of Anne, that even the efforts of Winifred Gerin, or of Ada Harrison and Derek Stanford, did not wholly succeed in surmounting the effects of Charlotte's oddly ambivalent attitude. She showed her sister a mixture of maternal care and sisterly jealousy. She would have suppressed *Wildfell Hall* if she could, and her editing of the poignant, tortured last poem of 1849 shows that she wanted her to be known as a calm saint. Anne *was* calm; she forced herself to be so. But just as Emily was subject to the devious attractions of her own inner Heathcliff, so Anne could have been subverted from her 'narrow way' by the arousing of an inner flirtatious Rosalie.[12] Her calm equilibrium was not easily achieved, as Charlotte surely knew. As a child Anne's favourite toy was a soldier known to the family as 'waiting boy'. We may well see Anne through much of her life as exemplifying this trait; she *waited*, with patience and hope, never entirely despondent even amidst bitter disappointment and crushing humiliation. In the end, she obtained what she waited for – an opportunity to 'do some good in the world before I leave it'.

1
Childhood

———◆◆◆———

'Exiled and harassed Anne', Emily calls her in a diary paper. All the Brontës for most of their adult lives felt exiled and harassed. It was inevitable from the moment that Mr Brontë, already divided in himself, left Ballynaskeagh, County Down, and set out for Cambridge. So much of his consciousness was Irish peasant that the Cambridge Tory veneer was hard to assimilate. He married a Cornish woman, Maria Branwell, a calm, pleasing, devout young lady, who fell in love with his enthusiasm and energy. Together they set up house in the West Riding of Yorkshire, at Hightown near Hartshead, where their warmth seems to have won the hearts of their neighbours. The friends they made in the district never forgot them.

In course of time Mr Brontë exchanged pulpits to become the incumbent at Thornton, where four children were born, in addition to Maria and Elizabeth, who had been born at Hartshead. Of the Thornton-born children, one was a boy, Patrick (after his father) Branwell (his mother's maiden name). The others were the three sisters who would one day become great novelists, and whom Charlotte Brontë's friend Ellen Nussey was to compare to three suns. Of these three, the youngest was Anne.

Fate thus thrust on Anne a role she never quite transcended. The youngest of six children will be petted and patronized, and expected to be a small-scale copy of the others. It will be hard for her to realize, beneath this smothering affection and condescension that she has her own life to lead. Yet Anne Brontë did realize it and was determined to be free of her family for the sake of her own development; but the need to

[15]

do this tormented her. She had to leave her beloved home, where she would have most liked to be, for other houses. She had to put aside her inclination to write 'soft nonsense' and portray evil 'as it really is'.[1] Her sister Charlotte could not believe that this was necessary or possible, and some later critics have agreed. Anne's attempts to 'de-Romanticize' the Byronic hero, so beloved of Charlotte and Emily, have often been ignored.[2]

Anne Brontë was born on 17 January 1820 at Thornton Main Street. The other children spent the day at nearby Kipping House with Elizabeth Firth, a friend of Mr and Mrs Brontë, who provided some alleviating comforts for the children as they grew up. Anne seems to have been a pretty child though eclipsed by her sister Emily. By all accounts the children were pleased with their new sister and saw something angelic in her. Charlotte once claimed that she had seen an angel at Anne's bedhead, and this turned out to be prophetic; despite the troubles brought on by her indifferent health Anne tried to live patiently, though beneath the surface her poems tell us of agony and sadness.[3]

Maria Brontë died on 15 September 1821, and Anne can have known little of her. But there remained seven members of the family to influence her, each a clearly defined personality. There was her father, 'eccentrick', enthusiastic, a passionate devotee of education and art, sometimes stern and sometimes playful, with a talent for telling stories that would scare the listeners out of their wits.[4] At 44, he now knew that his ambitions to move political or ecclesiastical mountains would never materialize. His great energy took him walking to the furthest limits of his moorland parish, and he continued to harry the authorities on all kinds of public matters.[5] His efforts at publishing literature had largely ceased; his Irish harp, which he had put at the service of God, had fallen silent.[6]

His wife's sister, Elizabeth Branwell, a Methodist with determined ideas on how children should be brought up, came from Cornwall to live with the family. She has been a controversial figure with biographers, and was certainly a strong influence on her youngest Brontë niece. Then there was Anne's eldest sister, Maria, clever, saintly and untidy.[7] Now that his wife was dead Patrick Brontë sometimes took Maria into his confidence and discussed his chief concerns with her. She had a withdrawn, intellectual air at times. She took her duties as surrogate mother seriously, and prayed with the younger children before they slept.[8] Elizabeth, the next eldest, was patient, and willing to engage in humdrum work.[9] She was thought of as more reliable than clever. Charlotte tended to confuse these two sisters and run their qualities together. Some careful disentangling has to be done before we can see that Elizabeth may have been more of a model for Anne than Maria.[10]

Next came little Charlotte, passionate and deeply imaginative. Her small stature has been remarked on many times, and in this context it needs to be noted that she would be outgrown by both Emily and Anne as they grew up; this lack of inches had an effect on the way Charlotte saw her youngest sister. Charlotte often stared at people, trying to fathom their inmost thoughts.[11] It is through these eyes that much of Anne's story is presented to us, and we need to remember that though she was enormously observant of external details, she did not always understand others' emotions, and certainly not Anne's. Charlotte invented racy and dangerous games, aided particularly by the intense and athletic Emily, who once leapt out of an upstairs window into a fruit tree, which broke and caused her to fall to the ground. She was often in a bad temper and her imagination knew no restraint.[12]

Branwell later tried to rule the roost. There seems to be no doubt that his sex would accord him special status, though Mr Brontë was determined to educate his girls fully.[13] Undoubtedly Branwell was very talented, quick and bright, but so mercurial that he could not be relied on; in fact, the antithesis of Elizabeth. We need to remember that Anne's early experience of males was made up of Mr Brontë, authoritative and kindly, but sometimes hasty, and Branwell, full of spirit, but inconsistent and self-opinionated.

With such a lively and diverse family, the young Brontës needed very little outside company. When they met other children, they found it difficult to understand them, for the others played unimaginatively at traditional games. The young Brontës seem to have found them boring and to have closed ranks against outsiders.[14] With five elder children to lead her, Anne naturally adapted to their interests and she does not seem to have had anyone of her own age to play with. Later, she found it hard to make close friends outside the family, but she persevered.

Anne Brontë would turn out to be Wordsworthian in her view of childhood, even though some of the real children she encountered seemed to deny her vision. Beginning in November 1847 she wrote a long, autobiographical poem, 'Self-communion'.[15] After lamenting the ravaging nature of time, she stalwartly maintains that time 'cannot touch the inward flame' and proposes a ransacking of her memory to recall what life had been like as a child.

> *I see, far back, a helpless child,*
> *Feeble and full of causeless fears,*
> *Simple and easily beguiled*
> *To credit all it hears.*

So Anne's first recollections of childhood stress her helplessness. This might well be so as the youngest of six. *All* the others could do things better than she could, and she was bound to feel 'feeble'. Although she accuses herself of 'causeless' fears, the effect of her mother's death, and those of her two eldest sisters in 1825, must have been to emphasize the impermanence of life. The phrase 'easily beguiled', while we should not read too much into it, reminds us of the plausible nature of Mr Brontë's breakfast table stories, and the air of verisimilitude with which the Brontë relatives in County Down teased their neighbours. The implication here is that Anne at first believed the stories he used to tell, and which Charlotte and Emily later produced. There is, however, condemnation in the word 'beguiled'; Anne is arguing that such imaginative flights are to be examined sceptically, something that as a child she was unable to do.

She goes on,

> *More timid than the wild wood-dove*
> *Yet trusting to another's care,*
> *And finding in protecting love*
> *Its only refuge from despair.*

Why does Anne use the singular, when she had many protectors? The answer may be suggested by a cautious inference from *Wildfell Hall*, in which Helen turns to her aunt for advice (though she speedily rejects it). The singular 'another' can hardly refer to her father, Branwell or Charlotte, and the evidence adduced in *A Life of Emily Brontë* suggests that it was only after Charlotte went to school at Roe Head that the alliance between Anne and Emily became significant.[16] The influence of her aunt is substantiated in a passage from Ellen Nussey's 'Reminiscences' of 1871, which will be quoted in chapter 2.[17]

Her heart, she next says, was tender, 'too prone to weep', and her love was 'so earnest, strong and deep/ It could not be expressed'. This tenderness of heart is a characteristic of Anne that distinguishes her from Emily and even Charlotte. In her novels, she refuses to cast Huntingdon into hell eternally, and she will not condemn Rosalie for her selfish flirtatiousness. This impressionable emotional basis forms a very good ground for a novelist, who will need to explore and understand very different characters without exercising harsh judgement.

> Poor helpless thing! what can it do
> Life's stormy cares and toils among; –
> How tread the weary desert through
> That awes the brave and tires the strong?
> Where shall it centre so much trust
> Where truth maintains so little sway,
> Where seeming fruit is bitter dust,
> And kisses oft to death betray?[18]

The implication is that among the multitude of kisses the little girl received from her adoring siblings, some were treacherous. She would not be very old before she read of the kisses and betrayal of Judas. However, she generalizes here in such a way as to show that she is not thinking only of the Bible passage: 'Kisses *oft* betray.' Her closest childhood and adolescent friendship, from about the age of ten, was with Emily and, from what we know of divided Emily's terrible obsession with treachery, it is reasonable to suppose that Emily kissed Anne and then betrayed her. While later on her father's curate William Weightman may not have kissed her (though perhaps he did), he certainly sent a valentine which seemed to promise too much. Her child's heart, says Anne in lines 66–7, was 'ready to believe' and 'willing to admire'. Her idols must have included Maria, Elizabeth, Aunt Branwell and perhaps her brother. Later, Emily would certainly be one of them.

Two other characteristics are mentioned by Anne in her self-analysis. Her love is 'so warm and deep' that it overflows at woe felt by another, not only for itself. In her first four years of life, she must have felt her father's grief at the death of his wife, and there would be many petty griefs too, especially perhaps from Emily who took life's reverses so hard. In particular, Anne records grief over 'a sparrow's death'. This may be influenced by the Bible reference, but there is plenty of evidence for the Brontës' great love of animals, and it seems likely that Anne shared this family trait very early.[19] A dead bird stirred her sadness and 'bitter tearfloods' followed.

Then there is Anne's very early religious sentiment. We shall return to the subject many times, as it proves an abiding influence on her, but it is clear that the Bible would have been read to her as a toddler, and that it would be the first of all books she was taught to read. The Bible would be a staple diet, mediated by Maria or by the sweet-voiced Emily, who could put beautiful expression into her reading before she was six.[20] Anne would be taught simple hymns, like those she recalled from Isaac Watts, and would attend church and Sunday school before she was five.[21] It is also likely that the elders directed her attention to what Charlotte, in early 1825, calls 'The book of Nature', the great world of birds, trees, animals and the skies above, which at Haworth were so close. Of these elements, Anne took almost as much notice of trees as of birds. Throughout the work of all the Brontës, trees are looked at both for themselves and for the metaphors they provide. Many of Anne's drawings include prominent or strangely characterful trees, which have not only been observed but distinguished as near-personalities.[22]

With his marriage to Maria Branwell Mr Brontë had secured the right to consider himself a member of bourgeois society. Now that his children were growing, he had to consider the matter of their education. In his youth he had been determined that girls and boys should be educated equally, and that talent should be fostered wherever it was found.[23] But to maintain these principles in the case of his own daughters would be very hard. He had taught Maria and Elizabeth to read, and was able to rely on Maria to give him an accurate precis of the news.

Now these two needed to move on to the next stage of schooling. There followed an episode in Brontë biography which has been little explored but which had its impact on the whole family.

Elizabeth Firth, Patrick's neighbour at Thornton, had declined his offer of marriage after the death of his wife, but she never forgot her position as Elizabeth's and Anne's godmother. She recommended for the two eldest girls her own old school, Crofton Hall, near Wakefield. It is not known whether she helped Mr Brontë financially, but she may have done so, especially perhaps in the case of Elizabeth. All the Brontë children would be excited about this new venture during the summer of 1823. Even Anne, at three and a half, must have realized that this was a turning point for the family, and a great opportunity, though she would have been reluctant to lose her sisters.

No record remains of the journey of the two sisters to Wakefield, or the send-off given by their brother and sisters. Perhaps we can imagine Charlotte and Branwell, Emily and Anne, running down Church Lane after the Haworth gig, waving as it disappeared down the steep slope of Main Street. We don't know if Mr Brontë went with the little girls, or by which route they went. As Elizabeth Firth was an influence on the choice of school, perhaps he went to Thornton with them and called at Kipping House, where the girls might have stayed, as they had done so many times before. They disappeared from Anne's sight and she would next hear from them through the letters they sent, which would presumably be read aloud by Charlotte, who might well have wished to share this pioneering venture.

Crofton was a two-storey mansion house, about three miles east of Wakefield. It had been altered to accommodate a girls' school many years previously and had been run by a famous headmistress, Richmal Mangnall, from 1808 to 1820. Though she had now been dead three years, there is no doubt that the school was still run on the lines she had laid down, and so were the same as those Elizabeth Firth had experienced earlier in the century. Richmal Mangnall had opinions rather at odds with the Tory views Patrick Brontë espoused. In 1798 his brother William had echoed family loyalties by fighting with the United Irishmen in County Down, but there was a complete change in his beliefs as time went on. By now, he might not have agreed with the bland acceptance of the French Revolution implicit in the answer given to one of the first 'questions' in Miss Mangnall's famous book *Historical and Miscellaneous Questions*: 'What was it? [the French Revolution]': 'A change in the constitution and government'.[24]

Miss Mangnall's book had originally been published in 1798, and was followed by an enlarged edition in 1800. Longman published their first edition in 1805, and the book was then reprinted many times. Miss Mangnall subsequently wrote and published verse and a geography book. It is probably significant that the whole Brontë family was so interested in this range of school subjects, history, geography and poetry, and that they accepted that it was natural for women to write and publish verse. Maria and Elizabeth would have seen a great deal of evidence of Miss Mangnall's literary talent, and would have reported this back to Haworth. The height of ambition for a woman wishing for economic independence must be to become a governess or keeper of a girls' school; she could then develop her literary talents and add to her income.

When the elder Brontës arrived at Crofton, they found their lessons taking place in a brick-built schoolroom, divided into two by an internal wall, each part with its own fireplace. The smaller room was a writing room, while instruction took place mainly in the larger room. Though by their time the school was run by a Mrs Hollingsworth, the school-room plan remained the same for many years. Sleeping accommodation seems to have been in the old hall itself. The pattern of the other boarding schools which the Brontës were later to attend is thus exemplified at Crofton: an old home altered by adding a schoolroom, with the girls sleeping in the upper rooms of the house. This was true of Cowan Bridge (though there the base was a group of cottages); and Roe Head was similar. When, many years later, Anne contemplated the delights of starting a girls' boarding school at Scarborough, she would realize that she must spend a considerable outlay on conversion and new building.[25]

The curriculum at Crofton was not particularly innovative. The cost of boarding and instruction in 'Plain and Fancy-Work' was thirty-three guineas a year. Access to 'English Grammatically, Writing and Accompts, Geography, Dancing, Drawing, French, Music and Italian' was through the use of visiting masters, at extra charge. It is not clear how far basic language or arithmetic instruction would be independent of the visiting masters and given as part of the thirty-three guinea package. One thing is quite clear: this was no forward-looking educational establishment. It seems likely that its appeal to Mr Brontë came solely from its recommendation by Elizabeth Firth, and the fees seem too high for him to have paid them on his own.[26]

However, if the curriculum was traditional, at least during Miss Mangnall's life the approach was humane. In the Preface to the *Questions* she writes approvingly of teachers who have time to 'converse with each [child] separately and lead them to a habit of reflection and observance for themselves'. During the evenings, if the habits of Elizabeth Firth's time continued, the governess would read aloud to the girls; while during the day pupils were sent off to research answers to questions they had been set individually. Though it must have been hard to obtain much attention from the teacher in a school of about seventy girls, the overall reputation of the school held steady for many years after the demise of Mrs Mangnall's own influence.[27]

Unfortunately we cannot answer the most important question about the young Brontës at school during 1823: there is no evidence whatever to show whether they were happy at school or not. But as Anne's passionate interest throughout her life in education must stem from this early time, showing that great emphasis was placed on it, it cannot have been made to seem worthless or unattractive to her. Maria was later accused of untidiness, and this is certainly characteristic of Emily too. It is not likely that this trait would have endeared her to her teachers or her conforming fellow-pupils. Elizabeth was more patient and mild, and Anne took after her rather than Maria. But even she may well have found that she failed to fit into Crofton Hall, either because of the rather closed educational aims of the teachers, or the social milieux of the girls. The Brontës never could compromise socially: they were shy and unpolished, felt deeply, and had little time for surface chatter. Even when she went to Roe Head, Charlotte spoke with a strong accent, which may well have been a mixture of Yorkshire and Ulster.[28] Maria, who was so close to her father in so much, must have had even more Irish in her accent. This may have caused another barrier.

The decision not to send the two girls back to Crofton may

have been determined by their failure to adjust, but perhaps it was also too costly for Mr Brontë's finances. What is more, they were never to recover completely from the whooping-cough they caught during 1823, possibly at Crofton, though it is impossible to be sure,[29] a circumstance which has to be borne in mind when we consider Charlotte's attitude to the health of both Emily and Anne at Roe Head.

It will not be difficult to make inferences about what the girls told their young sisters and brother about their stay at school. Maria would certainly have enjoyed the intellectual stimulation. Geography was to become a major preoccupation of the whole family, and they took it beyond the real to the creation of imaginary locations. The idea seems to have originated with Maria, and is explained by the loan of a geography book in Charlotte's account of the origin of the communal plays.[30] In view of her later performance, we may be sure that Maria was intellectually bright at Crofton and was able to perform the tasks of reading aloud and speaking in answer to questions with enthusiasm.

The story of Mr Brontë's next attempt to find a school for his daughters has often been told. Anne was too young to go with the other four to the Clergy Daughters' School at Cowan Bridge. Maria and Elizabeth were the pioneers, and were followed by Charlotte and then Emily. Anne was left in the care of Aunt Elizabeth, whose influence, especially in religious matters, we shall soon examine. Branwell was the only other child at home. He was undoubtedly privileged, learning directly from his father.[31] The contrast in educational treatment between boys and girls, though less marked in the Brontë household than most, was still sharp enough to cause Anne to attack the system years later in *Wildfell Hall*.

In due course very bad news came from Cowan Bridge. Mr Brontë set off in a panic to collect his beloved Maria, returning with her in deep pain and distress. She was terminally ill with tuberculosis but she sugared the pill for her father and sisters as was expected of a nineteenth-century child, and faced her death bravely; rather more uncomplainingly, so far as we can tell, than her own mother had done four years previously. This superhuman effort on the part of a courageous child Anne remembered all her life; she saw Maria as a shining example, and in due course emulated her. As Maria gasped for air during that spring of 1825, we may be sure that Anne, whose heart was so prone to overflow 'even at the thought of another's woe', felt her sister's pain. It is quite possible that the asthma symptoms often attributed to her were psychosomatic and developed in sympathy with Maria at this time.[32]

In turn, Elizabeth also failed and declined. Maria died on 6 May 1825; Elizabeth soon after. Charlotte and Emily were hastily recalled and, after deliberation, Mr Brontë decided not to send them back. It would be more than four years before any further experiments in schooling were tried. The world knows how Charlotte took on the mantle of the two dead sisters and rebuilt the family by her energy and imagination. For years, the surviving children wrote and wrote, weaving stories in the distant places that Maria had taught them about. They each identified with a toy soldier of Branwell's, though we know very little about Anne's choice. Charlotte says he was a 'queer little thing much like' Anne herself. The elders called this soldier 'Waiting Boy'. Branwell wrote in 1833 that Anne was 'nothing, absolutely nothing'; the other three were determined she should be so, and Anne, meanwhile, bided her time.

We have one tiny glimpse of Anne, written by Charlotte in 1829, by which time she felt she should try to systematize the 'plays' the family had by now invented:

> I am in the kitchen of the parsonage house Haworth [writes Charlotte]. Taby [sic] the servant is washing up after Breakfast and Anne my youngest sister (Maria was my eldest) is kneeling on a chair looking at some cakes which Tabby has been baking for us.[33]

A pleasant picture of Anne at nine, 'looking at' cakes and once again 'waiting', with an Elizabeth-like patience until they should be ready.

Anne's lot in life was cast: it was to be patient, passive, 'calm'. In the beginning of Charlotte's account of how the toy soldiers were first given to Branwell, it is she and Emily who are together in bed, where they shared secrets until morning, and they rushed to snatch up Branwell's new toys.[34] Meanwhile, Anne slept with Aunt Elizabeth and felt secure. It is unlikely that she moved out of her aunt's bed until Charlotte went to school. This intimate connection with an adult so early made Anne curiously more mature, less childishly excitable, and also more religious.

In 1836, when she met the Moravian clergyman, James la Trobe, he found her 'well acquainted with the main truths of the Bible respecting our salvation, but seeing them more through the law than the Gospel'.[35] Such theological definition is alien to the twentieth century, but we need to try to understand it if we are to follow Anne's religious development. She herself comments on it in 'Self-communion'. La Trobe's assertion is that Anne knew the Bible well, but saw its kernel as a code of law. This attitude is likely to have been gained from both her father and her aunt, though in neither case can we assume a Calvinistic element.

Mr Brontë's religious position was unusual. I have explored his early life in *The Brontës' Irish Background*, in which I showed that although he was attached as a teacher to Glascar Meeting, the Ulster Presbyterianism (which would have had a Calvinist element) in his own life was only skin-deep. His own father had been helped by the Presbyterians when an outcast, and this made him look kindly on them. He taught Patrick and his other children to read the Bible, Milton and Bunyan, but Patrick's mother remained a Catholic. In Patrick's sermons we find enthusiasm for Evangelical Protestantism, but not for its Calvinist extreme. At Cambridge, Patrick was close to the Wesleyan apostles. Undoubtedly, Wesleyanism was legalistic in various ways, but Wesley went out of his way to declare that 'Christ died for all'. There was no *a priori* damnation or rejection of part of his creation. Anne's antipathy to Calvinism did not come from reaction to her father, indeed, there are some hints that his dismissal from Glascar may have been due to the influence of a more rigidly Calvinistic minister than had occupied Glascar's pulpit previously. Patrick is likely to have been anti-Calvinist.[36]

Aunt Elizabeth is often suspected of Calvinism. This suggestion seems to originate with a misedited letter of Charlotte's in which the words '——'s ghastly Calvinistic doctrines are true' appear.[37] As Tom Winnifrith has shown, the reading is quite false.[38] The actual letter reads: '*your* ghastly Calvinistic doctrines . . .'. It is apparently Ellen who has suggested a Calvinistic interpretation of scripture. Aunt Elizabeth, in fact, was a Wesleyan Methodist. Her sister Maria had first met Patrick

Brontë at Woodhouse Grove, the newly opened school for Methodist boys. There the education was stringent and forceful, highly demanding of their belief and application, but it was not Calvinist, and neither was Maria or Elizabeth Branwell. Their origins were with Methodism in Penzance.

Elizabeth Branwell would have attended the new Methodist chapel in Chapel Street, Penzance, which had been built in 1814 on the site of a house once inhabited by Sir Humphrey Davy. Though their tradition descended in part from seventeenth-century Puritanism, by the early nineteenth century this was softening. In particular, the Calvinist doctrine of 'election', against which Anne writes in her poetry and *Wildfell Hall*, was not acceptable. In 1781 a conference of Cornish Methodists had debated whether even to 'hear' a Church of England preacher who spoke against 'the pardoning love of God and knowing our sins forgiven'. Doubtless James la Trobe was right in his view of Anne's legalistic understanding of the Bible, but Calvinism's belief in the inevitable rejection by God of numbers of his created mortals was not part of Elizabeth Branwell's creed, far less of Anne Brontë's.[39]

So Anne's understanding of religion included the duty of morning and evening prayer, church attendance and a moral way of life, which had to be learnt. Disobedience to this code was dangerous and could be visited with punishment. Ultimately, this punishment could be eternal, as the Bible allowed Christ a parable in which he talked of a final division into sheep and goats. The destiny of the damned was to be burnt in the eternal fires of hell. As a small girl, Anne would learn all this from Aunt Elizabeth; what she would not learn was the further Calvinist view that the 'Elect' had already been chosen, and that neither they nor the rejected could alter the situation. When the young Brontës started to read Cowper, they understood his fear in such poems as 'The Castaway' of eternal damnation predetermined, so that the victims could do nothing to avoid it. 'The Castaway' therefore became a crucial poem to at least three of the children: Branwell, who laughed at fate to hide his fear; Emily, who turned the world upside down and found heaven on earth; and Anne, who mourned for Cowper and nibbled away at the problem intellectually until she felt she had solved it.[40]

In 'Self-communion' Anne records that she was striving to find 'the narrow way'. Her 'inner strife and tears' were known only to God. She emphasizes this by adding that '*man* would scorn/ Those childish prayers . . . But God will not despise!' In this quest Anne differed from Emily and Branwell, since they both reacted with scorn to what they heard as children. Anne seems to have been less hasty in pondering both the Bible and *Pilgrim's Progress*; the metaphor of the hard and narrow road was very often in her mind. Anne's struggle was as 'mystical' as Emily's in that it involved the belief that she could communicate with an invisible power directly, though that power presented itself to her mind as more masculine than feminine, and more orthodox than pagan.

This leads me to another point to which I shall return. As a novelist, Anne is currently coming to be seen as a champion of female equality. Charlotte and Emily are also, in different ways, conscious of the penalties of being female in the nineteenth century, but there is nothing in their work quite comparable to the logical exploration by Anne, in chapter 3 of *Wildfell Hall*, of the assumptions on which boys and girls are differently educated. In Haworth parsonage, male and female roles were remarkably fluid: Emily dressed as King Charles, while Charlotte identified with male heroes in much of her juvenilia. Anne, however, takes a stronger line on the equality of woman *qua* woman.

Of the three sisters, Anne seems to be the one who saw herself in a female role beyond that of attraction and courtship. (Even Branwell never seems to have seen himself as potentially a father or husband figure; his Romantic notions of marriage to Mrs Robinson were otherwise expressed, as we shall see.) All the Brontës deal with 'love' in their work; Anne alone is concerned with parenthood, both in some poems and *Wildfell Hall*. That she can contemplate her own imagined baby and her own small children beyond the baby stage argues greater acceptance of her own gender than the others – in fact, greater acceptance of any gender. In this way she is able to think more concretely of the problems confronting women than Emily's supernatural statements. This acceptance of female identity may well have had something to do with Anne's closeness to Aunt Elizabeth in childhood. Emily perhaps saw adult life as intolerable, since mature constraints on freedom drove her back to the paradise of childhood. Anne, while still accepting that childhood was a special time, determined to struggle with the complexities of adult life directly, without flinching. Sleeping in the same bed as Aunt Elizabeth was thus a reassurance and a challenge, and a proof that adult life was livable.

The closeness between Anne and Aunt Elizabeth also sowed the seeds of Anne's disenchantment with the world of games and make-believe. The others had only children for companions; they believed only in the reality of children. Mr Brontë put few restrictions on them. He encouraged their love of the outdoor life where they were not held accountable. Anne, though in the 1834 diary paper she aids and abets Emily in not tidying herself, not making her bed and wanting to 'go out to play', must have had to acquire adult attitudes to housework before she was ten.[41] In the room they shared, Aunt Elizabeth must have exacted some semblance of social grace. Emily, Branwell and Charlotte put inner integrity first and thought the world should learn to accommodate them rather than the other way round. Anne would make genuine contact with others – William Weightman, the Robinsons and Ellen Nussey – while Emily repelled advances. This must be partly ascribed to Anne's childhood contact with Aunt Elizabeth.

But her artistic and intellectual attainments lagged behind the others, as they were expected to do. She finished her sampler just after her tenth birthday, on 23 January 1830. The previous year, we have seen her curiously examining and *not touching* the freshly baked cakes. Charlotte was trying to teach her copy-book writing, and she was proceeding in a concentrated but inaccurate way. 'Honour is purchased...' writes Charlotte; and Anne copies painfully beneath, 'Hour is purchased...'[42] She is already modifying Charlotte's script, using a plainer form of final *d*, eliminating Charlotte's backward loop. She signs her name, using an acute accent (as they all did at that point, instead of the modern diaeresis), Anne Bronté, and gives her age as nine.

In addition, we have a small group of drawings Anne made at the age of nine. One, dated in Charlotte's hand 7 April 1829, but apparently signed by Anne, shows a house in woods. There is the well-known picture of a bird and log which seems to anticipate chapter 17 of *Agnes Grey*, in which she discusses the love of a little girl for a pet bird. She 'would not hurt a toad [but] she cannot love it like the bird'. These pictures, and a further part-finished one dated 22 April, may have been drawn from copy-books. There is also a number of rather more accomplished pictures from about this date, such as the church dated 29 August 1828. I feel that they were presents given by Charlotte and Branwell rather than Anne's own; but all, taken together, show how the elder children were trying to encourage Anne in following the family's common pursuit.[43]

Anne's childhood, like that of the other young Brontës, was happy. Despite the traumas of losing her mother and two sisters, she was enclosed in a loving cocoon, with the bubbling stimulus of Emily and the dramatic imagination of Charlotte to guide her. Though the loss of this as a young adult depressed her, she would never lose her emotional buoyancy or her intellectual perseverance.

2
A Great Delight

———⟊———

The teenage years of any author are usually most important in his or her artistic development. They often provide a vital biographical clue without which the subject's writing cannot be understood. In the case of the two youngest Brontës this period is particularly hard to investigate and of the two, Anne proves the less accessible. Almost nothing is recorded about her between the ages of 11 and 17, except in conjunction with her sisters. Towards the end of this period she left Haworth for the first time since a childhood visit to Crossstone, with the rest of the family in 1829.[1] Throughout her early and mid-teenage years Anne was Emily's confidante at home. I shall therefore dispense with strict chronology, dealing with her Haworth experiences in this chapter and reserving her life at Roe Head for chapter 3.

Once again we are able to use a number of lines from 'Self-communion' to illuminate Anne's experience during these years. There is Ellen Nussey's visit of 1833 when Anne was thirteen, of which Ellen recorded various impressions at various times; there is the 1834 diary paper, though it was written by Emily, and the further one from 1837, also written by Emily but giving a small sketch which shows Anne working on one of her poems. I have used this material in *A Life of Emily Brontë* and there is not much more to be extracted from it. This is also the period of the Brontë portraits done under the aegis of William Robinson, who taught Branwell and Charlotte to draw. Recent discoveries by Dr Juliet Barker have helped to confirm some points made in *The Poems of Anne Brontë* and to modify others.

It ought to be possible to find strands to help us interpret

Anne's understanding of teenage girls like Esther Hargrave in *Wildfell Hall*, but the danger of circular argument precludes deducing anything about Anne's own youth from such passages. About the only thing that is clear is that the most important relationship Anne had as a teenage girl was with Emily. Emily told her what to do, almost what to think. At times, as Ellen Nussey said, they were 'like twins'.[2] There can be no doubt that this absorption in their own world was such as to exclude almost everything else. Luckily Anne deals with this phase very openly. We shall examine the whole section of 'Self-communion'.

> *Oh, I have known a wondrous joy*
> *In early friendship's pure delight, –*
> *A genial bliss that could not cloy –*
> *My sun by day, my moon by night.*

As children, Charlotte and Emily had been close to each other, leaving Anne to sleep with Aunt Elizabeth. But when Charlotte left to go to school, there was a shift in allegiance. The two younger girls lost their leader, and Emily came into her own. This is shown by the invention of Gondal, the imaginary island which was to be important to Emily for so long, and its sister island Gaaldine. Both were far from Africa, where Charlotte had launched imaginary expeditions for the whole family. Now was the time, the younger girls felt, to make a break from Charlotte's geographical constraints. Precisely when Gondal was invented is unclear, but it seems likely that it would have been developed during Charlotte's absence, and was so well established when she returned that her own world could not swallow it up again. Gondal had some similarities with the moorland world to the west of Haworth. The relationship is explored in *A Life of Emily Brontë*, and the dependence of Emily and Branwell on the library at Ponden Hall has been shown by various authors.[3] Anne would have accompanied Emily to Ponden, listening to her Gondal inventions, at first in total accord, wondering at and admiring her long-legged elder sister, whose physical courage has been established. This 'early friendship' was 'pure delight'. Emily, simply, was Anne's sun.

A great delight

The emotional chart is now filled in a little:

> *Absence, indeed, was sore distress,*
> *And thought of death was anguish keen,*
> *And there was cruel bitterness*
> *When jarring discords rose between;*

Emily is not known to have been 'absent' until 1835, when she went to Roe Head. Death is not nowadays expected of a teenage friend, but Anne had suffered this kind of deprivation too many times not to expect it again. She may be referring to her fears for Emily at Roe Head, fears that were plainly shared by the family to such an extent that Emily was allowed home. One gets a hint here that for all Emily's great energy there was something fragile concealed within her. This might chime with Romer Wilson's idea that Emily suffered a fit at some point.[4] Whatever Emily's physical power, Anne felt she had to disagree at times with her: this was 'cruel'; there were 'jarring discords'. In the end, such discords separated Anne from her sister like an ocean, but for the moment, as Ellen Nussey noted, the two were like 'united statues of power and humility'. Anne, when Ellen first met her, was thirteen.[5]

The next part of 'Self-communion' shows that Ellen did not seek below the surface of the relationship between Emily and Anne.

> *And sometimes it was grief to know*
> *My fondness was but half returned.*
> *But this was nothing to the woe*
> *With which another truth was learned: –*
> *That I must check, or nurse apart*
> *Full many an impulse of the heart*
> *And many a darling thought:*
> *What my soul worshipped, sought, and prized,*
> *Were slighted, questioned, or despised; –*
> *This pained me more than aught.*

Here Anne alleges that sometimes her fondness was 'but half returned'. In her closest relationship ever, Emily must some-

[33]

times have been dreaming of an ideal and rejecting Anne's actual love then and there.

Gradually, Anne tried to share her heart with her sister. Her soul worshipped in a literal way the Christian world-view and the 'narrow way' of the hymns. To Emily, already, this was not credible. She did not debate; she despised. We catch here the echo of conversations between the two sisters in Anne's amazingly accurate 'slighted' (Emily takes no notice of her young sister), 'questioned' (Emily thrusts rhetorical objections at Anne), 'despised' (Emily laughs scornfully). Tragically, what Anne did not pick up was Emily's own self-torture at her incapacity to control her own scorn.

These attempts by Anne to bare her soul to her sister must have taken place on 'the common' and at home. Between them, in the years 1832–6, they must have been writing something down on paper, in poetry or prose. It did not survive, while Charlotte's manuscripts for this period are copious. It seems likely that Emily and Anne destroyed their own work in the middle or towards the end of the decade, perhaps as a result of a joint decision.[6] The sharing of Gondal was at first most attractive to Anne, as we can tell both by this section of 'Self-communion' and by her poems, which are all Gondal-based until 1838. But Emily's very strong mind did not allow any influence by Anne, so it is likely that she felt excluded in this one-way mental traffic. At the same time we should not underestimate how much Emily gained from this closeness, in which she seems to have seen Anne as a confederate entirely loyal.

It seems likely that Anne did not seek emotional contact elsewhere before Emily left for Roe Head, and after that she preferred Emily to anyone else until 1839. A turning point was then reached when she thought she had discovered another person with more understanding of her attitudes. Ellen Nussey's descriptions of Emily and Anne in 1833 are quite consistent: 'She and Anne were like twins – inseparable companions, and in the closest sympathy, which never had any interruption.' Ellen's observation is doubtless totally accurate, but she is not competent to make the assertion of the final clause in the sentence. Anne tells us otherwise. We shall see her link with Emily becoming intermittent and finally fading.

It is fair, however, to believe Ellen's early observations, and the 1837 diary paper tells us a little about the time of twinship.

[34]

It has been examined many times, and I do not wish to repeat the account given in *A Life of Emily Brontë*. It is in Emily's handwriting and includes her drawing of herself and her sister sitting near a table with 'the Tin Box' of Gondal material in front of them. Anne's face is round and thoughtful, as she writes her poem 'Alexander and Zenobia'.[7] The principal characters in the poem, which has survived, are a boy of fourteen and his sweetheart, who are about to part. He promises to meet her after his exile, on her fifteenth birthday. As she is writing this Anne herself is seventeen, and we might be surprised at the young age of these lovers. It seems possible that Emily and Anne had acted out these parts, with Emily in the male role, as she had done earlier in such episodes as the escape of King Charles from the oak tree.[8] What is clear is that Anne was never heard of in a male role after the days of 'Waiting boy'. The dominance of her elder sister is obvious here, since she assumes the right to record their joint experiences in the diary paper. At the foot of the paper there is a small piece of dialogue. Anne asks: 'Well, do you intend to write in the evening?' There is a discussion, after which the sisters apparently agree to go out for a walk first.[9]

There is one firm piece of evidence of the reading of Emily and Anne before 1833. They called a confluence of two streams 'The Meeting of the Waters' after Thomas Moore's poem of that name. Perhaps they had encountered the poem in its musical setting, to a classicized Irish melody. Moore would later become a great favourite with Anne. We know their reading of Scott had begun before this, and that about this time Byron was becoming a favourite.[10] Emily and Anne both read Shelley, and this period seems a likely one for them to encounter him for the first time.[11] The use of Ponden Hall library does not seem to have been important for Anne, but she probably read some books from it.

It is not clear when Anne began to learn the piano. We may, once again, try to make inferences from Emily's piano playing, which became very accomplished. In view of the evidence of her music manuscript book of a later date, it seems that Anne was never such proficient player, but she was 'exercising' by 1834, since the diary paper of that year says, in Emily's words, 'Anne and I have not done our music exercise which consists of B major.'[12] 'Mr Sunderland', she adds, '[is] expected.' He was the Keighley organist who evidently gave

Emily and Anne keyboard lessons, which they do not seem to be taking very seriously. Yet Anne always enjoyed music and at Thorp Green it became a lifeline for her.[13]

Mr Sunderland was not the only professional to be employed by Mr Brontë to give lessons to his children. Charlotte and Branwell were both progressing with their drawing and painting, and there was an intention that Branwell would make his living by it. To aid them, Mr Brontë called upon William Robinson of Leeds, who seems to have been the stimulus for many drawings and paintings by both the older teenagers at this point. Throughout the Brontës' childhood and beyond, they drew from copy-books, but they all enjoyed using live models too. We cannot identify all the illustrations they copied from, and it is a fair assumption that some of the unidentified subjects are from unknown copies rather than life. But all the Brontës drew pictures of the animals and people around them. So it came about that Emily drew her thumbnail sketch of Anne in the 1837 diary paper, and both Charlotte and Branwell included Anne among their sitters.

Since 1979, when I wrote a section on Anne Brontë's appearance in my introduction to *The Poems of Anne Brontë*, there have been a number of exciting discoveries which help us to form an accurate picture of our subject. In the following pages I shall deal with the current state of knowledge in this area, taking into account recent meticulous work by Dr Juliet Barker.[14] Where there are still controversies I shall try carefully to establish probabilities.

There are now three authenticated portraits of Anne by Charlotte. The best known has been reproduced many times. It is a profile in the form of an oval miniature showing only head and shoulders. The date is 17 June 1834, when Anne was fourteen, and this profile, a watercolour, shows Anne's eyes to be blue. She has curly mid-brown hair, centre-parted and fairly long, but brushed so that her ears are visible. She is wearing a blue dress. Her neck and head shape are more vertically elongated than in the next picture to be discussed. Her prominent lips are pursed, and there is a hint of a smile. However, Charlotte's draughtsmanship is not secure enough for us to be certain whether this effect is intentional.

Another portrait, a drawing, was first printed in *The Bookman* in 1891. The 1981 edition of *Brontë Society Transactions* reported that it had been located and purchased for the society.

It is dated in Charlotte's writing 'April 17th 1833' and so was drawn when Anne was thirteen. In this profile, Anne faces right. She is seated on a chair and dressed in a cloak with turned-back veil, as though prophetic of Charlotte's later remark that she was hidden by a 'nun-like veil'.[15] It is interesting that Charlotte chose to draw her so, which suggests that at this time she was willing to play the role in which she had been cast. The drawing confirms Anne's curly hair, secured with a comb, her high-bridged nose and prominent lips, which are slightly parted as in some other pictures of her. It seems a lifelike portrait, though the hands and arms are not accurately proportioned.

A further portrait of Anne by Charlotte was discovered and returned to Haworth in January 1991 on loan from the owner, Mrs Phoebe Mitchell. Many of the features of the portrait, a three-quarter front, confirm the others. Once again we see Anne's strong nose, prominent lips, curly hair and large eyes. At this stage it would be premature to draw any firm conclusions from it, but it may well be the best indication we have of Anne Brontë's appearance as a young woman.

Branwell produced at least two family group portraits. The one that has been well documented is now in the National Portrait Gallery. It is considered to date from about 1835, the last occasion when all the four siblings would be together as teenagers before their departure for individual careers, and at a time when Branwell was painting a good deal in preparation for entering the Royal Academy in London. Anne appears at the extreme left of the picture, and is once again wearing a blue dress, though not the same one as in the earlier portrait, and her hair is shown as a medium brown. It is again centre-parted and curly. Her eyes are blue, and once again thoughtful, as are the eyes of the others. An article by Susan Foister in *Brontë Society Transactions* (1985) shows that Branwell sketched the girls in pencil first, then coloured his picture.[16] The original sketch lines show a straighter nose than the final picture. Anne was now fifteen, and her face seems to have filled out somewhat.

The second (because less known, but actually chronologically earlier) of Branwell's portraits is the 'gun group', first published in Horsfall Turner's *Haworth Past and Present* in 1879. In an article in *Brontë Society Transactions* (vol. 20, Part I, 1990) Juliet Barker shows how Turner's engraving came to be

produced, and successfully links it with the Greenwood tracings and the single profile of Emily, the sole remaining part of
it, which is also in the National Portrait Gallery.[17] In short,
the 'gun group' engraving is inaccurate because it was redrawn
by its engraver from a photograph of the original, of which a
copy was most astutely identified by Dr Barker in the effects
of the late Dr Mildred Christian. This she reproduces on page
9 of the article mentioned, and hence it is from this unclear
photograph supplemented by Greenwood's tracings, and not
from Turner's engraving, that we must try to obtain additional evidence of Anne's appearance in 1834, the date strongly
suggested by Greenwood's pencil note on his tracing of the
outline.[18] At fourteen, Anne is wearing a relatively low-
necked dress (to which the 'gun group' engraver has added a
collar), which may well be the same blue dress of Charlotte's
watercolour sketch. Her curly hair can be made out, again
centre-parted, and Greenwood's tracing once again shows
prominent lips and a high-bridged nose, though these attributes are invisible in the photograph. Greenwood has seemed
less interested in Anne than the other two sisters, and he seems
to have traced her dress wrongly. It is clear that the topknot in
the hairstyles of both Emily and Anne does not feature in the
original, and has been added by the engraver by analogy with
that of Charlotte, which is confirmed by the Greenwood tracing. Anne's face seems smaller in the photograph than those
of her sisters, and the engraver may be correct in suggesting
a fuller mouth than the others'.

Now that the National Portrait Gallery profile is proved to
be part of the 'gun group', its identification by Mr Nicholls as
Emily is confirmed by the pencil note on Greenwood's tracing, and Ellen Nussey's identification of the three sisters in
Turner's engraving may be set aside. There is therefore no
longer any reasonable doubt that Greenwood's identification
of Anne is correct.

Thus we now have five portraits of Anne Brontë as a
teenager, with which to compare other possible sketches.
These include a framed pencil portrait at Haworth (C 60 SB
1564–3) which is inscribed 'Annie Brontë' and is considered
to be yet another portrait by Charlotte. It was acquired by
the Brontë Society in 1950–1.[19] There is no indication as to
the date of this pencil sketch, but the clear authentication of
the other portraits now provides enough evidence to suggest

that we have a good drawing of Anne as a young woman. The high-bridged nose is characteristic, and her hair is now wavy rather than curly. Instead of looking straight ahead as on the earlier pictures, Anne now looks down, echoing Charlotte's letter of 20 January 1842, to which we shall later refer – 'Anne is so quiet, her look so downcast.'[20] A water-colour sketch, known as the 'Thorp Green' portrait, does not now seem to me to be of Anne, and I shall deal with it when we come to discuss Anne's period as governess at Thorp Green. In addition to these, there are two diary sketches by Emily, in the 1837 and 1841 diary papers. In the former, Anne's face appears round and her aspect thoughtful, but there is a hint of enthusiasm not exhibited in Charlotte's later drawing.

Anne drew many pictures herself, of which we have only a small collection left. Of these, three may be different kinds of self-identifications. They date from 1839, 1840 and about 1843 and will be mentioned in their chronological place. It needs to be made clear, however, that the first two, 'Sunrise at sea' and 'What you please', are both symbolic rather than realistic, and we cannot judge a great deal about Anne's appearance from either. However, I have now given details of no fewer than five authenticated pictures, two sketches and one probable portrait. This should give us a basis from which to deduce certain facts about Anne rather better than can be done in the case of Emily. A well-known description by Ellen Nussey may be added. It comes from her 'Reminiscences' of 1871:

> Anne, dear gentle Anne was quite different in appearance from the others, and she was her aunt's favourite. Her hair was a very pretty light brown, and fell on her neck in graceful curls. She had lovely violet-blue eyes, fine pencilled eyebrows and a clear almost transparent complexion. She still pursued her studies and especially her sewing, under the surveillance of her aunt.[21]

The final reference here is to the date Ellen is recalling, 1833. This is the date of Charlotte's first pencil sketch.

Anne Brontë, then, was well-enough looking, with attractive, violet-blue eyes and mid-brown hair, curly and quite long. She had a smooth, slender neck and (in Ellen's recollection) a clear complexion. One portrait may show a secret smile, and in another her eyes are downcast, an attitude which

[39]

may have been habitual after her teenage years, as it is confirmed by Charlotte's letter. None of the pictures shows her as tight-lipped: she is likely to be hesitantly sympathetic rather than condemning. There is an air of secrecy about the later portrait by Charlotte, and one of the self-symbolizing drawings is from the back. These harmonize well with the information conveyed by 'Olivia' in the poem written on 1 January 1840, to which we shall return, and Agnes Grey's description of herself as 'a resolute dissembler'. It will not be easy for us to reveal this shy person's character, and every use must be made of slight and apparently trivial evidence.

In 1836 we have our earliest extant poetic relic of Anne Brontë. It is a Gondal poem, the full understanding of which may always be impossible, since the background is missing. 'Lady Geralda' writes about the hopelessness of her home and that she wishes to leave it. Immediately, we are confronted with the problem of distinguishing Anne's personal feeling from the dramatic feeling of her Gondal characters. The whole tone of this poem is rather depressed, as Anne's will be during parts of her stay at Thorp Green. As she nears the end, 'Lady Geralda's' spirits lift a little, and she is able to write:

> But the world's before me now,
> Why should I despair?
> I will not spend my days in vain,
> I will not linger here.

Since this follows a stanza in which she complains that her father is long dead, her mother died more recently and her brother far away, this is not to be applied directly to Anne. But possibly the feeling of continuing to venture in the world (Anne was by this time at Roe Head) may be Anne's real attitude.

The period of Anne's adolescence, which had begun with enthusiasm under Emily's leadership, began to drag as she passed her fifteenth and sixteenth birthdays without any but pretend romance. Lady Geralda's cry is depressing, but it is not Anne's own; even so the tone of the poem may well represent Anne's staleness. At the start of her teens, Anne had been very willing to follow Emily across the moors, but there was a fundamental difference between their attitudes to Nature, shown in Anne's use of the word 'earth'. Emily's poems ring with praise of it, as though she were recreating the pagan worship of earth as mother. As we shall see later, Anne uses the 'Spirit of Earth' to represent dullness. In 'Self-communion' she cries out:

> *O earth! a rocky breast is thine –*
> *A hard soil and a cruel clime*
> *Where tender plants must droop and pine,*
> *Or alter with transforming time.*[22]

Lack of understanding was a two-way process. Emily failed to appreciate what Anne 'worshipped'; but Anne did not understand Emily's intense desire for Earth. By the time they were in their mid-teens, there must have been occasions when they returned from a 'ramble at liberty' on the moors with Emily justifiably feeling Anne was more like Edgar than Heathcliff. In any case, Anne, not dissatisfied to be a teenage girl, was looking for more conventional social outlets.

3

Roe Head

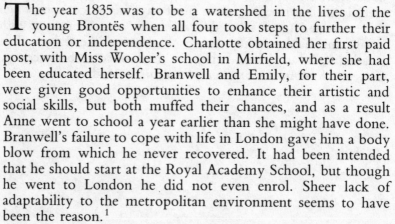

The year 1835 was to be a watershed in the lives of the young Brontës when all four took steps to further their education or independence. Charlotte obtained her first paid post, with Miss Wooler's school in Mirfield, where she had been educated herself. Branwell and Emily, for their part, were given good opportunities to enhance their artistic and social skills, but both muffed their chances, and as a result Anne went to school a year earlier than she might have done. Branwell's failure to cope with life in London gave him a body blow from which he never recovered. It had been intended that he should start at the Royal Academy School, but though he went to London he did not even enrol. Sheer lack of adaptability to the metropolitan environment seems to have been the reason.[1]

In a letter to his old friend Mrs Franks, dated June 1835, Patrick had stated his intention of keeping 'my dear little Anne' at home for a further year. Emily would go to the same school as Charlotte, but in the capacity of pupil.[2] Anne, doubtless fretful at her lack of experience, would have watched Emily leave. Though we have seen in 'Self-communion' that she did not agree with Emily in everything, she would have been sorry to see her go, and would have suppressed any jealousy that might stir in her sisterly fifteen-year old heart. Anne was waiting patiently for her own chance to come.

It came much sooner than expected. Emily, like Branwell, did not feel fit to undertake a course of tuition where she would not be free to express herself, and where she would be in the company of uncomprehending fellow-students. Psychological and physical symptoms assailed her. Charlotte became deeply worried and decided that Emily must return to Haworth as soon as possible.[3] Anne would be given the chance of an education instead. Her health was no better than Emily's, possibly worse, but she reacted differently to the need to subject herself to authority. If Emily bravely asserted in 1846 that 'No coward soul is mine', Anne proved that hers was of the same mettle during her two years at Roe Head.[4]

Charlotte had not been entirely happy during her own child-hood days at school. She had found two splendid friends in Ellen Nussey and Mary Taylor, but some of the girls were beyond her understanding. It was necessity that drove her to teach now; unlike Anne she had no desire to teach.

The regime at Roe Head was fair and disciplined, and Char-lotte would be given every help by Miss Margaret Wooler. She occupied a middle status between her and the pupils, and the evidence is that she kept her distance from Anne for most of the two years.[5] A gulf existed between the two sisters which was never quite bridged. Charlotte noticed Anne's physical condition and was alert for any sign of illness, but she did not want to enquire into her feelings, and in any case was absorbed in her own problems.[6]

Roe Head is the name of a hamlet on the northern edge of Mirfield. The school (also generally called simply 'Roe Head') was set up in a large, old house just one field away from the boundary with Mr Brontë's old parish of Hartshead-cum-Clifton. Maria herself had been christened at Hartshead church more than twenty years before. Anne must have felt that even if the area was not quite home, neither was it totally alien. She would have heard many stories about the school and its en-virons, from both Charlotte, who may have told her that there were ghosts on the unoccupied third floor, and from her father, who would have mixed the Luddites of Dewsbury and district with his Irish tales at the parsonage breakfast table. To be going to school at last would have seemed exciting to Anne, if rather unnerving. All the other young Brontës had been out in the world with mixed success. Now it was Anne's turn, and her determination is shown by her persistent return-ing to Roe Head in contrast with Emily's speedy and final withdrawal. For the next ten years she would spend much more time away from home than at Haworth; for her, as the youngest child, it was the only way she could escape the suffocation of family life.

[43]

When Charlotte wrote *Shirley* she gave this part of Kirklees a pleasing description. She laid emphasis on the rural background to the mills and occasional steelworks. Old woods surrounded Kirklees Hall, once supposed to be the haunt of Robin Hood. (His helmet was still preserved there. Anyone who tried it on would lose all his hair, as Mr Brontë's brother James proved on one of his visits.)[7] At the hamlet of Roe Head there was an inn bearing the sign of Robin Hood. But to the east and south of the small cluster of cottages, coal was king. The Misses Wooler did not own their school. The house was part of the estate of Mrs Marriott, a coal owner. In front of the house coal wagons would rumble past on their way to Huddersfield. Landed proprietors such as the Armytage (or Armitage) family would expect to gain as much from the 'mineral rights' to coal under their land as the crops above. There was hardship in the villages, leading to suppressed industrial turbulence and radical philosophy. The climate could be bitter, as the east wind roared across the Moor Top. On the surface this was a much kinder area than Haworth, but beneath this it could be bleak.

No registers have survived from Roe Head and our ideas of the school have to be built up in a variety of ways. We have no precise date for Anne's arrival, though she is thought to have been there by late October.[8] She may have reached the school by way of Hartshead Hightown, but perhaps she came up the hill from the Three Nuns inn and arrived by the main gate in the stone wall which still surrounds the school. The trees would have been shedding their leaves by then, and there were many trees close by the school house.

In front of her stood the three-storey building of which she had heard her sisters talk, set in five acres of ground. Two great bays projected from the south front. They were not part of the original house, but had certainly been added by the time Anne Brontë arrived at the school.[9] While Anne was there one bay window looked out from the schoolroom while the other seems to have been Miss Wooler's parlour.

Winifred Gerin calls this house 'rambling, roomy, solid [and] agreeable'.[10] It was certainly solid, but its accommodation was not substantial and perhaps there were no more than a dozen or so girls in residence.[11] When it was sold in 1876 it was described as having 'excellent cellarage' and 'entrance hall, dining and drawing rooms, breakfast room, library and two kitchens' on the ground floor. There were six bedrooms on the first floor with dressing rooms, but they were not very large and by 1911 had been reduced to four.[12] By this time it had long ceased to be a school, though a picture of Roe Head in an advertisement in the mid-nineteenth century shows that the Misses Hemingway ran it when the Woolers left. Probably there were some years in between when Mrs Marriott lived there herself.[13]

One might have expected that the top storey could be used as bedrooms for the girls, but from a remark Charlotte made this seems not to have been the case. Evidently the pupils slept in one or two of the first floor rooms, probably those on the north side of the house. Altogether the surface area of the house was 210 square yards, which compares with 912 at Blake Hall where later Anne would teach her first pupils.[14] In its modern form Roe Head presents a jumble of roofs and chimneys; there have been many alterations since the Brontës' time and many more pupils to be accommodated.

Part of the surrounding area was called the pleasure grounds, a term often applied to the less formal gardens belonging to a mansion.[15] These probably included the wooded walks to the east of the house where the children would exercise. One of these winding paths led to a small door through which they left on their way to Mirfield church or for walks. As the autumn skies clouded over Anne would wander here with the other girls among the young trees. She frequently used trees as metaphors for humans in her writings, and she may perhaps have seen a parallel between the growing trees and the 'great girls' around her, blown by winds which could excite but might stunt their growth.[16] Later, Blake Hall would also have 'pleasure grounds' of equal ambivalence for Anne.

Beyond the five acres of school grounds there was a cart shed, and the rate books of the later 1830s mention a dyehouse. As at Law Hill when Emily taught there, it would be a mistake to see these nineteenth-century girls' schools as untouched by the harsh world of industry. Law Hill had a working farm; Roe Head had its dyehouse and colliers' cottages, whose occupants worked at the colliery shown on the first large-scale Ordnance Survey map. In all these respects Roe Head was not unlike Haworth. It lacked the vast expanse of moorland stretching to Lancashire and bordered a soft vale, but some of the moorland enclosures were dank, with grey-brown grass a prominent feature. As at Haworth, the village houses were built of stone, by then darkened by industrial pollution. It should not be thought that the Brontë sisters' general avoidance of industrial themes (except in *Shirley*) results from a lack of acquaintance with industrial towns and villages.

It is likely that the same conveyance that brought Anne would take Emily back. Thus the erstwhile 'twins' may be assumed to have exchanged greetings as the younger supplanted the elder in exile.

Anne was to stay under Miss Margaret Wooler's guardianship for just over two years. This is a period when Charlotte's letters are particularly badly dated and muddled in printed editions. The manuscripts give some clue to their correct order, but there are many problems unsolved. In traditional biographies these facts are skated over very lightly so that the reader is not aware how much is conjecture and how many incidents treated vaguely because they cannot be dated or correctly placed. Charlotte mentions Anne very little in her letters or her 'Roe Head journal'. Two important events which present intractable problems are the removal of Ellen Nussey, Charlotte's friend, from Rydings to Brookroyd, and the removal of the school from Roe Head to Dewsbury Moor. Winifred Gerin's work therefore devotes a whole chapter to Anne Brontë's experiences at Heald's House, though it seems to me unlikely that she ever went there.

Putting together an impression of Anne's syllabus is not easy. We have some evidence relating to Charlotte's own education a few years earlier, and it seems reasonable to presume this regime was still in force. Charlotte also tells us in the 'Roe Head journal' some of the things she taught her very unwilling pupils.[17] There was certainly some ancient history, which was not exciting: it is notable that the work of the Brontës derives remarkably little from classical sources. It is possible that Miss Wooler based her curriculum on Mrs Chapone's *Letters on the Improvement of the Mind*, in which the author recommends Shakespeare's history plays, as Winifred Gerin says, because they will fix in your memory 'the reigns he has chosen more durably than any other history'. We have already encountered Miss Mangnall's *Questions* at Crofton; they were used at Roe Head also.[18]

So Anne settled into a routine that was secure if rather

boring. What her feelings were at this time can only be conjectured. Unlike Emily she was able to bring her emotions under control, and unlike Charlotte she could work at arid material without fretting greatly. At Roe Head, Anne must have formed some of the opinions on education which she would later express in her novels as well as her attitude to her own pupils. We hear nothing at all about her relations with the other girls; she brought no friend home to Haworth. She did not have a 'best friend' among them, it seems. To the others, she must have seemed very mature for her age, in some ways aloof, quiet-voiced, demure, but with an unbreakable will. To judge by the thoughts and actions of her female characters such as Helen Huntingdon, Rosalie Murray and Agnes Grey, she would have smiled ironically at times. The kind of homesickness and repressed rebellion that features in the poems may also be inferred.

The circumstances surrounding events of mid-1836 are quite well documented because a letter from Patrick has survived. Anne's godmother, Elizabeth Firth, and her husband, Revd. J. C. Franks, had invited Charlotte and Anne to stay with them at their vicarage for a week as soon as the holidays began. This was troublesome to Charlotte and probably to Anne, because they were longing to get away from Huddersfield and relax at home. So 'dear little Charlotte', as Mr Brontë called her, wrote to suggest they stayed only a few days.[19] When Patrick heard of this he was not pleased, and countermanded Charlotte's modifications. He esteemed the 'high privilege that they should be under your roof for a time', and promised to send over the gig at the end of the week, so Charlotte's plans were foiled: the two sisters stayed a whole week in Huddersfield.

The milestone on the old turnpike road at Robert Town read 'Huddersfield 5 miles', so the journey from Roe Head was rather less. This was no distance for Charlotte and Anne to walk, but if they took their baggage with them to avoid having to call back at Roe Head, they may have hired a gig or got a lift with another girl. The term ended on Friday, 17 June, and they set off that afternoon. It was a period of fine, warm weather, and they would certainly have preferred to be in Haworth. Still, leaving school must have cheered Charlotte, who was passing through a period of depression, finding teaching hard and lamenting her lack of time for imaginative

work. Sixteen-year-old Anne would have been looking forward to seeing Emily, but Mrs Franks had been a kind patron
and neither girl would want to offend her.

So they passed along the side of the Colne towards bustling
Huddersfield with its yards and its cloth hall, wearing its
recent prosperity jauntily. A major landmark, however, was
missing, and the Brontë sisters would soon be informed what
was happening and why. Mr Franks' church had been de-
molished and was in the process of being rebuilt. James Clarke
Franks had been instrumental in persuading the parishioners
that the old church was no longer good enough. By 1834 it
was being propped up on poles and the roof was delapidated.
Nonconformity had a stout hold on Huddersfield, as the fine
new Methodist and Calvinist buildings proclaimed. Franks,
however, was determined to fight back, and thus, by the time
Charlotte and Anne arrived in Kirkgate, they would be able to
see some evidence of the new church, a Perpendicular-style
building which was finished by October 1836 and exists largely unchanged today.

Huddersfield vicarage was rather less delapidated than the
old church had been. It occupied a site next to an old public
house called the Rose and Crown, which hired out chaises to
the chief families, doubtless including the Frankses.[20] The
Brontë sisters made their way there, perhaps with some ambiguous feelings about the church rebuilding. On the one hand,
as evangelicals they would approve any new enlargements
which would make the church fit to hold a larger congregation, but they also had a taste for the old and ruinous, as we
see by their reaction to Bolton Abbey on a visit which took
place in 1833. Charlotte then exhibited a correct Gothic
fervour.[21]

There is a good, extant description of the Franks' vicarage,
where Charlotte and Anne were to stay. There were two
major reception rooms downstairs, and no fewer than five
bedrooms above, together with 'another room built with brick
and covered with stone'.[22] It is certain that Charlotte would
feel gauche and ill-adapted to the social conventions as she was
greeted by Elizabeth Franks. A number of records testify to
this shyness.[23] Anne is likely to have been just as shy, or even
more so. A further ordeal awaited them as they went into the
vicarage, for in one of the downstairs rooms, 'floored with
deal' as P. Ahier tells us in the passage referred to above, they

[48]

found Charlotte's ex-school fellow, Amelia Walker of Lascelles Hall.[24] Charlotte considered Amelia a snob, but despite this the two sisters accepted an invitation to visit Lascelles Hall the following Tuesday.

The weather that weekend was hot and dry.[25] This must have inclined the Franks family to suggest walks about the town for Charlotte and Anne, and this in turn would cause Anne some physical distress as she sometimes found breathing difficult in dusty atmosphere.[26] Sunday services took place in St Paul's, now a concert hall, but in those days a new and ambitiously built church. The parish church would be reopened for worship during the first week of October. It is certain that the town rang with music during Sunday morning, since there were several very musically-oriented churches in the central streets.

The weather continued very warm, and on the Tuesday the sisters were to visit the Walkers at Lascelles. Charlotte had been at Roe Head with Amelia and her elder sister Jane: on the whole she preferred the latter. She found Amelia 'utterly spoilt by the most hideous affectation'. Charlotte knew what kind of society she was taking Anne into, and despised it.

All the evidence for the day's visit is external to Anne, but we cannot escape the attempt to understand her reactions to the experience. Charlotte's sole reference to her sister comes in her use of the plural pronoun in her letter to Ellen Nussey: '*We* spent the Tuesday at Lascelles Hall.'[27] It is quite typical of Charlotte that she says nothing whatever of her sister; her omission should be carefully observed, since it gives one clue to Charlotte's life-long attitude to Anne. She does not regard her as a companion with whom impressions can be discussed, but as an adjunct whose quiet behaviour can be taken for granted. Despite this, we can reconstruct the day quite well from external sources and Charlotte's letter.

Charlotte saw Lascelles Hall as an example of 'High Life.'[28] It is worth noting that this was Anne's first acquaintance with the kind of society she would eventually serve as a governess and discuss in her novels. We have to imagine her accompanying Charlotte and Amelia round the hall grounds, which were well shaded by plantations of trees. Later illustrations (there do not appear to be any contemporary with the visit) show clipped yews or cypresses, and there were both kitchen gardens and formal gardens. The 1841 census records six servants, two

male and four female.[29] Joseph Walker was, or had been, a
county magistrate. His son William, the 'booby', seems to
have had qualities akin to those of some of the men in Anne's
future stories.

We have to return to Charlotte's account of the day for
the surprising admission that it was 'on the whole ... very
pleasant' and that Amelia, for all her pretensions, was 'almost
enthusiastic in her professions of friendship'. It would be thirteen years before Charlotte and Anne went on another visit
together. On that occasion, Anne dutifully followed her sister
and gave the impression of supporting her.[30] Unless Charlotte's account of the present occasion wilfully suppresses
dissension with Anne, we may suppose that she too felt the
pleasantness of a warm summer day, though she would certainly be impatient to return to Emily at Haworth. There were
still three or four days to be passed at Huddersfield, during
which it may be assumed that the two sisters were shown the
cloth hall and visited the market. In her novels, Anne turns her
back on the industrial West Riding apart from Blake Hall, and
we may conclude that the experience of Lascelles Hall with its
Yorkshire gentry made more of an impression on her than the
crowds thronging the streets of Huddersfield.

At this point we must take time to explore the problems
already mentioned concerning the evidence for chronology
in Charlotte's letters to Ellen Nussey as printed in the
Shakespeare Head Brontë and other sources. As I have already
stated, I do not believe that Anne Brontë was ever a boarder at
Heald's House, where Miss Wooler's school was eventually
located, despite the fact that a whole chapter is devoted to it in
a previous biography. I have already indicated the problems in
Brontë Facts and Brontë Problems, and discovered solutions to
some of them.[31] If we are to make sense of the next eighteen
months in Anne's life, some of this discussion must be re-
capitulated here.

It needs to be pointed out that a key date in the period is
when Emily took up her post at Law Hill, near Halifax. Early
attempts to fix dates for these two years were strongly influenced by the mistaken dating of a crucial letter written by
Charlotte in which she records Emily's presence at Law Hill.
The letter was dated 1836, and when this was found to be an
error, the date was amended to 1837. This date too is incorrect; the letter is now known to have been written on 2

October 1838. Its heading, 'Dewsbury Moor', was never in dispute, but biographers had supposed that Charlotte had finally left Miss Wooler's employment earlier that year. This incorrect dating also carried the implication that Miss Wooler had moved her school to Dewsbury Moor from Roe Head between 29 May and 2 October 1837.[32]

In late 1837 Anne Brontë suffered an illness while at school to which we shall return, to discuss it in detail. Charlotte gives an account of it, rather briefly, in a letter to Ellen Nussey dated 4 January 1838.[33] Because of the misdating of the 'Law Hill' letter, the assumption has been made that Anne's illness occurred at Dewsbury Moor, but there is nothing at all in the account of the illness to indicate this. Anne's condition worried Charlotte so much that she argued with Miss Wooler, but where the argument took place is not given. However, we know from another source that Anne had a severe illness while she was at Roe Head.[34] If it had not been for the misdating of the Law Hill letter, the assumption would have been made – in my view correctly – that these two serious illnesses were one and the same and led to Anne's final departure from school. Though James la Trobe's evidence gives no date for his pastoral visit to Anne, there seems no reason to think, in the light of the re-dating of the Law Hill letter, that it was not at the end of 1837, and that Miss Wooler did not move her school to Dewsbury Moor until 1838. The move may, in fact, have been associated with the death of Mr Wooler, which took place on 20 April 1838.[35] My account of Anne at school will assume that the illness over which Charlotte worried and the illness during which la Trobe was called to see Anne at Roe Head were in fact the same.

The winter following Anne's visit to Huddersfield was most severe and there were deep snow-drifts at Haworth.[36] The old servant, Tabby, fell in the frosty street at Haworth on Thursday, 15 December. Luckily Charlotte and Anne had returned home from Roe Head the previous day and Charlotte was able to intervene to make sure Tabby was made comfortable. Anne must have been in good spirits, for she had been awarded a good conduct prize by Miss Wooler.[37] She wrote the poem, in the name of Lady Geralda already mentioned, about the 'stormy breath' of 'the wild winter wind', but it is not to be taken autobiographically. Charlotte and Anne returned to Roe Head, and on the next holiday during the summer Anne wrote the poem 'Alexander and Zenobia' which is featured in Emily's drawing on the 1837 diary paper.

But this time, the return to Roe Head does not seem to have been so happy. Events were moving Anne towards a psycho-somatic crisis, which had religious overtones. This resulted in a physical collapse, which proved to be the end of her school-ing. The evidence for the events and feelings of this term are as follows: (1) A poem written at Roe Head in October, entitled 'A voice from the dungeon'[38]; (2) Charlotte Brontë's letter of 4 January 1838; and (3) A letter from James la Trobe, Moravian pastor and later bishop, to William Scruton.[39]

We last saw Anne conversing pleasantly with her sister Emily on a fine July day, planning to walk on Haworth Moor, and writing a poem about young lovers. Her eager face looks out from Emily's sketch; she is at home and content, though it has been suggested that her imaginative interest in the lovers of her poem will not be sufficient to satisfy her for long. By the time she comes to write 'A Voice from the Dungeon' she sees herself, in the role of Maria Sabia, back in the summer:

> *The sun shone forth with cheering ray,*
> *Methought a little lovely child*
> *Looked up into my face and smiled.*
>
> *My heart was full, I wept for joy,*
> *It was my own, my darling boy;*
> *I clasped him to my breast and he*
> *Kissed me and laughed in childish glee.*

This vision is, however, as 'Marina' makes clear, a dream. She is, in fact, incarcerated for ever, and has 'done with life'. The child's father, too, appears in the dream, but Anne writes:

> *I gazed at him; I could not speak . . .*

In view of what Charlotte says about Anne's difficulty in verbal expression it seems that this nightmare may be an indication, voiced by Marina, of one of Anne's major worries.[40] Now almost eighteen, Anne found it hard to talk freely, though to judge by the reported conversation in the 1837 diary paper, she was happy enough talking to Emily.

At some point very soon, possibly while writing this poem,

Anne was ill in bed. Charlotte describes her symptoms as 'pain' and 'difficulty of breathing' the latter being assumed to be a symptom of asthma. The nature of this illness seems to be reflected in the poem where Marina talks of being unable to speak and gazing at the child's father 'in silent ecstasy'. In view of this, it may also be possible to extrapolate from the poem the suggestion that Anne was at a low ebb in October anyway, and may have thought of her school as a dungeon. Writing a year later at Law Hill, Emily employs the same metaphor.

The 'darling boy' of this October poem is paralleled by several drawings of babies made between August and November 1837. We have three examples.[41] All the children are naked, cherubic and have curly hair; they may all be the same subject. It is quite uncertain whether they are from a copy book or real life, though the differing dates of August and November suggest a picture book intermittently pored over. There is something idealized about the pictures which makes one inclined to see them as dream babies rather than real. We recall that Anne allows her heroine Agnes Grey to dream of the delight of teaching children before she encounters real ones at Wellwood House.

Though up to now these pictures of cherubic children have been neglected by biographers, it is interesting that Anne should draw them at this time, just before falling ill and at the same time as the 'Marina' poem was written. All these artistic expressions follow the romantic poem of the summer holidays; it seems that Anne must have followed it to its logical conclusion – typically for her – and seen that the imagined love must lead to imagined babies.

The next witness to her state is James la Trobe. He told Scruton that she was suffering from 'a severe attack of gastric fever which brought her very low, and her voice was only a whisper; her life hung on a narrow thread.' The two symptoms to which Charlotte alludes are thus confirmed: Anne suffered pain, which la Trobe locates in her stomach, and she could hardly talk. When we add these symptoms to the word picture of Anne as a child, looking at cakes but not touching them, and the pen portraits of the serious-faced teenager, with Charlotte's later pencil sketch of Anne with downcast eyes, we may well see this illness as a psychic crisis during which Anne subconsciously understood her feminine role as producer of children, and was both attracted and paralysed by it.

[53]

It is not clear why she should call for a Moravian minister rather than an Anglican. Anne's view of the Anglican clergy may be stated later in the character of Mr Hatfield in *Agnes Grey* and perhaps she felt more confident in approaching a Moravian, whose beliefs could be expected to approximate to those of her Wesleyan aunt. She had certainly passed Wellhouse, la Trobe's chapel, on many occasions on her way to Mirfield church with the other Roe Head girls. It must be recalled that Anne had tried to share her views with Emily, and according to 'Self-communion' had failed. Charlotte had been through her own recent difficulties, none of them shared with Anne. But Anne had to find a way out of her current dilemma, and her call for a clergyman would be a call to be allowed to confess and for guidance.

The need for emotional relief was expressing itself as a need for spiritual direction, and we may perhaps think that the reputation of la Trobe, whom she did not know personally, encouraged her to believe that she could talk openly with him on matters she found difficult. The third of the series of cherubic children, dating from December 1837, must have been drawn very shortly before la Trobe's visit. He was, he says, happy to attend Roe Head, 'where a Christian influence pervaded the establishment and its discipline', and was soon shown in to the patient, presumably in one of the first floor bedrooms.

Anne's voice was 'only a whisper'. According to Charlotte, Anne rarely said anything at all, as we have seen. However, perhaps Charlotte did not know Anne well enough for 'She soon got over the shyness natural at seeing a perfect stranger', says la Trobe. From that point on, the two seem to have conversed almost as equals, the thirty-three-year-old theologian who would one day be a bishop, and the insignificant but 'interesting' seventeen-year-old who would one day be a thoughtful novelist. In conversation, as well as on paper, she weighed her words. On this occasion, however, she seems to have found her voice quite quickly. La Trobe visited her more than once, though we don't know how often. He discussed the Bible with her and found her 'very well acquainted with the main truths of the Bible respecting our salvation', but evidently Anne saw Bible precept as a series of requirements rather than 'God's gift in His Son'. Her heart, however, 'opened to the sweet views of salvation, pardon and peace . . . and welcome to the weary and heavy laden sinner, conscious more of her not loving the Lord her God than of acts of Enmity to Him'.

For the evangelical Anne, this encounter may have provided a conversion experience, after which she could discard her theological worry. A good deal of the poetry of the next decade shows that she remained depressed, but la Trobe may well have provided a basis for her gradual physical and psychological restoration. For so warm-hearted a person, Anne's life at this time strikes one as remarkably friendless, and it would not be surprising if she greatly enjoyed these conversations with the young clergyman. It is worth noting that her first attempt to earn her own living in sixteen months from this occasion was to take her back to la Trobe's territory, though there is no record that they ever met again.

Nevertheless, if la Trobe had provided the turning point, it took some time for Anne's physical health to improve, and Charlotte became very alarmed. 'I looked upon her case in a different light to what I could wish or expect any uninterested person to view it.'[42] She remonstrated with Miss Wooler and the result was that Mr Brontë called the two girls home; in his mind as well as Charlotte's there was evidently the memory of the Cowan Bridge tragedy. Anne was out of danger by 4 January, but 'still requires a great deal of care'. Part of the therapy seems to have been immersion in Gondal, but the first of two poems written in January 1838 almost recapitulates the scenes of Marina's troubled dream. This time 'Alexandrina Zenobia' imagines the change in her lover, while she is held captive in a 'dark dungeon':

> *I struggled wildly but it was in vain,*
> *I could not rise from my dark dungeon floor,*
> *And the dear name I vainly strove to speak,*
> *Died in a voiceless whisper on my tongue.*

Like Anne's, looking up from her bed at la Trobe, Alexandrina's voice was 'only a whisper'.

In the second of the two poems Alexandrina converses with the north wind, thundering round her cell. The wind tells her that

The sweet world is not changed but thou
Art pining in a dungeon now
Where thou must ever be;
No voice but mine can reach thine ear,
And Heaven has kindly sent me here
To mourn and sigh with thee,
And tell thee of the cherished land
Of thy nativity.

Anne Brontë, who had reached the point of wishing for her own babies, has recoiled in confusion and tried to retrace her steps to her own childhood. Only a supernatural comforter can help. It would be more than a year before she could feel strong enough to brave the world again.

4

Disaster and Sunrise

It was often Anne Brontë's lot in life to step in where her sister Emily had failed. She had earlier taken her place at Roe Head, and later would write a novel dealing with topics Emily had, in Anne's eyes, handled misleadingly in *Wuthering Heights*. Emily had tried to be a teacher at Law Hill, struggled for some months with moderate success, returned (it seems) for a second term, but by early 1839 was back at Haworth, her patience exhausted. It was for Anne to fill the financial gap, leaving Emily to compose poetry to her heart's content.

'All true histories contain instruction,' *Agnes Grey* begins. The word 'true' has led to problems for biographers trying to write about this and subsequent periods of Anne's life. It is quite clear that Anne, writing through the pen of Agnes, a fictional heroine, does not intend us to suppose that the events of Agnes's life correspond in any literal way with those of her creator. There are close similarities at times, especially similarity of tone, but it is quite unsafe to suppose that what Agnes records is exactly what Anne did. In dealing with Anne's new venture, we shall begin by leaving the novel largely out of account.

It looks as if plans for Anne to go out as a governess may have overlapped with Emily's stay at Law Hill, for Charlotte mentions them as early as 12 March 1839.[1] Her letter suggests that there had been some difficulty in negotiating an appointment, but 'unless some further causes of delay' should occur, Anne would leave on 8 April. This she seems to have done, and had been some days away from Haworth when Emily, in the guise of R. Gleneden, wrote a mournful poem about the 'one absent' from the family hearth.[2]

[57]

This first venture of Anne's into the world of earning a living was made quite easy because she was to go back to Mirfield, the world of la Trobe and the Atkinsons. Reverend Thomas Atkinson, Charlotte's godfather, still lived at 'Green House', where perhaps Anne had visited during her time at Roe Head. Blake Hall was, so far as anyone knew, a godly house and should be welcoming to Anne. She need not be lonely there, as she could still meet some of those with whom she had been at school, and her father's old friends from Hartshead-cum-Clifton days were not far away. The Ingham family of Blake Hall had actually played a part in financing the foundation of la Trobe's meeting house at Wellhouse.

Some excellent research has been done on Blake Hall by John Nussey, Susan Brooke and others. I am basing my description of the grounds at the Hall largely on articles by Mr Nussay, whose help I acknowledge with gratitude. Susan Brooke's work has appeared in the *Brontë Society Transactions*. She was the granddaughter of a sister of one of Anne's pupils, and recorded some of the stories she heard from her grandmother.[3] There is no question of the authenticity of these stories and I have been able to supplement these sources by reference to Mirfield rate books and the 1841 census.

Anne's employer was Joshua Ingham, the third of that name, who was a local squire, magistrate and businessman. He was the inheritor of a Puritan and patriarchal tradition in which women were thought of as wholly subordinate. One of Joshua Ingham's daughters told how she was looking in a mirror at her ringlets one day. Her father, catching sight of her through an open door, cut off all her hair to punish her vanity. According to Susan Brooke, the same girl was so frightened of her father that when he appeared and stood motionless at the top of the stairs, she fell down and injured her back. Joshua would not let his girls go into shops; their clothes were supplied by a Huddersfield draper, who came out to Blake Hall when needed.

This tyrannical behaviour very much interfered with the liberty of the girls in the house. For example, they had to brush their hair for an hour every day, but without admiring the result. They were not allowed hand mirrors or perfume. Some of the older females revolted against such repression. Aunt Hannah Taylor, for example, kept up a feud with Joshua over church matters. She sought to curb his pleasures, which included breeding horses, by leaving evangelical tracts round the house.[4]

Mrs Mary Ingham, in the face of such cruelty, remained calm and mild. Charlotte told Ellen Nussey that she was 'extremely kind' to Anne when she arrived.[5] This was an initial impression, but it was still being maintained nine months later, when Ellen was told of Mary Ingham's 'mild, placid' nature. Evidently she was too mild to counter the delinquency of her children, of whom the two eldest, Cunliffe, aged seven, and Mary, aged five, Anne was to be in charge. By 1841 Cunliffe had been sent away to school. We may assume that Joshua had not intended to leave him at the whim of mother or governess for long. If he was to be brought up like his father, he would need to be placed in a much more male-oriented environment than the house could provide.

Blake Hall was a fine, imposing, stone-built mansion. It was not 'new' (like the Bloomfields' house in *Agnes Grey*) but had been rebuilt as long ago as 1747. Its southern aspect was well proportioned, looking out across parkland to the Dewsbury and Huddersfield road. It was approached by two carriage drives and there was a third entrance from the steep hill to the north, below Mirfield church. Some aspects of the house find their way into both *Agnes Grey* and *Wildfell Hall*; it was here that Anne first began to understand the lives and tensions of wealthy families, though she was perhaps never much concerned with the sources of their wealth.

Though the 1841 census was taken about eighteen months after Anne Brontë left, it sheds some light on the Blake Hall staff. Most important was William Partridge, the Grasmere-born gardener, living in the 'garden house'. He was a great innovator, who spent more than twenty years at Blake Hall, and the 'splendid dahlias' and 'other fine flowers' at Wellwood House in *Agnes Grey* may reflect his care for Mr Ingham's garden.[6] The Blake Hall gardens were always carefully tended; Anne would surely have gained some pleasure in looking at them that summer through the midst of her troubles. The porter at the lodge during Anne's time was Henry Peacock, said to be 62 in the 1841 census, and rated in the 1838 valuation for a cottage called the porter's lodge. The census records three male and two female servants, as well as a new governess, Mary Sugden.

Blake Hall's grounds covered over 64 acres altogether and in

[59]

Anne's time they were retained as the home estate, supervised personally by Joshua Ingham. By 1848, under the pressure of financial recession, he had let some of the fields to various tenants. The gardens and pleasure grounds extended to over 3 acres and the valuation mentions, as well as the gardener's house for William Partridge, the vinery, peach houses, stable, coach houses, barn and sheds. In 1848 there was a brewhouse, a wash house and a laundry, 52 square yards in area. There were also an orchard and two kitchen gardens. All this fine land gave a suitable impression, but its ownership depended on cut-throat commercial competition.[7] Financial fluctuations must have been partly responsible for Joshua Ingham's livid ill-temper.

In the house, the servants worked feverishly to clean the brass and silver. There were seventeenth-century oak chests which had been in the family before the front of the house had been rebuilt, and crimson carpets. The fine sitting room had tall bookcases, filled with leather-bound volumes and Chelsea china figures. It is doubtful whether Anne had permission or time to read any of these old books. The dining room had no curtains: oak shutters could be closed at night and there was a china cabinet with a dessert service, decorated with hunting scenes. On the walls were portraits of the Inghams and a stormy landscape near the window. Upstairs the rooms were similarly well appointed; one drawing room had a large blue-tiled fireplace, gold brocade curtains and chairs covered with *petit-point* embroidery.[8]

Two stories about the behaviour of Anne's pupils have survived independently of anything which may be deduced from *Agnes Grey*. Susan Brooke describes how some South American cloaks were one day received as a present. They were bright red and attracted the children at once. They put them on and ran screaming into the park, claiming to be devils and refusing to come back to do their lessons. Anne could not get them back, and eventually went off in tears to Mrs Ingham. The other story shows Anne unnerved at the results of such boisterousness. It is said that she tied the children to a table leg in order to get on with her own writing. In old age, Mrs Ingham described her as a 'very unsuitable governess'. If she really did tether the children, this is one of the few instances we have of fury in Anne, comparable to the anger both Patrick and Emily could exhibit. One may also ask what

Anne was writing. There is no poetry recorded from 1839 and no sign of any novel yet. As in Thorp Green later, I should not be surprised to discover that Anne kept some kind of journal or diary which she used in *Agnes Grey*.

Mary Ingham, Anne's pupil, grew up to be an eccentric woman, whose name was not mentioned to the younger members of the family. She is said to have been very dark and beautiful, but never married; she died in 1922. Cunliffe also grew up to be very determined, not to be beaten or gainsaid. He did not live at Blake Hall as an adult, but there is a story of a quarrel he had with a neighbour when the new church was being built in 1871. Cunliffe caused a memorial inscription to be altered so as to record his involvement and snub the other benefactor, Joseph Lee of Shillbank. The living of Mirfield church had been in the hands of the Ingham family for some time. These two obstinate adults had once been Anne Brontë's pupils; perhaps it is not surprising that teaching failed to come up to her expectations as a career.[9]

When Anne went to Mirfield church she would presumably have left by the north gate entering Pinfold Lane near the old rectory and walking up the sharp rise to the church along the side of the wood which still stands. Many of the faces glancing over the tops of the pews would be well known to her from her Roe Head days, and there may sometimes have been girls she knew. Edward Carter, whom Anne had met while she had been at school, had now been replaced by Reverend Ralph Maude. He had been presented to the living as long ago as 1827, but had suffered a severe spinal injury and was unable to take up residence at Mirfield. Now he was in full charge, planning to expand the church's activity in the area by building several new churches. The 1841 census shows him living in the vicarage house at Town Gate, looked after by his housekeeper Martha Waterhouse and a young maid. He was the only clergyman whose sermons Anne heard who remained unmarried. He may possibly have contributed to her portrait of Mr Hatfield, though an alternative model will be suggested later.[10]

Some of the background discussed here undoubtedly makes its appearance in *Agnes Grey*. The ages of the four children at Wellwood House mirror exactly the ages of the Ingham children. Cunliffe is the same age as Tom, Mary Ann is 'Mary', Martha at Blake Hall is Fanny in *Agnes Grey* and Emily is

Harriet. This similarity cannot be coincidence, and it must be a possibility that some of the incidents related in the novel really happened. One would not be surprised to find that the cussed and spiteful Cunliffe really did torture birds in his childhood, or that all the children went dabbling in the dirtiest parts of the garden just when dinner was ready. Joshua may well have made a rare intervention, and the nurse, 'Betty', to whom Agnes turns for support, may be Elizabeth Crowther, one of the names from the 1841 census.[11]

It is unknown when or why Anne left Blake Hall. It may have been as a result of the 'tying the children to the table' episode, since that is what stuck in Mary Ingham's memory. There is no doubt that *Agnes Grey* reflects Anne's deep disquiet at facing unruly 'desperate little dunces', as Charlotte called them.[12] A strong believer in authority, but too inexperienced to know how to use it, Anne may have reached desperation quite quickly. In these cricumstances it would have been difficult for her good qualities as an educator to be discovered, and no progress could be made. Thus, whether she was dismissed or resigned, she must have left Mirfield, her 'Wellwood' – the promised land near Wellhouse – with a sense of humiliation and disappointment.

But when she reached home there was a new circumstance, which turned out to be a delight. William Weightman, Mr Brontë's new curate, had arrived in mid-August (he first signed the register on 19 August); and he was to prove an exception to the general run of Haworth curates in many ways. How far Anne allowed her feelings towards him to develop has been hotly disputed, and this question has become confused with another one – the degree to which he is represented in *Agnes Grey* in the personality of Edward Weston.

To find some guidance in answering these questions, it will be necessary to anticipate Anne's history and move straight to a letter written by Charlotte to her friend Ellen Nussey, and dated 20 January 1842:

> Your darling 'his young reverence' as you tenderly call him – is looking delicate and pale – poor thing, don't you pity him? I do, from my heart – when he is fat and jovial I never think of him – but when anything ails him I am always sorry – He sits opposite Anne at church sighing softly and looking out of the corners of his eyes to win

her attention – and Anne is so quiet, her look so downcast – *they are a picture.* (My Italics)[13]

This is Charlotte's view of two of the congregation as they sat
in the vicarage box pew on a Sunday (presumably 16 January
1842), a pew where these two, with others, had sat on many
occasions between 1839 and that January. Anne is modest,
Weightman trying to attract her; Charlotte sees that both are
conscious of each other. She does not consider it necessary to
enlarge on the situation to her friend, so we must assume that
Ellen would not have found the link between Anne and Weightman particularly surprising.

Already Weightman is said to look ill. Eight months later he
was dead. A few weeks later still, we find Anne writing a
lament for an unnamed man who has just died. His life is
likened to sunrise 'athwart the glittering main'.[14] The poem
was omitted from all collections until the 1950s; Charlotte had
begun the process of ignoring it though perhaps the word
'suppressing' is too strong. There is no case for considering it a
Gondal poem. Its subject is a real young man, and it fits into a
series of 'love' poems, though the love is mildly expressed and
opportunities for possessiveness are deliberately rejected. The
man about whom the poems are written has some constant
characteristics: a sunny smile, a light heart, a voice (silenced at
last), and he is buried in the old church. The reader will make
up his or her mind as to who is the subject of this series:
but did *two* young men whom Anne knew well enough to
romanticize both die in late 1842? It seems to me that all the
circumstantial evidence fits William Weightman and no one
else.

The first of the poem series is dated 1 January 1840, as
though by a new year resolution.[15] This poem, 'Maiden, thou
wert thoughtless once', describes a change in attitude that has
come over a young girl, ostensibly a Gondal heroine (but her
name is not found elsewhere in Emily's poems or Anne's).
Once, this girl was careless of her appearance but now she
keeps on smoothing her 'hazel' hair. She takes pains over her
dress and loves to sit at the piano playing over and over again
a few simple tunes.

Why does 'Olivia Vernon' do this? She tells her inquisitor
that she has grown up. Each year new feelings are apparent.
'Olivia' then adds to herself and her friends that she is glad no

one can see into her heart. Many young people exhibit their feelings in their faces, but not she. You might gaze on her face 'for hours' and not realize how her emotions change from 'joy to bitter woe' according to the presence or absence of a young man. 'Last night', for example, the family group was sitting round the fire when she heard the footsteps of 'one well known to me'. The man, however, did not come into the room, and Olivia records her anguish and her 'bitter, aching woe'. The vocabulary is strong enough for Emily.

This poem, written a few weeks after her return from Blake Hall, constitutes a great change in Anne's style of writing and tone. The self-analysis in it is evident. It plainly records the arrival of a person who can excite in her feelings of sexual attraction and makes her realize that childhood is past. She is almost twenty. The scenario of the poem, a family group chatting pleasantly round the fire on a winter evening, sets this at Haworth, 'Olivia' notwithstanding.

About six weeks before, Anne had drawn an allegorical picture unfortunately untitled, but strongly reminding us of the poem written after Weightman's death in which a young man's life is likened to sunrise on the sea.[16] The drawing, dated 13 November 1839, shows a girl or young woman staring out to sea, her eyes shaded against the intense light of the sun which appears to be rising there. (It could possibly be *setting*, but the individually drawn rays suggest *rising*: sunsets are more often diffused patches of light.) The girl has a hand-kerchief in her left hand; she is obviously going to greet someone, and there does appear to be a tiny sail across the water.

The significance of this picture and one or two later ones requires consideration. Both in *Jane Eyre* and *Wildfell Hall* the Brontë sisters give a strong indication that they understand painting and drawing to have symbolic content. Jane shows Rochester her strongly metaphorical pictures soon after she reaches Thornfield. In *Wildfell Hall* Arthur Huntingdon comes across Helen painting a vivid landscape in which two turtle doves are sitting in a 'brilliant golden green' tree and being watched by a 'young girl who was kneeling on the daisy-spangled turf with head thrown back and masses of fair hair falling on her shoulders, her hands clasped, lips parted, and eyes intently gazing upward in pleased yet earnest contempla-tion of those feathered lovers.'[17]

Huntingdon wishes to lay the symbolism totally open. 'Sweet innocent!' he comments, 'she's thinking there will come a time when she will be wooed and won like that pretty hen-dove by as fond and fervent a lover . . .' He also embarrassingly teases Helen for not giving the young girl black hair, her own colouring. The picture lets the reader, and Huntingdon, know how Helen feels. It is minutely described, and one would not be surprised to find that Anne had drawn such a picture herself, as the 'large forest tree' appears in several sketches of hers. The point to grasp is that she knew perfectly well the technique and value of pictorial metaphor, so that when we look at 'Sunrise at sea' our interpretation may legitimately follow that of Helen's painting in *Wildfell Hall*. Of course, elements of the sunrise picture may have been drawn from a copy-book, but it seems as though the Brontës had learnt to compose allegories in their pictures after the manner of Hoffmann and other German Romantics.

In particular, a comparison might be drawn between Anne Brontë's allegories, particularly this one, and several paintings by Carl David Friedrich (1774–1840). 'Morning Light', for example, shows a silhouetted woman, rear view, holding out her hands in salutation to the dawn, which is breaking over distant mountains. Once again we have a single figure, whose concentration is on the far distance, though the sun is not yet visible in Friedrich's picture, and the whole tone is more solemn than that of Anne's. A later painting by Friedrich is entitled 'Moonrise over the Sea', and features three grouped figures, two female and one male, sitting on a rock not unlike that in Anne's picture and gazing out at a mysterious moonrise. Like Anne's girl the figures are pictured from a three-quarters rear view. Carl Gustav Carus (1789–1869) wrote that it was often very effective to introduce figures into a landscape painting because 'a lonely figure lost in contemplation of the silent scene will prompt the spectator to think himself in his place'.[18] To which it might be added that the lonely figure could, and in the case of Anne's picture surely does, represent the artist, and the emotional content of the painting relates very closely, in a symbolic way, to her.[19]

The girl in the drawing is more like Anne Brontë than Helen's young girl is like her. We can hardly see the girl's face, but her hair is in the ringlets that Anne sometimes wore. She is waving to a new element in her life. The sun is rising as she

[65]

peers across the sea, and although Anne had not yet seen
the actual sea she would grow to love it. As in Yeats' poem,
she sees the sea-shore as portraying potential and the sea, life
itself.[20] The sun represents the new warming force in her life;
exactly the same symbol is to be used in the poem written in
December 1842 after Weightman has died. Thus Anne's actual
experience of William Weightman opens with a drawing of
sunrise and closes with a poem in which a young man's life is
likened to sunrise.

Between November 1839 and January 1840 the subject
matter of the allegorical picture has been stripped of its metaphor and can be written with nothing but a Gondal name to
cover it. Though we cannot prove that both these reproduce
Anne's feeling about Weightman, there are too many coinci-
dences here for us to believe anything else. There simply is no
other young man whose influence over Anne grew between
November 1839 and January 1840, who died in late 1842, and
was coupled with Anne in Charlotte's mind in January 1842. It
may fairly be stated that Anne was powerfully attracted to
William Weightman. There is a good deal to be written about
that young man.

William's grandfather, Walter Weightman (the family name
is given with various spellings in various documents) was born
at Kirkby Thore, north-west of Appleby, Westmorland, about
1738. On 22 November 1777 he married Margaret Jack-
son, spinster, aged 21, at her parish of Penrith. Their first
child, Jane, was baptized on 5 April 1778 at Penrith. William
Weightman senior was baptized the son of Walter and Margaret
at Penrith on 9 November 1783 when Walter was described
as 'husbandman'. The social standing of William Weightman
and his forebears is illuminated by this. William grew up and
moved to Appleby where he became a brewer, perhaps also
carrying on other trades in food supply. He married Hannah
Topham at Penrith on 19 February 1810. William, later to
become curate of Haworth, was christened on 29 May 1814,
and was the second in the family, the eldest being a girl, Mary.
Their brother Robert was baptized on 17 March 1816. William
became a pupil at Appleby grammar school.[21]

There is some mystery about how long he stayed at school,
since he is said to have entered Durham University 'from
school', though by this time, 21 October 1837, he was twenty-
three. He took the course for a Licentiate in Theology, re-

maining at University College from Michaelmas 1837 until summer 1839. There was not a great deal of classics included in the course, though William would later gain a reputation as a classicist. Tradition says that William Weightman was an MA, but this cannot be right, as he would have been allowed remission on his licentiate if he had been so.[22]

While Anne had been at Blake Hall Mr Brontë had been seeking a curate, and by June the negotiations had reached the point where William Weightman could give notice at St Mary-le-Bow church in Durham that he intended to offer himself for ordination. The licence was granted on 19 June, and term ended at Durham that day. He could now practise as a curate, but would need a further process to become fully ordained. This would take place a year later, and we have both Charlotte's view of it and the official record.

By August 1839 William has arrived at Haworth, when we have presumed that Anne was still at Blake Hall. He makes many subsequent appearances in Charlotte's letters to Ellen Nussey, though precise dating of these letters is sometimes in dispute. It appears that Weightman quickly became a favourite at Haworth, pleasant to all, and certainly not thought of by Charlotte as in any way particularly interested in Anne. Her enthusiasm for him at this point was secret. It seems fairly certain that the new curate soon announced that he was engaged to a certain Agnes Walton of Crackenthorpe near Appleby. Charlotte tried to draw a picture of her for him and thought she saw delight at her attempts. Actually, however, 'his reverence' (as he was humorously called) may have been laughing up his sleeve. Agnes would almost certainly have been very surprised if she had known Weightman was claiming to be engaged to her and her family might have been alarmed. We can discover a certain amount about Agnes, who was just one month younger than Anne. The Walton family came from a higher social stratum than the brewers of Appleby. An elder sister had been born in London and their father, John Walton, was described in directories as 'gentleman'. After Weightman's death Agnes married a prosperous farmer, and was in Islington, London, for the birth of her first child. William Weightman is likely to have met and proved attractive to Agnes Walton, but whether her family would have agreed to an engagement is doubtful.[23]

We can, however, notice the superficial similarity between

[67]

the names Agnes and Anne. As the flirtatious William paid court that winter to dumpy Charlotte, lanky Emily, bland Ellen Nussey and dissembling Anne, who was later to use the name Agnes for her novelistic self-identification, it would not be surprising if he preferred Anne. We naturally look to Charlotte's letters at this time to see what early impression William made. Some of them are hard to date, but one dated 17 March 1840 provides an interesting account of his activities. By this time, it appears that Ellen had been to stay at Haworth (she had been invited in January, but had apparently not been able to come before February). In the letter Charlotte is in a teasing mood, scolding Ellen for telling their mutual friend Martha Taylor some gossipy details which Charlotte had wanted to keep secret. Just what these details were we do not know, but they do seem to have something to do with Weightman since in the midst of her scolding Charlotte retracts and tells Ellen to go straight to Martha and tell her everything, including the valentines they have all received from him.[24]

It seems, then, that the censored stories concerned Weightman and the events of Ellen's visit. We learn that by now he had earned himself a female name, Celia Amelia. (Another barrier against emotional attachments, along with Agnes Walton.) 'Celia Amelia' had his portrait painted by Charlotte during Ellen's visit. The valentines had been sent, mysteriously, from Bradford. Weightman had given a lecture at the Mechanics' Institute in Keighley on the value of a Classical Education, to which all the four girls had gone, returning to Haworth at midnight. At some point Anne caught a cold, and was still not better by 17 March, when Charlotte also had caught cold. Charlotte also mentions William's pride in his academic gown, as he pointed out its adornments and material to the admiring young women.

A certain amount can be added to these bare facts but some mysteries remain. For example, that there were four valentines, no one doubts. But Charlotte records the wording of only three: 'Fair Ellen, Fair Ellen', 'Away, fond Love' and 'Soul divine'. 'Fair Ellen' must have been written to Charlotte's friend. 'Soul divine' could be Emily's, if Weightman was sharp enough to understand her preoccupations, as he may well have been. But what about 'fond Love'? For whom was this written and why was the 'Love' bidden to go away?

Does 'fond' mean 'dear' or 'foolish'? There are two ways of approaching the mystery, though they yield no firm answers.

It may be that in writing to Ellen, Charlotte might modestly omit the valentine she herself received. In this case 'Away, fond Love' was written to Anne. Alternatively, Anne may have removed her own valentine, and Charlotte could not remember it. If 'Away, fond Love' *was* Anne's, this may imply that her going to Thorp Green was being regotiated by February 1840, and it had already been settled that she would be leaving. Later in the letter to her friend, Charlotte seems to be trying to fan a spark of interest in the curate on Ellen's part. But if Weightman, even jokingly, was calling Anne 'fond Love' Charlotte might well be concerned to divert everyone's attention from this.[25] As we have seen, on Anne's side there was some feeling for the curate, and if she did receive a warmly worded valentine from him, it would have been hard for her to disregard it.

It has been impossible so far to discover which newspaper Charlotte sent to Ellen a little before this, containing a 'notice of "her" [Weightman's] lecture at Keighley.' The lecture was pronounced 'very good' and this verdict says a good deal for Weightman's communication skills since he was not a classical scholar. Ellen remembered the return of the lecture party at midnight, accompanied by the Rector of Keighley, and how Aunt Elizabeth lost her temper when she found she was two cups of coffee short. On the walk back there were four girls and two gentlemen; it would be interesting to know how they paired off during that four-mile walk and whether anything particular was said to Anne. In later years, February often seems to have been a good month for her, and though this fact may have nothing to do with this walk back from Keighley, there may be a causal link.

Anne Brontë's relations with William Weightman, if we could only trace them, might illuminate our understanding of the thought behind *Wildfell Hall* rather than *Agnes Grey*. But whatever they had been or were going to be, they were now to be interrupted. Somehow – and it may even have been through Weightman, with his links with Durham – she had obtained a post in the house of a daughter of Thomas Gisborne, the Prebendary of Durham. It may well have suited Charlotte for Anne to be leaving. Ellen, on her return to

Birstall, wrote that she was considering marriage to a Mr Vincent. Emily was not interested in marriage. As Weightman's fickle reputation became clearer, Charlotte may have wished to protect her young sister from heartbreak, though 'Olivia Vernon's' strong and secret poem shows she was too late. Once Anne was away, Charlotte encouraged the curate to think of Agnes Walton and noted his interest in Caroline Dury of Keighley. Any danger to Anne's feelings, she may well have thought, was over.

5
Thorp Green, 1840

———✦———

The next five years were to prove exceedingly influential in setting the tone for Anne's literary career. These years have been underestimated and even diminished in length by biographers, though there was nothing comparable to them in the lives of Charlotte, Emily or Branwell. Anne would get to know the area gradually; we must not confuse her feelings in 1840, when she was newly arrived, with her comments in the 1841 diary paper, or again those in the 1845 diary paper. In most accounts there has been no room for the wide variations of experience and fluctuations of feeling that Anne encountered in these years; they were a lifetime of learning and should not be telescoped. In each of the five years Anne was with her sisters for about five or six weeks and with the Robinsons the rest of the year. A profound change was effected, as was almost inevitable. Emily could be seen objectively; Gondal viewed at a distance. The element of realism Anne so strove for became imperative to her at Thorp Green; her two novels are thus worlds away from Emily's and even Charlotte's.

She probably went to Thorp Green (nowadays often spelt Thorpe) on Friday, 8 May 1840, a mild, overcast day with light flurries of rain in the offing.[1] The youngest of Anne's pupils, Mary, had not long ago celebrated her birthday; she was born, according to George Whitehead's register, on 21 March 1828,[2] and was therefore twelve. It may have been this birthday that had caused Mrs Robinson to look for a governess, and if so one can understand that the reluctant friendship that grew between Anne and her young pupil had a special basis; it was because of Mary that Anne was at Thorp Green.

However, there were two other girls for Anne to teach in 1840: Lydia, who had almost reached the age of fifteen and Elizabeth, thirteen. In addition, it seems that she was expected to tutor Edmund, aged eight. Almost three years later he would be entrusted to Branwell. A fourth Robinson sister, Georgiana, was still a baby. A few certain facts about the Robinsons are known and we shall deduce more. But here once again we need to remind ourselves to set aside the novels as sources of biographical information for the time being. Of course, Anne Brontë used her life to build the stories of these books, but they should not be taken autobiographically without great caution. As with Blake Hall, Thorp Green will need to be looked at in the light of external source material, of which there is more than is often realized. At times we shall need to delineate the locality in some detail from this material in order to set this against the fictional description in the novels and to help to fill in background which we cannot gather from Anne herself, because of the absence of any directly autobiographical writing.

There was certainly no snow the day Anne Brontë went to Thorp Green, unlike Agnes Grey's arrival at Horton Lodge. The approach to Thorp Green was not by a private road and there would be no lodge-keeper to unfasten the gate for the impressive drive to the mansion. (It seems possible that here and elsewhere in *Agnes Grey* Anne was using some of the characteristics of Kirby Hall, the neighbouring property at Ouseburn.) Anne would have arrived at Thorp Green Hall up Score Ray Lane from the main road, crossing the little beck at the sharp bend and passing the dark windbreak on the right. On the left was part of the park, but Anne would not be looking at this for long before she turned up the short carriage drive and came to a halt in front of the portico of Thorp Green Hall.

This was altogether flatter and less exciting country than at Blake Hall. Anne would soon discover that the mansion had extensive views from its upper windows, and walking about the fields would be easy, with no steep hills such as the one that led up to the church from the rear gates at Mirfield. The Vale of York, with its lush watermeadows, forms the background to the second half of *Agnes Grey*, and some characteristics of the Ouseburn district are transferred in detail to the novel. Anne's new home was not built of stone like the houses in the Pennine country, but of the typical pink and yellow brick which can still be seen so frequently in the area. Entering the stone and plaster portico, she would find herself in a spacious entrance hall, with stairs ahead and a long rear window not unlike that at Haworth parsonage. Thorp Green Hall had, in fact, been built at much the same time, though it had an additional storey and the high sash windows at the front were more imposing.[3] It looked, and in many ways was, a peaceful house, with enough room for the inhabitants to get away from each other when they needed to. It seems likely that Anne was shown to her room by a servant, and the arrival scene in *Agnes Grey* may well be based on Anne's arrival. Part of the description of the inside of Horton Lodge corresponds with that of Thorp Green. It is likely that Anne was led up the back stairs and down the dark corridor that provided access to rooms in the east wing, just as Agnes was in the novel. Anne's bedroom probably looked out over the farm buildings at the side of the house.

If Friday, 8 May was the date of her arrival, she would probably have her first outing on the following Sunday, to the village church at Little Ouseburn, which she would get to know well. Another overcast day, it would make the Robinsons decide to travel in the carriage. It is likely that Anne went with them, as she did not know the way on foot. They would traverse the twisting and narrow but flat lane past the Stripe Houses, little cottages where some of Mr Robinson's tenants lived, and along the edge of the Brickkiln Field.[4] Beyond this were the woods of Kirby Hall, and across a flat meadow, the home farm, then being rebuilt. A turn in the lane disclosed the fingerpost pointing to Little Ouseburn village. The present ornamental gates opposite the village were not yet erected. From here on the lane was called Church Lane and ran almost straight until the Moat House was reached, with the small Norman (perhaps even Saxon) church beyond it.

This church must surely have pleased Anne. In its very open situation, it looks the epitome of peace. The original church from which Kirby (formerly Kirkby) was named, its harmonious outlines had not been greatly changed or spoilt since the middle ages. The peaceful churchyard has its complement of old graves, but they do not crowd and jostle as at Haworth. Though she did not describe it in detail in *Agnes Grey*, she did sketch it. She left out the unusual mausoleum of the Thompsons, though she could not have helped being impressed by it. Outside the churchyard a grazing field sloped away to the beck, which had been artificially widened here to provide an ornamental pool continuing under the bridge to become the park pool at Kirby Hall. Most of the pool has now dried up and the beck has shrivelled to its normal size.[5]

The service is likely to have been taken by the vicar, Reverend Edward Lascelles. In 1840 he was thirty-one and still unmarried. He had been the incumbent of Little Ouseburn for three years, but he was not to prove a popular parish priest; it must seem probable that Anne drew on him for her picture of Mr Hatfield. At this time Lascelles, who was London born, lived at Green Hammerton and must have had to walk to his church along Moss Hill Lane, which ran near the back of Thorp Green Hall. (In *Agnes Grey* Mr Hatfield walks along 'Moss Lane'.) To understand more about Mr Lascelles and his relations with his parish, it will be necessary to jump to an occasion in 1854, when Anne had long left the district and some of the other participants in the saga had died, as she had.

On Sunday, 28 May of that year there was a shocking exhibition of defiance against Mr Lascelles, brought on, it seems, by his own hastiness. For some unknown fault, he stopped the clerk, William Sadler, and ordered the constables and churchwardens to turn him out of the church. They advised Sadler calmly to go, which he did, but was followed by almost all the congregation who 'shouted in the church', and after the service had finished 'shouted the parson up to his own house'. George Whitehead, the Little Ouseburn diarist, commented, 'There was a regular row in the town.' Sadler clerked the following week but was then replaced.[6] There are other hints of the high-handed and erratic nature of Revd Lascelles. In 1847 and 1849, he was ending tenancies in glebe property, and on 11 February 1849 he 'fell down in a sick fit in the reading desk' at church. By this time he had married, but for Anne's first few years he was an aristocratic bachelor with London manners, apparently unsuited to his parish. It is perhaps ironic that she borrows his christian name, Edward, for her ideal clergyman in *Agnes Grey*.

During the next few weeks after her arrival Anne would be learning about the family for whom she had come to work. By the time of the 1841 diary paper she was confiding, 'I dislike the situation and wish to change it.' She never did so; as we continue with her story we need to ask why this was so. Meanwhile, her first impressions may well have been mixed. It is unlikely that she formed a good opinion of Revd Lascelles, whose attitude and responsibilities were so different from those of her own father. Lascelles had a compact, small, rural parish; Mr Brontë's was large and populous, with industrial problems compounding the unhealthy state of Haworth itself. The inevitable comparison would be much in Mr Brontë's favour; however, it is not necessary to suppose that all Anne's first judgements were against Thorp Green and its inhabitants.

At this point we need to return to the opening of *Agnes Grey*, to begin to discuss its relationship with Anne's actual life in the Vale of York. As we saw in the Introduction, she cannot be taken literally as she attempts to set a realistic scene for her heroine. The first person narrator Agnes stresses her 'obscurity' in a way very congenial to Anne Brontë, and the author then skilfully adapts the circumstances of her own life in such a way as to provide little ironic distance between herself and her narrator. But we must stress that Anne does not simply use her own life history unchanged. For example, Mr Brontë had no 'snug little property of his own'. Mrs Brontë had not been a squire's daughter, and her superiority in social status has been exaggerated in presenting Mrs Grey. There *were* six children in the Brontë household, but four, not two, survived. Mrs Brontë, unlike Mrs Grey, did not teach the girls since she had died when they were small. Mr Brontë did not lose his money through speculation. There were 'heath-clad hills' in the Brontë background, but no weeping birch in the garden. The Brontës did do most of the cooking and gardening and their clothes were patched, like these of Agnes Grey.

In general, then, Anne Brontë presents Agnes's circumstances as like her own, but the detail is invented. The family's patronizing attitude as well as their genteel poverty is Brontë-like, but 'Mary' is not based on either Charlotte or Emily: she is a lay-figure without much character, and Anne seems uninterested in her. However, some of the characters in the book do have a vivid life. Of the children at Horton Lodge, John and Charles are very briefly sketched, but both Matilda and Rosalie are full portraits lovingly described, even when their actions merit censure. While John, Charles, Mary, Richard Grey and others are flat, Rosalie and Matilda are alive and drawn almost from the inside. They must surely be based on the Thorp Green girls.

Certain hints suggest that Rosalie may be based on Lydia Robinson and Matilda on Elizabeth (called 'Bessy' by the family). Mary does not seem to appear in *Agnes Grey*, but she may be written into *Wildfell Hall*. External evidence about the characters of the Robinson girls is hard to discover, and we shall make the most of what is available. Though Charlotte was most disparaging about them before she had met them, both Bessy and Mary obtained some marks of respect in later life. Charlotte may have had a jaundiced view of them, but Anne, whatever she thought of them on first sight, gradually became very close to both. The actions of the Murrays do not correspond precisely with those of the Robinsons, and we shall sometimes be able to distinguish between points where Anne is drawing from life and where she is using invention. It is worth recalling too that the action of *Agnes Grey* covers only the first part of Anne's experiences at Thorp Green, as we shall see when we come to consider its writing in more detail.

In the course of time Lydia Robinson proved herself as headstrong as Rosalie, but more romantic. While Rosalie is always cautiously aware of the ultimate need to marry money, Lydia married as she wished. Yet the marriage she made suggests that she was dashing and pretty, quite willing to hurt her relatives and willing also to act for herself. These are Rosalie's characteristics. Elizabeth seems to have fallen under the spell of Anne Brontë, postponing her marriage in the search for a likely partner. She resembled Matilda in her enthusiasm for riding, and we may think that Anne portrayed her accurately in her early teenage as frequenting the stables at the farm.

Mrs Lydia Robinson had been born Lydia Gisborne in Staffordshire and was christened on 25 September 1799. This is a date worth remembering in view of the traditional notions of her age relative to her husband.[7] We shall return to her antecedents and status later, by which time Anne will have learned much more about her employer's wife. The character of Mrs Murray has been thought to mirror Mrs Robinson's, but there are ways in which the two differ. We shall later notice some passages, however, in which Anne seems to be reporting accurately. She would soon learn that Mrs Robinson was rather on the defensive in Yorkshire, exiled from her roots and submerged to some extent by the elder Robinsons. She had been the family's second choice for Edmund, who might have married one of the Thompsons of Kirby. Anne would find him rather remote and unlike her idea of a clergyman. He rarely seems to have officiated at Little Ouseburn church, and only once christened a child whose surname was not Robinson.[8]

Of the children, only Georgiana would not be in Anne's charge. She would be confined to the nursery, though perhaps Anne would show some interest in her, to judge by her baby drawings of 1837 and her poems at various points. In later times the nursery was on the top floor facing south, in the east wing.[9] The nursery at Grassdale in *Wildfell Hall* is not very clearly located.[10] Anne's tasks would be performed in the schoolroom, also apparently in the east wing, but on the ground floor. To judge by the contents it seems certain that this had been the room used for the education of Mr Robinson and his two sisters about he time of Waterloo. Not much addition to the bookstock had been made since.

Our impression of the contents of the schoolroom, as with so much of the interior of the house, comes from an inventory taken a few years later, when the Robinsons had let the house to a family called Woodd. On the floor was an old carpet cover (a drugget) and in front of the fire, a hearthrug. On one wall was a mahogany chest of drawers and in the centre a dining table where Anne could have her meals with the children or by herself, as Agnes does in the novel.[11] There was a small stand or 'what-not' on which books and ornaments could be placed. A couch, with its cover, and six chairs were also in the room. The inventory mentions a 'Book Case' and 'Set [of] Painted Book Shelves'. The former would presumably have had a glass front. A mahogany 'Pembroke' table completed the furnishings. The hearthrug is specifically stated in the inventory to be old as were the books; so it seems that the schoolroom furniture had not been changed since Edmund and his sisters had been instructed there. This room was to be Anne's realm for the next few years.

Less than a fortnight after she arrived at Thorp Green the district was overwhelmed to hear of a disastrous fire at York Minster, on 20 May. Anne later became very fond of the Minster. It seems likely that her enthusiasm may have been kindled on visits to the city where she must have seen the restoration work. Later the Brontës owned a little miniature of the church during the fire reproduced on glass.

In later years Anne was able to spend part of June each year at Haworth. She would then rejoin the Robinsons to go to Scarborough, where they took their annual holidays. It seems unlikely that she would be allowed much time at home in 1840, having so recently joined Mrs Robinson's staff. Quite possibly she went direct to Scarborough with the family, travelling by coach or in the Robinsons' own carriage. In course of time Anne made many discoveries at Scarborough; but we shall leave most of these for a later chapter. To understand her state of mind that summer we need to look at a poem written when she returned to Thorp Green alluding to her experience, and a further one also written at Thorp Green in which the mood changes sharply.[12]

After her essay into personal poetry of 1 January, a new strain enters Anne's poetry. Whereas the Gondal poems of 1836 and the following years had sometimes merely reflected a mood that Anne Brontë felt at the time, the poems of the next five years are more directly personal. Some clearly record direct experiences of their author, as I have shown in my introduction to *The Poems of Anne Brontë*. Both Anne and Emily distinguished, as the years went by, between Gondal (fictional) verse and personal poetry. There is a good deal of variety, especially in Emily's work, within the non-Gondal category, but it is certain that a clear division should be drawn between these two types. From 1840 onward, Anne almost never wrote Gondal verse away from Emily: left to herself she wrote ruminative, philosophical poems or hymns, and when we can discover external evidence about the circumstances in which they were written, we can see that they are, as Agnes Grey says of her poems, 'pillars of witness' to feelings and events encompassing Anne Brontë at the time.[13]

The first poem is called 'The Bluebell' (22 August 1840). In it, Anne describes a summer expedition in scenery that is later recalled by the setting of some early scenes in *Wildfell Hall*. The sea lies behind the poet and a range of hills ahead. She is walking 'all carelessly' along a sunny lane. She laughs and talks with 'those around' – presumably her pupils – and does not feel as harassed as usual. The sudden sight of a blue harebell on the bank by the road recalls her own childhood.[14] She had then been dwelling 'with kindred hearts' and did not have to spend her life looking after others, as she now had to. In writing the poem Anne at one point describes her employers as 'icy hearts' despite the cheerful tone at the start. The sight of the harebell recalls lost happiness.

Apparently while at Scarborough Anne drew another allegorical picture. Entitled 'What you please', a title which perhaps echoes an instruction of Mrs Robinson ('You may do what you please, Miss Brontë') it depicts a young girl of Anne's age, but with rather more conventionally pretty features, exploring in a wood. There are summer flowers nearby, perhaps foxgloves, which begin blooming in June and continue into July. Trees overarch on both sides and the girl lightly rests her hand on a sapling. The background shows more trees and bushes, and the girl appears to have crossed a clearing to reach her present look-out point.

The girl of Anne's romanticized self-portrait has dark hair, falling in ringlets like Anne's own. She is unlike Charlotte's dashing heroines, but while she shares Anne's attentive, keen eyes, her mouth is a pretty rosebud and her face rounder than Anne's. She wears a cloak over a low cut, long dress. It is Anne's idea of what she would like to be, doing 'what she pleases', peering intently out of the wood for a glimpse at life beyond. This first Scarborough holiday, as shown by 'The Bluebell', was an introduction to a fresh world and so Anne symbolically represents it. We note the harmony of the girl with her surroundings. Her creator sees human nature as part of Nature itself (a view shared by Emily). The girl shelters among the trees; she is not yet quite ready to dash out of their shade and encounter whatever adventure she can see. She leans very lightly on the sapling, moving it gently so that she can observe the world. It is a congenial obstruction, but she means to put it aside. The girl's other hand is raised and the fingers slightly curled in a nervous gesture of potentiality; the attitude reminds one of a wild creature that looks out of the wood in anticipation, but is ready to turn back at the slightest sign of danger. The sapling might symbolize the Robinsons, or her own childish self. In various ways Anne shows herself still intertwined with this young plant but looking out beyond it. To some this interpretation will seem fanciful, but it builds on the view of 'Sunrise at Sea', which has previously been suggested.

After the poem inspired by the bluebell, Anne's next is very much starker:

> *O! I am very weary*
>   *Though tears no longer flow;*
> *My eyes are tired of weeping,*
>   *My heart is sick of woe.*
>
> *My life is very lonely,*
>   *My days pass heavily:*
> *I'm weary of repining,*
>   *Wilt thou not come to me?*
>
> *Oh didst thou know my longings*
>   *For thee from day to day,*
> *My hopes so often blighted,*
>   *Thou wouldst not thus delay.*

It is, in a way, an expansion of 'Olivia Vernon's' final lines. In the earlier poem a drooping heart is in anguish because a young man has not come. The 'bitter, aching woe' now recurs. But there is a great deal more implied in the poem.

The poet, writing at Thorp Green as the title confirms, has been hoping for the arrival of a visitor.[15] 'Lines written at Thorp Green' is anchored by its title to a place and a particular set of feelings. Like the poem of 1 January, it must refer to Weightman. If during this summer Weightman remained at Haworth carrying out his clerical duties, we might argue that any hope Anne could have had that he might arrive in Little Ouseburn was necessarily a delusion. But as Charlotte's letters make clear (though he has misled her somewhat) he was not able to stay at Haworth that summer. He had to travel on business to fulfil the conditions for his ordination, which would take place at Ripon, not all that far away from the Vale of York. This fact was known to everyone.

According to a letter of Charlotte's, Weightman left Haworth on 14 July.[16] He did not sign Haworth registers from 12 July to 13 September. It appears that he had told Charlotte, and presumably Anne, that he had to pass an examination to be ordained. Charlotte wrote in the same letter to Ellen, 'I have no doubt that he will get nobly through his examination, he is a clever lad.' His cleverness was rather like Branwell's; it consisted partly in subtle exaggeration. In fact, there was no examination to be taken. He had already submitted documents to the Bishop of Ripon and a testimonial signed, among others, by Mr Brontë; these were quite enough to secure his ordination.[17] If the poem of 28 August is taken with Weightman's absence from Haworth and his claim to be in the Ripon area, it seems probable that he had made some kind of promise or half-promise to Anne. Charlotte was by now beginning to suspect that Weightman was a rogue, though she knew less about him than we do today. Broken promises to Anne would be quite consistent with his warm but inconstant character.

In due course we shall be examining Anne's motivation in writing *Wildfell Hall*. Its central core is the story of a young woman who is beguiled against her better judgement to marry a handsome rogue. It is true that Arthur Huntingdon, unlike William Weightman, is cold-hearted and sly, but he is hardly more unreliable than Weightman. After his death Anne romanticized the young curate, but if he had not died she might have begun to discover his flaws in more detail. As it was, in August 1840 she still seems to have been expecting him to fulfil the promise of 'Sunrise at Sea'. However, he did not visit Thorp Green, then or ever.

The third poem of the group under discussion is undated and only survives because of its inclusion in *Agnes Grey*. It fits badly into its context there and was clearly not written expressly for the novel:

> Oh, they have robbed me of the hope
>   My spirit held so dear;
> They will not let me hear that voice
>   My soul delights to hear.
>
> They will not let me see that face
>   I so delight to see;
> And they have taken all thy smiles,
>   And all thy love from me.
>
> Well, let them seize on all they can; –
>   One treasure still is mine, –
> A heart that loves to think on thee,
>   And feels the worth of thine.

The date of this must be conjecture, but the rhyme scheme is that of 'O! I am very weary', whereas later poems more often use the ABAB pattern. Who, then, are 'they' who have tried to divide the poet from the beloved? There is no evidence on this matter. We could speculate that Weightman had written blaming his non-appearance on either the Robinsons, who would not entertain him, or the Brontë family, who required his service at Haworth. There is not the faintest shred of evidence for either of these suppositions, or even anything to suggest that Weightman wrote at this time to Anne. In a letter of June 1840, however, Charlotte claims to have discovered letters being exchanged between him and a girl in Swansea, though in the same letter she mentions a proposal that he stay at Crackenthorpe with the Waltons.[18] Whether or not early Victorian convention allowed it, William Weightman wrote letters to any young girl he fancied. It is quite possible that he wrote to Anne, even though Mr Weston does not write to Agnes Grey.

At this point in her life Anne was plainly a naive if very sincere young woman, whose sincerity will not be mirrored by most of her acquaintances and whose enthusiasm will lead her into disappointment. Her later poems, and some parts of her novels, are full of the sadness of disillusion as the bright expectations of youth fail to be realized. This naive sincerity is being deployed in two areas: relations with a potential marriage partner and the role of governess. In the long run Anne's directness and genuine concern were to make headway with the girls at Thorp Green, while fate would interrupt her relations with Weightman. At the moment, it seems, the failure to communicate was leading Anne towards a crisis of confidence in both these situations.

In such circumstances Charlotte's antidote would have been to unfetter her imagination and retreat to Angria. Anne had shared Gondal with Emily, and we might have expected her to enter keenly into the Gondal world now. By 1840 Emily had taken to poetry very seriously, but its content was (as it always would be) often concerned with Gondal. This solace was open to Anne, but she rejected it. Instead, she returned to her encounter with James la Trobe, and to her own hard-won insights about her personal need for religion. This was to prove not so much a consolation as a weapon with which to overcome her distress.

One Sunday in early December she found herself alone at Thorp Green. In similar circumstances at Law Hill, Emily had wondered whether to imagine a visit to Haworth or to envisage herself in Gondal.[19] Anne writes:

> *O let me be alone awhile,*
> *No human form is nigh.*
> *And I may sing and muse aloud*
> *No mortal ear is by . . .*
>
> *One hour, my spirit, stretch thy wings,*
> *And quit this joyless sod,*
> *Bask in the sunshine of the sky,*
> *And be alone with God.*[20]

Thorp Green is as 'joyless' as she has suggested it is in her Scarborough poem. Plainly there is, as yet, no return of love from the Robinsons. In the second stanza she mentions 'restless, wandering thoughts', perhaps implying thoughts which wandered in space to Haworth, but not to Gondal. Anne's solution is to *sing*; in due course we shall be able to discover what she sang. Within a week or so after this poem was written, Anne returned to her family ('friends', as Agnes Grey would later call them) for Christmas. Here she found Charlotte keenly searching for another post for herself. Branwell, who had left his employment as a tutor in the Lake District, was now away at Sowerby Bridge railway station in a new kind of post, and Emily was deeply engaged in Gondal mist. It was not difficult to fall under her spell again, and to Emily and Gondal Anne duly returned.

6

The End of
Romantic Hopes

Charlotte had told Ellen Nussey in a letter generally dated 24 January 1840 that Anne would not return to Blake Hall. After this, none of her extant letters to Ellen in 1840 mention Anne by name; it is with a letter to Emily of 2 April 1841 that Anne re-enters her correspondence. With such a gap in our evidence it is little wonder that previous biographers, with the exception of Mrs Gaskell, have lost a year from Anne's life and begun her stay at Thorp Green in 1841.[1] It is, of course, possible that some of the letters Charlotte wrote to Ellen in that year have been destroyed, but there is also the probability that Charlotte was little interested in Anne's career and unwilling to talk about it until she had herself obtained a similar post. In the letter to Emily she records having received a letter from Anne, in which she 'says she is well', though Charlotte doubts this.

The main content of the letter from Anne to her eldest sister may have been news of the death of the baby, Georgiana Jane, a sad event which would have left an impression on Anne. She died on 15 March and was buried a week later, Mr Lascelles officiating at the funeral.[2] News of the death was announced in the Yorkshire papers and as far away as *The Derby Mercury*. Even without the melancholy note introduced by the death of this toddler (though she was not Anne's responsibility) it is likely that Anne was not happy at Thorp Green. Even by July, when she wrote her 1841 diary paper, she was asserting, 'I dislike the situation and wish to change it for another.'[3] There are no further references to Anne in Charlotte's letters for the first part of 1841, though in the latter part of the year Charlotte had begun to discuss tentatively with Ellen the proposal that two of the three Brontë sisters (Charlotte and Emily as it would soon become clear) should go to the Continent to perfect their French, so that in due course they might set up their own shcool.[4]

As in later years, Anne would have returned home for a fortnight in the summer of 1841, before writing her diary paper. Charlotte was away from home until 1 July, by which time Anne had returned to the Robinsons. William Weightman had also left by this time – he did not sign the register again until the middle of August. In late June, however, Weightman, Anne and Emily would have been at Haworth together. No poetry was written by either of the Brontë sisters during this time; perhaps they were concerned with Gondal prose. It would be most valuable to know about Emily's attitude to the incipient or fitful relationship between Anne and the curate. Her nickname 'the major' has been thought to refer to her capacity to chaperone her sisters, and those who consider this to be the case may suppose that she would have tried to dampen any warmth there might have been between them. But there is no real evidence to confirm this origin for Emily's nickname; it might just as well stem from her height and her striding gait over moorland.[5] Given the feelings and misunderstandings of 1840, and the reference in Charlotte's letter of January 1842, Anne may well not have been indifferent to the curate at midsummer 1841. Any rapprochement would have had to have Emily's approval. Beyond this point it is impossible to go without straining the evidence, but the significance of Charlotte's absence should not be missed.

Anne now accompanied the Robinsons to Scarborough, which had lost none of its charm. The sea breezes would banish Anne's asthma, and ease of breathing would bring a relaxed attitude. On 30 July, she wrote the first individual diary paper of the well-known series (the 1834 and 1837 papers had been almost wholly written by Emily). She notes that she has 'the same faults' as in 1837, but 'more wisdom and experience and a little more self-possession than I then enjoyed'. The manuscripts of both Anne's diary papers are not available, and texts derive from Shorter's *Charlotte Brontë and her Circle*, where he prints transcripts. We cannot therefore be sure whether Anne actually wrote, as she is always quoted, 'I am now engaged in writing the fourth volume of Solala Vernon's life.' 'Solala' may be an invented Gondal name, but it looks suspiciously like a misreading by Shorter. We may recall that 'Olivia Vernon' was a thinly veiled disguise for Anne herself in January 1840, and it is possible that if the manuscript again becomes available, we shall find that the mysterious Solala is really Olivia. Even if this does not prove to be the case, we may suspect that the four-volume life that Anne was now writing contained autobiographical material and an attempt to work through the problems and feelings of a young woman: in short, it may well have been an early attempt to treat the themes that surface in *Agnes Grey*.

The diary paper was apparently written late at night: 'My pupils are gone to bed and I am hastening to finish this before I join them.' All we know of the Robinsons' accommodation at Scarborough dates from later years, and will be better dealt with in a subsequent chapter. If Lydia was in bed, Anne must have been writing deep into the night, for surely Lydia would not be one to leave social gatherings early. Anne also mentions the possibility that the three Brontës might set up a school of their own. There are suggestions in *Agnes Grey* that if there was to be one, Anne knew where she would have liked to situate it. It would have been on the landward side of Scarborough, perhaps in Westborough Street. This was presumably the route to the bluebell lane of 1840, and it looks as if the Robinsons took Anne for drives to the moors beyond Hackness. Return was perhaps via the celebrated Scalby Mill tearooms. Here on the moors she was to locate the scene of her second novel. With the sea breezes blowing across there was no sign of her asthma: 'the unspeakable purity of the air!' she allows Agnes to write excitedly.[6] The school project never came to fruition. To judge by Agnes Grey's attitude, Anne may well have been disappointed at this, for she seems to consider the profession of schoolmistress much preferable to that of governess.[7]

Back at Thorp Green depression set in. On 19 August she wrote a melancholy poem regretting that she would not see her home until the winter wind had replaced the 'whispering breeze' of August. Many of Anne's Thorp Green poems bear witness to this depression. It is as though the outlook exhibited to la Trobe in 1837 had recurred and could not be shaken off. We may compare it with Charlotte's state of mind in 1843, during the summer she spent alone in Belgium, which would become the basis of Lucy Snowe's near-breakdown. Anne calls her malaise 'lethargy'. It will be worth paraphrasing her poem 'Despondency' to see what feelings she records.[8] She complains first of a 'drowsy and dull' spirit, 'heavy and dull as lead'. It is bound by 'iron chains'. In the past she has been moved to anguished repentance over her sins, but she cannot now feel any such zeal. After repenting she has been filled with a strength of spirit and has been 'full of love'. Now, 'my sins increase' and 'Faith itself is wavering'. It is a miserably unhappy poem, though at the end she has enough confidence to throw herself on God's mercy, calling herself, in Wesleyan mode, a 'wretch'.

Evangelical Christianity encouraged the believer to *feel* love for God, and taught that this would be as a result of genuine repentance. In cosmic terms, there seems little which needed repentance, but we need to recall the high tone preached by Wesley and others, by which standard Anne always judged herself. She may have been displeased at the way she chafed at her routine of teaching and did not always respond to the Robinsons' needs. Her discontent with Thorp Green may have appeared sinful. Helen Huntingdon repeatedly argues that her love of God should be higher than that for her husband, and if Anne could not rid herself of her affection for home, including Charlotte and Emily, and perhaps Weightman, she may have supposed such a love was idolatrous and ought to be replaced by a love of God which would make her happy to work in whatever circumstances he chose for her. Her close communion with Emily while they were together may not have precluded a degree of envy while she was miles from home and Emily safe at Haworth. As we have seen, Anne had been willing to substitute herself for Emily at Roe Head in 1835, and had done so again, by coming to Thorp Green after Emily's return from Law Hill. This is not to say there was no element of self-sacrifice in her actions. Charlotte's plan to set up a school required that the sisters should go to the Continent to perfect their French: as time went by it began to be clear that while Anne had proved a more persistent teacher, Emily would be chosen for the honour. Jealousy could well have been a spiritual sin of which Anne accused herself.

Anne's motives are sometimes obscure and have to be deduced from the kind of motivation she praises in her poems and novels. A splendid chance now presented itself to be rid of

Thorp Green and the Robinsons for ever. Charlotte and Emily were to go to Belgium in the New Year. When Anne returned to Haworth in December, about the time of 'Despondency', this plan must have been presented to her. It must have been suggested that she should stay at home to look after her father. Yet she passed over this opportunity to leave her post with honour and returned to Thorp Green. On the face of things, this was against all practicality and she must have had overwhelming reasons for her decision.

We have now returned chronologically to the point where we began to detail Anne Brontë's relations with William Weightman: January 1842. In Charlotte's letter of 20 January, Weightman is reported to be sitting opposite Anne in church and sighing 'to win her attention'. In response Anne is quiet and downcast.[9] If she was to return to Thorp Green, she would have to do so within a few days. There were many good reasons for not returning, including the fact that she would be able to enjoy a few more weeks of Emily's friendship before Charlotte and she left for their school in Belgium. Anne's behaviour in church might be described as modestly evasive, but the attraction between the two is certainly noted in Charlotte's account. The psychology of this is hard to penetrate with certainty but it looks as though Anne may have been subconsciously aware that Weightman would not make a suitable permanent partner. Yet at the same time she did not entirely trust the suppressed flirtatious side of herself, (such as we see expressed in her creation of Rosalie and of Annebella) not to provoke a situation in which they would become close.

During the holiday she and Emily had made strides with Gondal. According to Anne's 1845 diary paper as transcribed by Shorter they had begun 'Gondal Chronicles' at this time.[10] This fascinating statement has been ignored by most commentators, and it is indeed slightly dubious what is meant by it. Certainly Anne did not mean that 1841 was the date when Gondal invention itself was begun, since we have many records of it dating at least from 1834. In all likelihood it had begun even before that, after Charlotte's departure to Roe Head, possibly in 1831. By this time the two sisters had accumulated a mass of uncoordinated and perhaps self-contradictory stories and poems, such as the great saga of A. G. A., Emily's Gondal *persona* from about 1837, and now

Anne's life of Miss Vernon. It seems that they decided they must take a grip on the tales and try to sort them out as 'chronicles', that is a coherent history in chronological form. Both sisters were interested in accurate dating, as is shown by the way in which they carefully date their poems and celebrate anniversaries by the ceremonial of writing and opening diary papers. To have the Gondals adrift in a mass of uncoordinated material must have been annoying. Both sisters were also very interested in the question of Time (Emily uses a capital in her manuscripts once or twice) and its effect on personality. Both must have agreed to clarify this matter in relation to their Gondal inventions. From December 1841 to mid-January 1842, we may see them as collaborating fully on systematizing Gondal, though the work was not finished by 1845, and was probably never finished.

What is not clear is whether there was any positive feeling, apart from the reluctance to stay at Haworth unchaperoned with Weightman, recalling Anne to the Vale of York. The action of *Agnes Grey* is mainly based on events in 1839–42; in it we see a gradual growth in understanding between Agnes and her pupils. It would be hazardous to assume that this reflects accurately the growing sympathy between Anne and hers, but certainly there was such a growth, and it may have begun as early as this. Though Anne would hardly look forward to returning to Thorp Green, she may have had reasons other than the feelings of delicacy (and perhaps mistrust of her own emotion) which removed her from Weightman.

On Tuesday, 8 February Mr Brontë set out with Emily and Charlotte for Belgium. William Weightman was left in sole charge of the curacy at Haworth, though the registers suggest that he had little work to do baptizing or marrying parishioners. It is possible that he was already suffering from his final illness, as Charlotte's letter also mentions that he did not look well. This year there was no quartet of girls at the parsonage to whom he could send valentines, but did he possibly send one to Anne? Certainly she was much elated in mid-February and wrote a buoyant poem much different from 'Despondency' of two months earlier. Entitled 'In memory of a Happy Day in February', it begins: Blessed be Thou for all the joy/ My soul has felt today . . .'

Ostensibly the poem has a religious tone. After writing that all those she loved were far away (travelling to Belgium, as we know) and then describing the wind blowing freely over the withered grass, she denies that her happiness emanates from Nature, but asserts,

> *It was a glimpse of truths divine*
> *Unto my spirit given*
> *Illumined by a ray of light*
> *That shone direct from Heaven!*

Here was Anne's equivalent of the ecstatic experiences felt by Emily at the sight of a full moon or the caress of the west wind. She speedily wrote the first stanzas but was then interrupted and concluded the poem nine months later in very different circumstances. Of course we cannot deny Anne her divine revelation, with its psychological uplift. But it must be a possibility, surely, that softly sighing William Weightman, deprived of all female admirers, and possibly even regretting Anne more than the others, had sent a valentine and thus aided the psychological uplift.

Anne's ecstasy did not last. Seeing a dove, apparently kept as a household pet, she pitied it and wrote a sad poem in which she uses the dove as a symbol of herself confined in a cage. Loneliness makes the dove wilt; it is the lack of a companion, not the wires themselves, that weighs upon its spirit. In *Wildfell Hall* too she will use a pair of doves symbolically to suggest a girl's thoughts and so make Helen vulnerable to Huntingdon. There were doves kept in a pigeon cote by the Robinsons, but they could fly round the grounds. Anne's solitary dove is more likely to have been kept in a cage by one of the neighbouring farmers or in a cottage such as those she mentions in *Agnes Grey*.

Easter arrived, and with it enough time for Anne to begin, on Easter Monday, 28 March, a new manuscript book for her poems. Like Emily, she seems to have been in the habit of writing on rough scraps, then copying neatly into a fair copy book. Anne's fair copies were written in normal handwriting, unlike Emily's, who generally used the Brontë small script. Even this small detail highlights a difference in temperament and outlook between the girls: Anne so often tends to the 'normal', the anti-romantic, the social and communicating, despite her extreme shyness. With the systematization of the Gondal chronicles may have gone a discussion of the possibility of one day publishing poetry or fiction. If so, her observations of the Robinson family may have been confided to a diary such as Agnes Grey claims to have kept.

It is necessary to stress again here that even if such a diary ever existed, it has not survived. Personal records of Anne Brontë's five-year stay at Thorp Green do not exist, except for the laconic comments I have quoted from the 1841 diary paper and shall quote from the 1845 paper, together with the content of her personal poems. In this situation the biographer has to work through all kinds of local documents quite unconnected with the squire's governess to understand what events she must have witnessed. Of these, Anne herself gives no report whatsoever, but if we are to judge how her life-experience affects her poetry and novels, and in the case of *Agnes Grey* make some kind of judgements about its degree of autobiographical content, we have to examine whatever local records tell us of life at Thorp Green while Anne was a governess there. It has to be emphasized that Thorp Green is a tiny hamlet, not like the large village of Haworth. The term 'Thorp Underwoods' is slightly more inclusive, but even this covers only twenty or so buildings in the 1841 census. Whatever went on in Thorp Green, and especially at Thorp Green Hall and its farmhouse and cottages, Anne Brontë would have witnessed.

In May 1842 a minor scandal burst over the house, the details of which are still a mystery. Reverend Edmund Robinson almost never officiated at Little Ouseburn church in whose parish Thorp Green Hall was situated. He did baptize his own children, but when Georgiana died, he did not conduct her funeral service. There can be no doubt from this evidence and other documents from Thorp Green, both within and without the house itself, that he was thought of as 'squire', not 'clergyman', and his ordination could for all practical purposes be disregarded. I have not been able to discover any occasion during Anne's time at Thorp Green when he christened a child, except that on 15 May 1842 he baptized William Kettlewell, the illegitimate son of Jane Kettlewell, spinster. No father's name is given on the birth certificate, on which the date of birth is anomalously given as 16 May 1842, and the mother's place of residence is given as Thorp Green. As has already been explained, this description applied only to the Hall itself, the farm and a few cottages. It is quite inconceivable that Anne was not as aware as everyone in Thorp Green of the birth of this illegitimate baby.[11] 'Thorp Underwoods', the slightly wider term, is given as the place of birth. Could this shock have been registered by Anne in any known document, and how serious was the scandal? In her 1845 diary paper Anne wrote 'during my stay I have had some very unpleasant and undreamt-of experience of human nature.'[12] Though it is fairly supposed that some of this unpleasant experience was connected with Branwell in the years 1843–5, and some connected with Lydia and her other pupils, the nature and attitudes of the hunting parson Edmund Robinson must have been shocking to Anne. Unfortunately it is impossible here to be sure on which side of the credit balance this baptism falls. As Edmund Robinson only baptized his own children, does this mean that William Kettlewell was his? Or does this show a compassionate side to the 'squarson' who is prepared to christen an illegitimate child born in his house or its dependent farm and cottages when the high-handed Reverend Lascelles would not?

One might look for the clue to the child's father in his Christian name. There were two servants at Thorp Green whose name was William. William Lambert is shown as a 'male servant' in the 1841 census and was living in Thorp Green Hall itself. In 1846 he is described by George Whitehead as the 'farmer', presumably working on the home farm which was across the garden from the Hall and overlooked from her window, so far as we can tell, by Anne Brontë. In 1846 he married a dairymaid, Elizabeth Pannett, and set up in farming elsewhere. William Allison is not featured in the 1841 census but children of his were christened by Edward Lascelles after 1845. Allison appears to have been the coachman, and will re-enter our story later. The name Kettlewell is common in the Ouseburn area, the most likely candidate for the mother of William being Jane Kettlewell, dressmaker of Great Ouseburn, who in 1841 was aged about thirty, and lived next door to the house where Edward Greenhow, clergyman, lived with his family.[13]

It would probably be unfair to suspect Edmund Robinson, Anne's employer, of fathering William Kettlewell. His account books give many examples of benefactions to his servants, and perhaps his action in baptizing the child was a similar act of patronage. Nevertheless, the whole episode must have constituted part of Anne Brontë's catalogue of 'undreamt-of' experiences. I have not been able to trace anything about the life of William Kettlewell, who does not seem to feature in the accounts of Mr Robinson, or his wife's continuation of those accounts after his death.

We must here discuss another matter relating to Anne's period at Thorp Green. In 1950 the Brontë Society purchased from a Mrs E. Foster a small watercolour of a girl, which was at the time attributed to Charlotte Brontë.[14] A note with it read: 'My husband's mother in her young days lived at Great Ouseburn, near both Green Hammerton and Thorp Green and she knew the Robinsons of Thorp Green Hall when Anne Brontë was a governess to the children who gave her the portrait. It has been in my husband's family for over sixty years. His mother's maiden name was Anderson.' The assumption seems to have been that this was a portrait of Anne by Charlotte, as I recalled in my 1979 introduction to *The Poems of Anne Brontë*.[15] It is now necessary to review the evidence carefully, taking into account the note quoted above and our greater knowledge of Anne's stay at Thorp Green.

There certainly were Andersons in Ouseburn during the relevant period, as is shown by the 1848 directory, in which William Anderson is given as a tailor and draper.[16] It would seem, however, that any Anderson contemporary with the painting must have been Mrs Foster's husband's grandmother, rather than his mother. There would have been no reason for the local draper to have been given a picture of Anne Brontë by Charlotte and to have treasured the picture, though once Charlotte's name (but not Anne's) became famous, the chances of the picture being kept would have been greater. The subject of the portrait, a young girl of about twelve or thirteen, does not look much like the portraits of Anne which we discussed earlier, but the style of painting is very much like that of both Charlotte and Anne. Mrs Foster may well be right to write that 'the children' to whom Anne was governess gave her husband's ancestor the portrait, but it is more likely that it is a portrait by the governess of one of the children than of the governess by her sister. The portrait may well be of Mary Robinson, drawn and painted by Anne.

It is almost certain that Anne spent her summer fortnight at Haworth in June 1842 as in the previous years, before going to Scarborough with the Robinsons. While at home she had drawn a portrait not unlike the small water-colour we have just been discussing, this time writing on it, 'a very bad picture, drawn 24th June 1842 by Anne Brontë.[17] 'Bad' presumably means it was a bad likeness. The sitter was a young woman, rather like the subject of the watercolour just described, but apparently rather older. It may be that this was another attempt to draw one of the Robinson girls. It is interesting that Anne did not throw it away.

The Robinsons were in Scarborough by 7 July. There is no evidence for this year from Anne's poetry, but an investigation into centemporary Scarborough papers shows that members of the Ingham family were also staying at the Cliff; it is impossible to determine from the *Scarborough Herald* which members, but the presence of Cunliffes and Listers shows that it was the same family.[18] (This raises the question whether the Inghams and Robinsons knew each other, and whether Anne's employment at Thorp Green owed anything to a recommendation from the Inghams. On the other hand, we may wonder whether, on the contrary, Anne would be petrified when she saw them, in case they told stories of children tied to table-legs.)

Late in August William Weightman caught cholera. Cholera epidemics were a frequent occurrence at Haworth because of the poor sanitation and the dominant position of the churchyard, which meant that the virus was washed down the hill to reinfect the population. As we saw, Weightman was unwell in January, and there may have been more to his death than cholera. He signed the register in the fourth week of June, and so would have been able to meet Anne that last summer. Now, his disease progressed rapidly, and he died on 6 September, being buried four days later. Branwell had watched by his bedside and Mr Brontë paid him many visits. The whole family had been attracted by his cheerful talk and humour, and he had a serious side too, as Charlotte once found when she discovered he had been assiduously visiting the poorer members of the parish.[19]

Emily was not at home to write to Anne about Weightman's death, even if she had been interested to do so. The news would have come as a shock, and would later give rise to the poem already mentioned, dated December 1842:

> *I will not mourn thee, lovely one,*
> *Though thou art torn away.*

The end of romantic hopes

'Tis said that if the morning sun
Arise with dazzling ray

And shed a bright and burning beam
Athwart the glittering main,
'Ere noon shall fade that laughing gleam
Engulfed in clouds and rain.

And if thy life as transient proved,
It hath been full as bright,
For thou wert hopeful and beloved;
Thy spirit knew no blight.[20]

In selecting for the 1850 edition, Charlotte avoided publishing
this poem, which alone was not published until 1959. This
strange omission suggests that the elder sister knew quite well
to whom the poem was written, and understood the circumstances of its composition. Emily, writing after Branwell's
disaster in 1845, refers dreamily to the way in which she has
refrained from personal attachments while all her 'compeers'
have 'seen their morning melt in tears'.[21] She knew, presumably, of Charlotte's hopeless attachment to M. Heger, and
considered Anne to have been attached to Weightman.
However, the sunny youth of Anne's later poems is not the
real Weightman, but a much less complicated and idealized
version of him.

Any view of the reality in Anne Brontë's relations with
William Weightman must be tentative. I have shown that by
January 1840 Anne was writing in such a way as to indicate
that she had fallen under the curate's spell, and by February he
had sent her (but also the other girls) a valentine. Her hopes of
that year were dashed, though it seems he had given an indication that he might visit Thorp Green. Charlotte knew that he
was philandering with other girls in and around Haworth, but
his alleged engagement to Agnes Walton at Appleby cannot be
substantiated as the social classes of the two were not the
same. By January 1842, Anne and William are seen as a pair by
Charlotte, and that February, Anne is very cheerful when she
could have been expected to be in a despondent mood with her
sisters in Belgium. The same summer, Anne and William were
together in Haworth, and at his unexpected death, she wrote a
poem which can only refer to him, though in idealized terms.
All this has to be matched with the evidence in *Agnes Grey* and

Wildfell Hall of an understanding of the process of falling in love which seems far removed from Emily's account of the same emotion in *Wuthering Heights*. However, as we shall see later, the two novels bring on stage very different lovers for their respective heroines.

At the time of his death William Weightman was twenty-eight. He had presumably given up the possibility of being married to the superior Miss Walton, but even if he had not died of cholera, Anne's story might not have been any happier. Weightman's brother, Robert, was ejected from his living on grounds of habitual drunkenness. Though Arthur Huntingdon is stony-hearted and William Weightman warm, Charlotte does criticize his dealings with the alleged 'enamorata' at Swansea as 'heartless'.[22] Weightman is often taken to be a model for Edward Weston, whom he does not much resemble; the experience which he provided may even have given rise to one aspect of Arthur Huntingdon. However, in her poems, Anne continued to allow herself to dream. Meanwhile, another loss was imminent.

Aunts feature very strongly in Brontë novels. In *Wildfell Hall* Helen's aunt is seen as a cautionary influence on enthusiastic youth. Just such an influence had been exerted over her youthful flock by Aunt Elizabeth Branwell. She had represented the voice of female authority for all of them. Now, unexpectedly, in November 1842, she died. Of her surrogate family only Branwell was at home during her last illness, and he recorded dreadful suffering on her part. Charlotte and Emily were summoned at once from Belgium. In *Agnes Grey* Anne Brontë records a bitter discussion between Agnes and Mrs Murray, which has no particular function in moving the plot forward. Its accurate dialogue and speech rhythms suggest that it is based on a real discussion, and it may be a record of Mrs Robinson's response to a request for leave on the present occasion.[23] Mrs Murray tells Agnes that she has 'influential friends ready to continue their patronage and to show you every consideration'; this in spite of her reluctance to allow her home in time for the funeral.

At a later stage we shall be examining this passage and others in order to try to understand the relationship between Anne and the Robinson family. Meanwhile Anne returned to Haworth in weary distress, the only positive outcome of the summons home the chance of meeting Emily and Charlotte again and hearing directly all about their stay overseas. But this death was crucial to the whole family; for twenty years Aunt Elizabeth had taken the place of their mother, and her loss now precipitated them into a stage of uneasy independence and young adulthood.

Anne returned to Thorp Green for a few weeks before Christmas. It was presumably at this time that she made cheerful notes for another poem exulting in the wildness of the wind. It was completed on 30 December, while Anne was at Haworth for a few days. When I wrote the notes to *The Poems of Anne Brontë* in 1979 I had been unable to locate 'The Long Plantation', where Anne claims to have seen scudding white clouds above the bare branches of the wind-tossed trees. However, the first edition six-inch map of Ouseburn shows that it was the name of a wood at Kirby Hall, not far from the River Ouse. The implication is that the Thompsons of Kirby allowed Anne into their park, and that she took advantage of their permission gratefully.

7

Branwell Joins
his Sister

———◦∘◉∘◦———

A splendid opportunity to leave Thorp Green had presented itself with the death of Elizabeth Branwell. Again, Anne refused to do so. Instead, she introduced her brother to the family at the Hall. In late January 1843, probably on the twenty-first, she returned with Branwell, who was to have the responsibility of tutoring Edmund.[1] Though Anne could not have suspected it, this move was to prove disastrous for Branwell and cause upset and scandal to the Robinsons. But in early 1843 it must have seemed a good idea. By employing him the Robinsons showed their confidence in Anne and were prepared to extend their patronage, while Anne showed that she trusted them and put some reliance in Branwell too. Through parts of 1843 Anne felt happy and expanded her interests.

Up to 1843 Branwell's record had not been a good one. He had been an extremely bright boy, learning quickly and taking the lead in the children's literary games. But when it came to earning his living he had failed. Portrait painting had been his original choice of career but he had botched his entry to the Royal Academy. This crucial failure led to a series of different posts. He had tried writing poetry, tutoring, and working on the railway. In each occupation unreliability had caused him to be dismissed. He had proved boastful, neglectful and sometimes drunk.[2] The general impression of him was that of a generous man, good company, but lacking determination. Anne, whose poetry shows how unwilling she was to abandon all hope for sinners, must have thought that in a sheltered environment, with little to distract him, he could redeem his past. But she was wrong: there *were* things to distract him, even at Thorp Green.

It is likely that the arrival of the governess and her brother at Thorp Green in January 1843 was greeted with more interest than Anne's own had been nearly three years earlier. The girls, as well as Edmund, would be keen to see this fiery-headed but diminutive Irish lad, with his ready flow of conversation. He could be just the person to stimulate the stolid young Edmund. Bessy was now seventeen, having celebrated her birthday during Anne's holiday. The bulk of the governess's time would now be spent with Mary. There is a hint of such a reduction of duties in *Agnes Grey*.[3]

The crucial role of the Robinson family in providing a scenario for Branwell's ruin and for Anne's poetic and literary reaction to that ruin has been an important concern of all Brontë biographers. Winifred Gerin, Daphne du Maurier and Ada Harrison have been among those who have tried to depict the family accurately in order to explain how it came about that Branwell's association with them turned to disaster.[4] Biographers were late on the scene, treading warily after Mrs Gaskell's rash assertions caused the threat of a libel action and subsequent changes to be made in *The Life of Charlotte Brontë*.[5] The problem turns on the characters of the members of the family and their family relations, since Branwell would declare that he was in love with Mrs Robinson, and that she had encouraged his love. Careful study of topographical and social documents throws some light on these matters, but we must also try to see the family through the eyes of Anne – a hard task since she leaves us few clues to her thoughts except the contents of the fictional *Agnes Grey*, which we are for the moment disregarding.

By the beginning of 1843 she would have been long enough at Thorp Green to be able to piece together something of the connections and background of her employers. The Reverend Edmund Robinson was the son of an older Edmund and had been born in January 1800 and baptized at Little Ouseburn. His elder sister Jane lived at York but was often at Thorp Green. Another sister, Mary, had married Charles Thorp, a canon of Durham. On the evidence of the 1841 census Edmund Robinson liked to consider himself older than his wife, though he was actually a little younger. His age would have been given in his own words to the census enumerator, though ages in this particular census were often rounded up to the next 5. He is recorded as 45 years of age, when he was actually 41, and Mrs Robinson as 40, though she was actually 42. Rumour later suggested that he was much older than his wife, and this seems to stem from his attitude, though his health too may have been poor. His account book, in which there are entries for 'soda water', suggests dyspepsia, and he would die many years before Mrs Robinson.

Other biographers of Anne have mentioned the suggestion that the Robinsons were related to the Earls of Ripon, one of whose seats was at Newby Hall, the other side of Boroughbridge.[6] It has so far been impossible to prove or disprove this rumour, though often Edmund Robinson gives the impression of belonging to the squirarchy rather than the aristocracy. But Branwell's erstwhile pupil Edmund was eventually drowned in 1869 in a boat belonging to Newby Hall, so it does seem as if further research might confirm the link.[7] Mr Robinson had a hunting stable and seems to have enjoyed riding to hounds.[8] Later, Mrs Robinson was to call him her 'angel' but successive biographers have detected tension between the Robinsons, and it is possible that there were financial problems during Anne's stay: in October 1842 Edmund Robinson sold Lylands Farm, an outlying part of the estate.[9]

I have already explained in the Introduction that all Brontë biographers have considered the background of the Robinson family critical to an understanding of Branwell's downfall and Anne's unhappiness while there. In the nature of the case, we do not have any statement from Mrs Robinson about her feelings for her son's tutor, though we do have the very sharp reaction to the version of the story which Mrs Gaskell had heard from Charlotte. Beyond this, I shall contend that Anne Brontë's view of the aristocracy and gentry as exhibited in *Wildfell Hall* is based on the circle she encountered at Thorp Green and Scarborough, and of whom she heard from members of the Robinson family. We therefore need to follow all previous biographers of Branwell or Anne into the family history of the Robinsons. By 1843 Anne would know that Lydia had been born far from Yorkshire, and still owed her allegiance very much to the family she had left behind in the north Midlands. She was baptized at Barton-under-Needwood, Staffordshire, on 25 September 1799, the youngest child of Thomas and Mary Gisborne. Their eldest,

Mary, thirteen years Lydia's senior, had married William Evans
of Allestree, which may be in part a model for Grassdale in
Wildfell Hall. William Evans was to rally strongly to his sister-
in-law's cause when Branwell lost all rationality. After Mary
came Thomas, like William Evans a Whig politician. Then
followed John; William who emigrated; James, who was now
a clergyman in Derbyshire; Matthew, who divided his time
between Derbyshire and St Leonard's-on-Sea; Francis; and
Walter Joseph, a country landowner in Chapel-en-le-Frith.[10]

The Reverend Thomas Gisborne's life and opinions were
just such as to commend him to Mr Brontë. Though not an
aristocrat, he had married into an aristocratic family. An able
man, he had a brilliant Cambridge career. He was a friend of
William Wilberforce and frequently entertained him at Yoxall
Lodge where he lived the quiet life of a perpetual curate and
country squire. There he wrote poetry, sermons and pseudo-
philosophical inquiries, just as Patrick Brontë wrote and published verse and sermons and moralistic novels. His retired life
allowed him to live into his eighties; his wife, one Mary
Babington, died in January 1843, four years before her husband. From the life story of Thomas Gisborne we may reasonably infer the outlook of his youngest child, Lydia Robinson;
she would have a taste for poetry and a respect for the arts that
would predispose her to favour the gifted Branwell. Gisborne
was also very alive to the beauties of nature and like a pale
shadow of John Clare he protested against the enclosure and
'disafforestation' [sic] of Needwood, though since he himself
profited from it, one cannot take his protest quite at face value.
Brought up in this Wordsworthian tradition, Lydia Robinson
would have been able to strike a chord with both Branwell and
Anne.

We have already noted that, like Anne Brontë, Lydia was
the youngest in the family. Anne had conscientiously tried to
escape from the feeling of inadequacy the cosseting of her
elders had engendered, but Mrs Robinson remained dependent
on others throughout her life. Undoubtedly she had been
mothered and indulged by her sister and tribe of brothers. An
early miniature shows her as a sprightly, dark-haired and
bright-eyed girl, who is said to have been the belle of the ball
in Lichfield society.[11] Setting aside for a moment her relations
with Branwell and Anne, she shows herself petted, spoilt and
incapable of making any decision for herself. The tritely reli-

gious and moralistic speeches put into the mouth of Mrs Murray in *Agnes Grey* could well be based on the words of Lydia Robinson, well drilled in evangelistic terminology but self-seeking and impetuous.[12]

There is still more in the Gisborne background which Anne Brontë was able to use in her novels. Hugh Bateman, Thomas Gisborne's brother-in-law (he had married Thomas's sister Temperance) was knighted in 1806 and Hugh's daughter Catherine married a baronet, Sir Edward Dolman Scott. A more distant relative and trustee of Thomas's father's will was Sir Robert Wilmot, who is one possible source of the name in *Wildfell Hall*. Both the Gisbornes and the Robinsons were on the fringes of high society rather than an established part of it; hence a streak of snobbery in Lydia which combined oddly with her motivation to charity, seen in the account books, and her literary-artistic streak. It is important to note that this attitude would have ruled out any question of a marriage between herself and Branwell, even had money been no consideration.

A copy of Gisborne's sermons was to be found in the schoolroom at Thorp Green.[13] Doubtless Anne picked it up and at least scanned it during the weary hours she records spending there. His prose works were long-winded and sententious, enquiring pompously into the duties of the middle classes and the position of females; Jane Robinson is alleged to have called him 'pious, canting Gisborne'. Clerical and upper-class hypocrisy are both targets for Anne Brontë in her novels. The final word on Lydia comes from Mrs Gaskell, who heard disreputable tales from her cousin, Lady Tevelyan. She did not repeat them in detail, but said she had been 'a bad woman for long and long'.[14] It is this final verdict that has stuck in the minds of Brontë biographers and influenced all judgements about her. The evidence which I have so far summarized and which is still to come suggests that she was weak and deceitful, but she clearly had a generous side, and had enough in common with Branwell for the two to enjoy each other's company. His own view of the situation must be taken into account as it develops, but it is clear that Anne would not have wished to introduce him into danger if she had thought Lydia's character a risk.

That spring Mr Brontë was entertained at Thorp Green. This news is contained in a letter from Charlotte to Branwell in which she says she has heard that he is doing well and is 'in good odour'.[15] Relations between the Brontës and the Robinsons were reaching their high point. The invitation suggests that Branwell was an immediate success, and Anne would be pleased to foster signs of this.

Mr Brontë's stay went well, though he would not have been an easy guest in some ways; well enough as a talker and happy to exchange anecdotes with his hostess, with whom he would have been charmed, but less happy at a dining table. He would enjoy strolling among the pastures to be shown the River Ouse and learn about the shooting potential of the pheasant coverts. (Branwell, to judge by his custom at Haworth, would actually take part in pheasant shooting, but probably with such friends as Dr Crosby from Great Ouseburn rather than with the Robinsons.) We need to remember that when the storm broke over Branwell, Patrick Brontë had met and presumably been charmed by Mrs Robinson; he could rely on his own memory of her character. Meanwhile as Anne walked the fields that spring she could watch ploughing (February to March), drilling wheat (March), well-sinking, sewing oats (late March) and barley (April), setting potatoes (May) and drilling swede (June), all recorded in George Whitehead's diary.[16]

Charlotte describes Anne as 'pretty well' in the letter just mentioned. News of her health would have been brought by Mr Brontë. Charlotte's cautious phrase, suggesting an upturn in Anne's health and powers, may be accepted as correct, especially since we know Anne started to take a stronger interest in music, buying a music manuscript book in which she was to copy some of her favourite hymns and songs during the next eighteen months.[17] Mr Robinson's later account book (none for this year has survived) shows that Lydia and her daughters liked to go shopping in York, where Anne might have purchased the manuscript book. One summer Anne drew a small sketch of Little Ouseburn church from the opposite bank of the little beck. Evidently she sat in Townend Field to draw it, and it is fair to see from the drawing evidence of a fine afternoon with the trees in full leaf. There is also a drawing by Anne of a romantic dream castle, but the bridge in front of it resembles the river bridge at Little Ouseburn. Her drawing of the church omits the Thompson mausoleum and shows the church roof as it was before alterations in the mid-nineteenth century. It was this summer that Anne brought home Flossie, the lively dog that Charlotte later drew sitting on a window-ledge at the parsonage, a gift from the Robinsons. Flossie may be the dog that appears in another of Anne's sketches, in which a girl leans towards the dog in a friendly way, while in the far distance is a mansion house, which could be Kirby Hall.[18]

That year's visit to Scarborough, the first when Branwell was present, was cut short by a week.[19] The reason may have been the impending wedding of Harry Thompson, son and heir at Kirby. This took place amidst a 'monstrous stir' on 24 August.[20] Henry Stephen Thompson was a busy, industrious man, who had been in the army, but had since taken on the role of pioneer agriculturalist. His coachman is said to have been amazed at the energy of his master; in his place, said the coachman, he would 'put his hands in his pocket and look at his property'.[21] Anne's scapegrace gentry in *Wildfell Hall* are unlike what we know of Harry Thompson, but it must have been at gatherings such as this 'great stir' that she gained her knowledge of the rich and their attitudes. Charlotte is less successful with her house party in *Jane Eyre* than Anne with various social gatherings in *Wildfell Hall*. One week after the wedding the harvest began at Ouseburn, while the Thompsons went on a continental tour from which they returned on 15 November.[22]

Anne's religious considerations kept her busy during this year. On 28 May she wrote a poem called 'A Word to the Calvinists', foreshadowing her discussion in *Wildfell Hall* on the fate of sinners after death. The poem is a strong plea to counter the Calvinist idea of themselves as beyond the struggle of good and evil, from which exalted position they could look down on the rest of mankind, certain of their own salvation. Anne expresses the hope that 'even the wicked shall at last/ Be fitted for the skies'. In her novels she shrinks from making her villains utterly repulsive; even as she condemns Rosalie, she portrays her attractively; Hattersley reforms. The family at Thorp Green did not live up to Anne's expectations; Lydia was certainly a wayward flirt, Bessy (to judge by Charlotte's later comments) self-seeking. In the end, however, Anne reassured herself that, like her wayward brother, they would be saved by God.

By September, however, her poem 'The Doubter's Prayer'

shows that she was struggling against the prevalent view of Branwell that her 'light of life' – faith in the Christian message – was 'vain delusion'. Branwell never made any secret of his atheism, from which he was only jarred on his deathbed. He himself wrote very little at Thorp Green, unless his poems for this period have been destroyed. It is suggested that he chose his friends from the Thorp Green servants, an action unlikely to please Anne.[23] On Thursday, 14 September Anne bought a German dictionary, for which she would certainly have to travel to York. As on the previous occasion, we can assume that she went with Mrs Robinson and one or more of the girls. The dictionary may indicate that she was beginning to teach her pupils German, but we need also to recall that she was sharing the teaching with Branwell, who was in charge of the young Edmund, and that Elizabeth, like Lydia, was now rather old for a governess. The lighter load that resulted from their complete or partial removal from the schoolroom perhaps encouraged Anne to follow Emily in her enthusiasm for German.[24] It would in any case be fair to see Anne as much more particularly engaged in supervising Mary Robinson than previously. Despite the somewhat gloomy 'Doubter's Prayer' (which however ends rather more positively) the year has shown many signs of increasing leisure and confidence for Anne.

On 7 November she wrote 'The Consolation', which suggests that she still did not feel accepted by the Robinson family. Referring in it to 'Cold stranger glances' and the difficulty of being discouraged in her 'kindly thoughts', she wishes for the 'warm hands' of her friends at Haworth: Emily's, of course. For all her work with Mary, and still to some extent with Bessy, she could not feel that they were 'warm friends'. However, this cold feeling was perhaps influenced by the actual weather. Snow had fallen as early as 17 October, and the next day it was 'such a snowy day' as never was seen.[25] Heating a large house in those days was not easy, and clearly the schoolroom, with its old hearth rug, was less than welcoming.

In *Agnes Grey* and *Wildfell Hall*, as well as her poems, Anne is most concerned with the way in which youthful hearts grow cold.[26] All the Robinsons seem to have possessed a polite but cool veneer, which Anne could not quite penetrate. On Tuesday, 21 November (Tuesday was her poetry day at this time) she was in nostalgic mood, writing of the mirth, laughter and frequent smiles of her childhood. Speech then expressed 'the inward thought' and the happy young Brontës did not welcome the end of the day. Hard as she would work for her young ladies, they were not her kin and did not share her views. She continued to draw from memory or already existing sketches. In October, a man sits resting with his dog, beneath an enormous tree overlooking a lake, both figures dwarfed. In December, she drew another water scene, this time a winding stream with a church behind and large trees in the foreground.

Anne came back to Haworth in time for Christmas. Charlotte was still in Brussels and Branwell was occupied with his own strange dreams. Internal evidence suggests that at this time Emily and Anne discussed their poetry, perhaps considering the differences in tone and content between the Gondal and non-Gondal poems. As a result Emily began to keep separate new-copied notebooks for Gondal and non-Gondal work, and seems to have made efforts to order the Gondal episodes into a coherent narrative.[27] Emily was still the leader in poetic composition; apart from hymns, which Emily did not write at all, Anne's work often echoes her sister's. The similarities that occur for the rest of the two sisters' lives are not coincidental. For the next year or two, the girls are expressing similar points of view; after that they are dealing with the same problems but seeing different solutions. Just now there can be no doubting their united attitude to the vital need for literary composition.

Returning to Thorp Green at the beginning of 1844, Anne was most regretful to leave Haworth. She revolted against the Robinson milieu in the short poem 'Fragment':

> *Yes I will take a cheerful tone*
> *And feign to share their heartless glee,*
> *But I would rather* weep *alone*
> *Than* laugh *amid their revelry.*

The poem is very similar in tone to the *Agnes Grey* passage in which Rosalie tries to interest Agnes in her coming out ball.[28] 'I was charming – wasn't I, Matilda?' askes Rosalie, and both passages may reflect Anne's experience now on arriving after a painful leave-taking from Emily and finding the guests still everywhere in the house, with the young Robinsons elatedly boasting of their conquests. If the general view of Branwell's behaviour at Thorp Green is correct, he would have joined in the 'heartless glee', thus displeasing Anne even more. Despite her reserve, both she and Branwell, according to a letter Charlotte sent Ellen, were 'both wondrously valued in their situations'.[29]

An inspection of her music manuscript book shows that when the Robinsons were otherwise occupied Anne would use her time by playing and copying out hymns and songs. The previous June she had bought the book for three shillings and sixpence. By October 1844 she had reached page 73 in copying, and assuming a fairly regular rate of work, she could be expected to reach about page 27 by this time. Sure enough, the previous pages contain Hood's poem 'I remember, I remember, the house where I was born', an extremely popular verse about a childhood home. Though Anne was not actually born at Haworth parsonage, it was this home she recalled in selecting the Hood poem for transcription, and there is further circumstantial evidence of her feelings at this time if the date proposed for composition of her own poem 'Home' in *The Poems of Anne Brontë*, early 1844, is correct.[30] Next to Hood's poem in Anne's selection comes 'Ye banks and braes of bonny Doon', a melancholy song recollecting departed happiness. These secular and nostalgic poems reflect Anne's mood in departing from Haworth that winter. Prior to this, she had copied mainly hymns or religious music. Anne's music copying is not expert. Harmonies seem conventional, as though possibly made up by Anne herself after copying the air. She writes laboriously, sometimes making errors, but the book is an important indicator of her musical taste, which finds its reflection in her poems.

Anne was still learning German, and may well have been teaching it too, if there is any parallel between Rosalie in *Agnes Grey* and the situation of one or more of Anne's pupils. Rosalie continues to learn German with Agnes even when she is technically out of Agnes's care. On 7 March Anne bought *Deutsches Leserbuch*, Rosalie's lessons perhaps reflecting Bessy's. Chapter 11 of *Agnes Grey* begins in early February and a bright day with a 'glorious canopy of bright blue sky' is described. The feel of the passage is much like Anne's previously mentioned poem 'Home', in which the sun has silver rays reflected back from the beech bark. The poem describes a 'fair and wide' garden with long winding walks and trim borders round a 'high mansion' with fair halls within. Anne contrasts this 'lovely scene' – Thorp Green or Kirby Hall – with her home at Haworth. No manuscript of 'Home' has survived, so that attempts to date it must be made on internal and circumstantial grounds. February or March are the most probable dates.

The next poem to be started is vigorous and unusual. According to the manuscript, it was at this time that Anne began to write 'Views of Life', in stanza 2 of which an imaginary interlocutor is introduced. This *persona* holds youthful, romantic views, which are gently set aside by the older, more worldly-wise second voice. It is, says this voice, 'the glow of youth' which gives the impression of a 'false light', which has to be replaced by 'the naked truth'. There are similarities between this poem and Emily's early poem 'I am the only being', in which the demise of 'the hope of youth' is chronicled. This poetic influence may suggest that Emily's is the voice of the interlocutor, but the idea that Emily could have represented the feelings of youth in early 1844 should probably be rejected. The first sixteen stanzas of the poem were copied into the 1844 copy book and the poem was then apparently abandoned until mid-1845, by which time, after a despondent spring, Anne had become more confident.[31]

It had been nearly two years since she had last seen William Weightman. At Easter she returned to his memory with a poem that celebrated his sunny smile and 'angel form'. Now, frozen below the 'cold damp stone' was 'the lightest heart that I have ever known' and the kindest. Anyone who doubts that William Weightman was of special interest to Anne Brontë has to account for her celebration of a 'light heart' belonging to a man now buried beneath the floor of an old church, *not* in a churchyard, and this not only in the present poem, but in a later one too. 'Yes, thou art gone' of April 1844 seems almost to be an extension of Heber's 'Thou art gone to the grave', which Anne copied about this time into her music manuscript book. That spring Mary Robinson reached the age of sixteen. Anne's residence at Thorp Green was entering its final phase. However much the Robinsons saw themselves as patrons to the Brontë family, there must have seemed little future for Anne as a governess in their house.

Both Anne and Branwell were at home in Haworth by 23

June, but they soon set out for Scarborough. Anne's holidays in Scarborough have seemed important to Brontë scholars, both as forming the basis for the settings of parts of her two novels, and also as providing the scene for Branwell's pursuit and possible conquest of Mrs Robinson. There is no extant diary of Anne's to provide an understanding of her impressions of Scarborough, and we have to illuminate the text of *Agnes Grey* by reference to many external documents. The chief of these are contemporary newspapers, which have already been used extensively by Winifred Gerin, but which provide even further detail on closer inspection. The Robinsons rented 7, Cliff, owned and advertised by William Wood. These buildings have featured in many Brontë biographies and have been illustrated on a number of occasions. Mr Wood's 'lodgings' were some of the most prestigious in Scarborough, and were in the best location. There were other lodging-houses on St Nicholas' Cliff, but Mr Wood owned the finest, of which he could say in his advertisement that they 'command an uninterrupted view of the sea'. The prestige of these lodgings gives us additional information about the Robinsons' self-esteem, and indicates Anne Brontë's taste in holiday accommodation when she chooses them for what turned out to be her final seaside holiday in 1849. This prestige is greater than appears in some Brontë biographies. The buildings owned by Mr Wood were three storeys high on the landward side, where they overlooked a pleasure square and small garden.[32] But the elevation facing the sea was grandiose, with elegant Regency style windows, pilasters and balustrades. Wood's lodgings, where Anne stayed in 1844, and to which she returned five years later, were the chosen holiday homes of the very rich.

It is even possible to build up a picture of the inside of Anne Brontë's temporary home. In 1844 Mr Wood's 7, Cliff contained a breakfast parlour as well as a dining room, drawing room and twelve bedrooms. The Robinsons did not rent it all. On 1 August, for example, Mr and Mrs Holbrook and family occupied part of No. 7, with the Misses Riley and two Wheelwright sisters. These other families replaced Mrs Abbotson, who had been at No. 7 the previous week, and Edward and Henry Brook with their relations. Mr Robinson's mother, who presumably could have rented the rooms tenanted by the Brooks and Abbotsons, preferred to live at No. 3, where she had stayed for several years. With her were Revd. J. Eade and Revd. W. Eade, later to become a member of the family by marriage and to take on the education of the unintelligent young Edmund. (The presence of Edmund is not specifically noted by the Scarborough papers until 1845.) This year Miss Jane Robinson seems to have stayed in another lodging-house altogether.[33]

In front of the lodgings was a grassy slope leading straight down to the sea. All along the beach were bathing huts, and it seems likely that Anne would try sea bathing, though this is nowhere recorded. At the rear of the house two paths led away to pleasure. One descended to the left, down a gentle incline and under a bridge to the museum. This little, round building is described by Branwell in a partly finished novel.[34] It housed geological specimens and fossils, a matter of keen concern to the people of the 1840s, who sought feverishly to understand how the antiquity implied by these ancient stones could be reconciled with the suggested dating of the Old Testament. The other path led to a marvellous bridge across the Mill Beck. At the entrance one bought a week-, fortnight- or month-long ticket, and was given the freedom of the spa and grounds, together with the right to 'parade the bridge', as the 1848 directory puts it. Lydia, Bessy and Mary would have enjoyed this greatly, but Anne too in her way would have liked the heights of the narrow iron bridge, with the fresh sea breezes gusting in from the east.

Scarborough Spa was famed for the healing quality of its waters. Their medical properties were considered to help the body's regularity: 'the waters of these wells are a compound of vitriol, iron, alum, nitre and salt, and are both purgative and diuretic,' the directory claims. In 1844 the buildings of the Spa were not as imposing as they later became, but they already included a 'saloon' in which orchestras performed and which drew crowds on rainy days. As her music manuscripts show, Anne had a discriminating taste in music, and she would certainly have enjoyed chaperoning her charges to concerts at the saloon, and perhaps to the Town Hall in St Nicholas Street. A typical concert, held on Tuesday, 16 July, included a Mozart symphony (one of the D major ones), an air from Weber's 'Der Freychutz' (according to the advertisement), a quartet by Pleyel, a Rossini overture, and various lesser works such as quadrilles and a flute duet. The repertoire was similar to the kind of music Anne was practising for her own benefit, and apparently with Mary Robinson. Her heightened interest in music that autumn may owe something to the Scarborough concerts.[35]

In St Thomas Street was the Theatre Royal, owned and run by a family named Roxby, who were destined to play an unexpected part in the Robinson story. They also had theatrical interests in Manchester. At the start of the season Mr Samuel Roxby would take up residence at 10, Huntriss Row and deploy his strategy for the year. On Thursday, 1 August the company performed *King Richard II* , and there was also an extravaganza called 'Tom and Jerry'. On Saturday there was a 'fashionable night', including the first appearance of Mr Robert Roxby, manager of the Theatre Royal, Manchester, a celebrated comedian. These programmes sound more like Branwell's choice than Anne's, but Lydia's later history shows that she was attending these theatres, with or without her ex-governess.

One thing we can be sure of is Anne's observation of her fellow visitors. Not only in Wood's lodgings, but along the whole of the Cliff the nobility and gentry rented rooms. There were absentee clergymen, captains and colonels; there were Lady Selina Henry, the Marchioness of Hastings, landed gentry turned manufacturers, and at No. 9 of that year, four Misses Willmott. Many of these guests hailed from Yorkshire, but there were others from the Midlands and South, and even as far afield as Cornwall and Dublin. When she came to write *Wildfell Hall* Anne had considerable experience of the gentry to draw on.

It is clear from Anne's two novels that she had walked about Scarborough and its neighbourhood. Such walks took her up the steep hill of the castle, past St Mary's church, though the names of these places are omitted in *Agnes Grey*.[36] In the novel, 'the ——hill' is just outside the town, and some way up it (for the walk takes some time) the hero and heroine see 'the venerable old church' on their way to the vantage-point from which they can look out over the sea. The paragraph is couched in such a way as to suggest personal knowledge. The 'venerable' church was in fact in a very run-down state, with a confusion of box-pews and various internal structures detracting from its medieval architecture. However, Anne's choice of adjective indicates that she knew of the history of Scarborough's parish church, which had been used as a gun post in the Civil War, fired on by a canon from the castle. The castle is not mentioned in the novel, though it is implied that Agnes and Edward Weston will stand there looking out romantically to sea. Anne's understatement in the novel should not lead us to ignore her choice of detail in scene-setting. However, it is doubtful whether she would attend services in St Mary's, since the new and nearer building of Christ Church, Vernon Road, in which her funeral service was later conducted, appears to have been the Robinsons' choice of church.

A very curious poem, written at Scarborough and dated 2 August 1844, is 'Fluctuations'. It seems to use various meteorological constituents as symbols for Anne's objects of affection.

> *What though the sun had left my sky;*
> *To save me from despair*
> *The blessed moon arose on high*
> *And shone serenely there.*

We may confidently suggest William Weightman as the person associated with 'the sun'. He had indeed 'left' Anne's sky by September 1842. But who is signified by 'the moon'?

> *I watched her with a tearful gaze*
> *Rise slowly o'er the hill;*
> *While through the dim horizon's haze*
> *Her light gleamed faint and chill.*

> *I thought such wan and lifeless beams*
> *Could ne'er my heart repay*
> *For the bright sun's most transient beams*
> *That cheered me through the day.*

> *But as above that mist's control*
> *She rose and brighter shone*
> *I felt her light upon my soul,*
> *But now – that light is gone!*

The moon appears to be a friend known to Anne between late 1842 and 1844. 'She' is to be replaced by 'a little star' and then a meteor before returning in stanza eight. The poem ends:

> *Kind Heaven, increase that silvery gleam*
> *And bid these clouds depart;*
> *And let her kind and holy beam*
> *Restore my fainting heart.*

This is a poem for which we do not have enough clues. Reading and re-reading it, we feel it must describe in code Anne's friendships. The sun has already been equated with Weightman; even his 'transience' has been mentioned. But the hints at a social life which we cannot understand are most tantalizing. The 'moon' is someone whom Anne first found in 1842, but who later fades, only to return in 1844. As the poem was written in Scarborough towards the end of the summer holiday this year, the 'moon' may be another Scarborough visitor, or a resident. Unlike Emily, Anne was a competent and charming letter writer, though only a tiny handful of her letters have survived. The person coded now as 'the moon' seems likely to have been a correspondent, but there is little chance of any further clue to his or her (almost certainly her) identity becoming known.

It is the opinion of Branwell's biographers that at Scarborough he further ingratiated himself with his pupil's mother, Lydia Robinson. This seems likely. Mrs Robinson's charitable and kindly, patronizing attitude to her governess would have taken on some warmth when directed at a male object. Looking back from October 1845 he wrote:

> This lady (though her husband detested me) showed me a
> degree of kindness which, when I was deeply grieved one
> day at her husband's conduct, ripened into declarations of
> more than ordinary feeling.[37]

It is easy to see that Branwell, inexperienced as he was, might easily fall under the spell of such dashing confidence. He could also begin to see himself in the role of a knight in shining armour. Because Anne felt responsible for Branwell, we cannot evade an attempt to chart the course of events between him and Mrs Robinson.

Mr Robinson's objectionable conduct could have been of various shades of inconsiderateness. Like Mary Ingham at Blake Hall, Lydia would have been brought up to endure degrees of masculine rudeness or even oppression, attitudes that would not have been tolerated at Haworth under the matriarchal rule of Aunt Elizabeth, and supported by Charlotte. Though at home Branwell always tried to be cocky, he was unable to lord it over the females in the house, and Mr Brontë, though eccentric, was always noted for his courtesy. In this scene, reported later to Branwell's friend, he reacts quickly in support of Mrs Robinson's honour. Whenever we date the scene, it is likely to have been before 1844, so that on this holiday while dyspeptic Mr Robinson stayed in the lodgings Branwell escorted Lydia round the flowery walks across the Mill Beck bridge. Neither Mr Robinson nor Anne Brontë need have noticed any impropriety at this stage. Half a sentence in a later letter Charlotte asserts that Branwell had been 'irritable' during his stay at home in June; one could interpret this to mean that he was anxious to be back in Mrs Robinson's company.[38] But Anne too was happy at Scarborough; she would not have seen any incongruity in Branwell feeling so.

The party returned to Thorp Green during the second week of August, and from that time Anne's interest in her music developed. There are a number of extant music books with clear dates of purchase and some which are not so clear. By 13 October Anne had reached page 72 in her manuscript copybook and here wrote a copy of her hymn 'My God! Oh let me call thee mine' to a tune then well known, titled 'Justification'. The hymn was very much in the Wesleyan tradition, requesting faith in the coming trials and mourning over the past. Its tone suggests that Anne Brontë's cheerful experience at Scarborough had been replaced by another period of self-doubt.

Most of the music Anne bought was vocal with piano accompaniment, though 'Solfeggio for young pupils' is purely instrumental. Among the collection was one of Moore's airs, arranged by Henry Bishop, 'Come, chase that starting tear away'. This was not one of Moore's Irish songs, of which both Anne and Emily were fond, but a light and melancholy song from his later collection.

Among the pieces copied into the book about this time is a duet, 'Time around his dial stealing'. The implication is that Anne would be joined in performing it by a second female voice, and the most likely person to have sung with her must be Mary Robinson. Such a relationship as this indicates is portrayed in *Wildfell Hall*, where Helen and Esther talk readily with each other and exchange confidences despite the difference in their ages. In view of the relationship which later developed between Anne and Mary Robinson, when Anne was sought out as a counsellor, it is reasonable to suppose a developing friendship at this time. We shall explore the further progress of this friendship in chapter 10.

A day or two after the purchase of 'Come, chase that starting tear away' Anne and Branwell returned to Haworth, and on 16 December Anne wrote a Gondal prison poem much like those that enchanted Emily. Once again her close friendship with her sister was renewed. Branwell was 'less irritable', perhaps because he was increasingly confident that Mrs Robinson returned his affection. But the bleak tone of Anne's poems during the next six months may be interpreted as awareness of his ambiguous position. This could also result in strain between Anne and the Robinson girls. Returning to Thorp Green in late January Anne viewed her prospect with hatred:

> *Call me away; there's nothing here*
> *That wins my soul to stay;*
> *Then let me leave this prospect drear,*
> *And hasten far away.*

> *To our beloved land I'll flee,*
> *Our land of thought and soul,*
> *Where I have roved so oft with thee,*
> *Beyond the world's control . . .*

For the first time for years Anne seems enthusiastic about Gondal while away, and yearning for Emily. Such pleasure as she had felt the previous autumn in Mary's company had evidently evaporated. In any event, January was a bad time at Thorp Green; she had remarked on the 'heartless glee' of Thorp Green society the previous January. Her manuscript book was full, and no later one has been found. From external evidence we know that the pleasant walk to Little Ouseburn church, the source for the scenes in *Agnes Grey* where the heroine converses with the curate Mr Weston, was now radically changed by the grubbing up of the roadside hedges to be replaced by new quickthorn, set in straight lines. The resulting disturbance changed the walk from a meandering lane to a desolate track that emphasized the bleakness of winter.[39] There is a curious report on Anne's health that spring in the pages of

A. M. F. Robinson's *Emily Brontë*. She had heard that Anne had written letters home telling of 'health worn out by constant agonizing suspicion'. She also implies that Anne's final return from Thorp Green that summer was due to her feeling of degradation on realizing Branwell's situation with Mrs Robinson:

> Many letters had passed between them, through her hands too. Too often had she heard her unthinking little pupils threaten their mother into more than customary indulgence, saying: 'Unless you do as we wish, we shall tell papa about Mr Brontë.'[40]

This is an interesting and unique piece of apparent information which requires discussion.

As we have seen, Anne had been occupied for some time now in teaching Mary Robinson alone. She was certainly not 'little', being now almost seventeen. Bessy may have been taking German lessons with Anne, but the epithet 'little' is even less likely to have been applied to her. A. M. F. Robinson's remarks, therefore, have generally been glossed over and could be taken to show her lack of primary information. However, they require careful consideration in the light of an entry in Mr Robinson's account book for 1845. It reads: 'Apl. 11th. Mr G. for Governess 25 0 0' (i.e. £25). 'Mr G' is identifiable from other entries as Edward Greenhow, a local clergyman who had the living of Nun Monkton from November 1844.[41] The entry implies that he was paying Edmund Robinson for a share in Anne's services, and we must assume that she was teaching some of his children as well as Mary Robinson. The Greenhow children are much more likely to have been the source of A. M. F. Robinson's remark than Mary Robinson. The eldest, William, seems to have been almost adopted as a friend for young Edmund; if anyone were to teach him, it is sure to have been Branwell. However, Eliza Greenhow was twelve, Eleanor nine and Sophia seven. Charlotte was only five. If Branwell taught William while Anne taught the four girls, details of Branwell's habits could have been reported by her brother to Eliza and used in some form of blackmail. Thus the discovery of the account book entry may go some way towards vindicating A. M. F. Robinson's story and increasing credence in her other information.

At this time the Greenhows evidently lived at Great Ouse-burn. It looks as if Anne might be expected to walk across the fields there on some days of the week; it is possible that the strain of teaching young children revived feelings of Blake Hall and contributed to the tone of despair that invades the poems during this spring.[42] During the walks to Great Ouse-burn Anne might well gather further material which would be used later for the Vale of York sections of *Agnes Grey*. Teaching young children evidently made her think again of her own situation, unlikely as she now was ever to have her own baby. In 'Dreams', dated in the manuscript 'Spring 1845', she imagines 'an infant's form beloved and fair' at her breast. Not for the first time we see how Anne yearned to be a mother.[43]

A. M. F. Robinson's suggestion that Branwell and Mrs Robinson had exchanged love letters through Anne seems hard to substantiate, though if we take the view that the account book entry makes sense of the record of small children being taught by Anne, it may be that an informant of A. M. F. Robinson had special knowledge. On the other hand, Anne was certainly stirred and bewildered that spring, as is shown by the series of poems of which 'Dreams' is one. It appears to contemplate a real lover, appearing in a vision at night; whether the reference is still to William Weightman or not the text gives no clue. Just as Weightman had died and destroyed a former dream, so in the poem when the author feels herself 'beloved at last' she records waking to find the dream 'of happiness destroyed'.

> *A heart whence warm affections flow,*
> *Creator, thou hast given to me,*
> *And am I only thus to know*
> *How sweet the joys of love would be?*

8

An End and a
New Beginning

———◦◦◦◦———

Summer and autumn 1845 were dramatic times for both
Anne and her 'friends'. Anne left Thorp Green 'of her own
accord', as Emily's diary paper puts it.[1] The circumstances of
this departure will need to be discussed, as also will the departure of Branwell, not 'of his own accord'. Lydia Mary Robinson left Thorp Green later, eloping with her lover to Scotland.
Emily and Anne went on the first of what should have been a
series of journeys together. Both sisters turned to writing
novels with a Yorkshire instead of a Gondal background.
Charlotte made a raid on Emily's privacy and discovered
remarkable poetry. All three young women stood on the
threshold of publication. Some or all of these events were
interrelated and formed a complex web of event and consequence. It is important for the reader to understand how
flimsy is the evidence surrounding these undisputed events.

Anne left Thorp Green on or about 12 June, which date
appears to accord with those of previous years.[2] Mr Robinson,
meticulous about the salaries of his employees, as the account
book shows, paid her final month's money the day before.[3] It
is quite clear from the accounts that her decision not to return
had been made, or she would not have been given one
month's salary; normally she seems to have been paid quarter-
ly. It was time to leave Mary, who was seventeen and was too
old for a governess, and the small Greenhows who had either
worn Anne out or had insufficient claim on her to keep her in
Great Ouseburn. There seems to be no mystery about Anne's
departure: she had finished her task with the Robinsons and
needed a summer holiday. In the course of time she would

presumably have considered another teaching post, but for the moment she was exhausted.[4] The fact of her arrival at Haworth, but no reason for it, is laconically recorded by Charlotte in a letter to Ellen, which uses the terse words, 'Anne is come home, and her presence certainly makes me feel more at liberty.'[5]

In the event the summer was to be clouded by Branwell's disgrace. Since this final débâcle of Branwell's unsuccessful career is often indicated as the catalyst which precipitated the writing of the Brontë novels, and since Anne alone of the three had observed his conduct at Thorp Green, a discussion of the whole episode is important. There is some new evidence to present, which will modify the accounts given in Winifred Gerin's *Branwell Brontë* and Daphne du Maurier's *The Infernal World of Branwell Brontë*, though some of the facts detailed in these two accounts remain acceptable. A more thorough examination of the cash book produces data which were not fully explored by earlier writers, who did not have the benefit of cheap photocopying which allows fragmentary evidence to be sifted continually. The date of Branwell's final payment is correctly recorded by Winifred Gerin.[6] Under the date 11 June an entry reads 'Mr Brontë due July 21st 20 0 0' [£20]. The word July is underlined. This payment represented a quarter-year's salary for Branwell, who had last been paid on 21 April. His January payment is not recorded, and the book begins only at the beginning of January, so we cannot show conclusively that he took his previous salary before Christmas, though this is probable, since his payment date would fall within the Christmas holiday. However, the early payment in June instead of July suggests that he was being paid off. It does not support Branwell's story, told to Charlotte, that he had only a week at Haworth and was then required back at Thorp Green.[7] This time the early payment seems to be 'in lieu of notice'.

In previous years Branwell and Anne had returned to Thorp Green after about a fortnight's holiday at Haworth to go with the family to Scarborough.[8] This time Branwell told Charlotte he must go back within a week, though the Robinsons would not be going to Scarborough for three weeks yet. If he was to return within a week, why did Mr Robinson have to pay him on 11 June? Why not wait a week until he came back from Haworth? On balance it seems that Branwell lied to Charlotte in telling her that he had to go back to Thorp Green after only a week. One motive for this might be that he was afraid to say that he had yet again lost his job.

Charlotte's letter to Ellen Nussey adds further complications.[9] She tells her friend that Branwell will come back to Haworth again when the Robinsons go to Scarborough. This is another departure from the usual custom, as both Branwell and Anne would normally have accompanied the family for their seaside holiday. Charlotte went to stay with Ellen, but when she returned she found Branwell at home, apparently talking of a letter from Mr Robinson 'sternly dismissing him and intimating that he had discovered his proceedings, which he characterized as bad beyond expression, and charging him on pain of exposure to break off instantly and for ever all communication with every member of his family'. These are Charlotte's words, apparently quoting from Branwell's letter of dismissal as Branwell had quoted it to her. He claimed that he had received the letter the previous Thursday, that is 17 July.[10]

But Branwell must have known in June that he would not be going back to the Robinsons before 21 July, if ever. Instead of telling Charlotte the truth, he had apparently invented a story that he was needed back at Thorp Green in mid-June. If he stayed at Haworth a week, he must have gone back to Thorp Green on about the 19th. Mr Robinson would have been greatly surprised to see him, but Charlotte records that he did go back, though of course she had only his word as to where he was going and why. Branwell's only possible motive in going back was that he had by this time become obsessed by Mrs Robinson and thought he would be able to see her. If, as seems likely, he had already been dismissed, his behaviour can be explained partly by his need to keep up appearances at home, and partly by an infatuation with Mrs Robinson.

The Robinsons 'set off to Scarboro'' on 4 July, according to George Whitehead; they had a full day there on 5 July, with the purchase of bridge tickets and a whip for Edmund being recorded in the cash book.[11] Daphne du Maurier thinks Edmund did not go to Scarborough with the rest of the family, since his name is not recorded in the *Scarborough Herald* on that date.[12] But over the years he is rarely singled out for any mention in the local papers and her inference is unsafe. Her notion that Branwell might have been needed at Thorp

1 Unfinished drawing, attributed to Anne Brontë. The
dog resembles Flossie, the King Charles Spaniel given to
Anne by the Robinsons in 1843. The house in the
background may be Kirby Hall. © Brontë Society,
Haworth.

2 Little Ouseburn church, drawn by Anne Brontë. © Brontë Society,
Haworth.

3 Little Ouseburn church as it is now. Alterations to the roof of the east end date from about the 1860s. Photograph by author.

4 A romanticized view of a bridge and castle. The bridge may be based on the Ouse bridge at Little Ouseburn. © Brontë Society, Haworth.

5 Anne Brontë's drawing
of an elm tree. © Brontë
Society, Haworth.

6 Roe Head House,
Mirfield, drawn by Anne
Brontë. © Brontë Society,
Haworth.

7 A Watercolour head of a girl, probably painted by Anne Brontë. It was given by the Robinsons to the Anderson family at Ouseburn. © Brontë Society, Haworth.

8 Anne Brontë's grave at Scarborough. Photograph by author.

9 Branwell's 'gun group' portrait. © Brontë Society, Haworth.

10 Anne Brontë's symbolic drawing of 1840: 'What you please'. © Brontë Society, Haworth.

11 Scarborough in 1845. 'Wood's lodgings' is the building on the Cliff at the right of the picture. North Yorkshire County Library.

12 The 'monk's lodgings' at Thorp Green. Photograph by author.

13 Anne Brontë, drawn by
Charlotte. The picture was
returned to Haworth from
America in 1991. © Brontë
Society, Haworth.

14 Map of Thorp Green in the
nineteenth century.
Photograph by author.

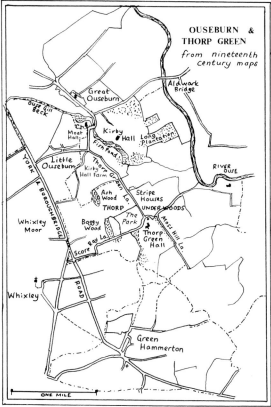

15 Kirby Hall the nextdoor estate to Thorp Green. Royal Commission on the Historical Monuments of England.

16 Wellhouse Chapel, Mirfield. Anne Brontë's use of this as a basis of the name Wellwood House in *Agnes Grey* suggests she found a special interest there. Photograph by author.

Green to look after Edmund until he went to Scarborough does not have a basis in probability.

On 26 June, a week after Branwell had returned to Thorp Green, Charlotte went to stay with Ellen Nussey. She stayed more than three weeks, extending her holiday after Ellen received a letter from Emily at the parsonage in the second week of July, laconically suggesting she should keep Charlotte an extra week; 'all are well at home,' Emily says drily.[13] But who, precisely, were the people 'at home' on the day Emily wrote? Was Branwell already back, as he certainly was a week later, finally admitting that he had been forbidden ever to contact the Robinsons again? We have to remember that no one has even seen the letter Branwell claimed to have received from Mr Robinson, 'sternly dismissing him', on 17 July. It could be an invention. It is even possible that Emily connived at Branwell's story in the end, having played her part in keeping Charlotte away an extra week in the hope that some solution might be found to Branwell's problems.[14]

The following is a possible reconstruction of events, taking into account the known character of Branwell and the evidence of the cash book. Branwell had received his pay for the quarter on 11 June, perhaps in lieu of notice. Returning to Haworth, but considering himself still employed until the end of the quarter, 21 July, he would have two thoughts on his mind: he would have wanted to conceal from his father and Charlotte that he had lost his job, and he would have wanted to find a way to rescue Mrs Robinson, as he saw it, from the clutches of a tyrannous husband. It is unlikely that he would tell Anne the truth, but his muddled lies would seem lame, and she might in any case have heard rumours of his imminent dismissal from Bessy or Mary. She would have been full of unease as she and Branwell returned together on 12 June. At home, Branwell told Charlotte that he would be going back to Thorp Green for a time, but admitted that he would not be going to Scarborough. It seems certain that he did go back, but he could not have been openly received at the Hall itself. It looks as if he must have taken lodgings or stayed with a friend in the Ouseburn area, possibly with Dr Crosby. There he would plot to run away with Mrs Robinson. This sounds silly, but it is the kind of romance into which Branwell sometimes dreamed himself.

We may theorize that one day he turned up at the Hall itself.

Mrs Robinson, who had perhaps amused herself with her personal patronage of this fantastic young poet, realized in some alarm that he was serious. She had no alternative but to inform her husband, telling him that she was being pestered by her son's former tutor. The evidence is that she was relieved and delighted at the way he dealt with the situation; clearly he did not blame her. At his death, less than a year later, Lydia would write 'my angel' as her characterization of him in the account book. Now, at this critical point in June 1845, he must have sent Branwell packing, possibly saying to his face the words that are recorded in the letter supposed to have been on 17 July, or possibly reserving them for paper, if we believe Branwell's account and accept that the letter was not a fiction. That June, with his final pay in his pocket, Branwell could have afforded to stay at Ouseburn. He must have believed that Mrs Robinson's behaviour, friendly and perhaps flirtatious as it was, indicated her willingness to elope, but he sadly misunderstood her attitude and motivation.

We must now return to Anne, whose embarrassment at the whole affair must have been mortifying. Just as Branwell's departure may have drawn tears or misleading protestations from Mrs Robinson when he left on 12 June, so when Anne stepped out of the front portico for the last time, the young Robinsons would have promised to write to her. This they did, copiously. It seems likely that their correspondence would have started that summer, and that they would report to Anne all that had transpired on Branwell's unauthorized return. Some of this she would share with Emily.

It is interesting that the first half of 1845 was such a buoyant time for Emily, though so depressing for Anne. Her elation rose to a peak when the two sisters decided to make a journey that summer to the two places that Anne loved: York and Scarborough. The purpose may have been to try to restore Anne's spirits, though Scarborough was eventually dropped from the programme, and Anne would not revisit it until 1849, in very different circumstances. Once Charlotte was safely away with Ellen Nussey, the two younger sisters set out, on Monday, 30 June. Whether Anne, or both she and Emily, knew that Branwell was up to some kind of mischief is not certain. The change of plan to omit Scarborough could possibly have something to do with a wish to follow him and to try to save him from whatever folly he was about to commit.

As evidence for the journey, we have Emily's fragmentary account book and the two diary papers written at the end of July. On the Monday night the young women stayed at York and spent some of Tuesday exploring the city. They undoubtedly visited the Minster, with which Anne had fallen in love. She certainly knew the York shops, and it is regrettable that the account book stubs do not mention any purchases they made there. The fragment does mention the hotel bill and that the girls travelled back to Leeds by train.[15] This was their 'first long journey by ourselves together', and Emily says that despite 'broken' weather 'we enjoyed ourselves very much'.[16] Amazingly, Anne does not even mention the expedition in her own diary paper, to which we shall return.

The twenty-five-mile journey from York to Leeds was straightforward, and they then took an omnibus to reach Bradford. Some problem or obstacle was encountered there, for Emily says in her diary paper, 'we enjoyed ourselves very much, except during a few hours in Bradford'. The account book records payment of one shilling for glass of wine that evening in Bradford, so it looks as if the problem provided a shock. After the wine, they were restored enough to go on to Keighley, perhaps again by omnibus, since payment for two is recorded in the account book. A night's rest cost them a total of three shillings and sixpence, and they walked back to Haworth in the morning.[17]

Reading Anne's diary paper, which says nothing about these adventures, we may feel that her sister, high-spirited as she had been in her teenage years, had jollied Anne into this excursion. On the way, she told Anne that they were Gondal princes and princesses escaping from 'the palaces of instruction' to join the Royalists. Anne's omission of the whole episode suggests that she found it hard to be a princess that summer. 'The Gondals are not in first-rate playing condition,' she wryly remarks. 'Will they improve?' For Emily, they did; for Anne they did not. She was now too enmeshed in the concerns of the real world to gain any solace from Gondal. She must have tried to get Emily to take the situation at Thorp Green seriously, and show practical concern for Branwell, who was to be sent on a recuperatory tour of north Wales.

Later, Emily said he was a 'hopeless being'. It was her belief that character was fixed, and just as she herself wished 'to be as God made me' so Branwell was as he was, and that terminated all discussion. To Anne, this was soul-destroying; for her sinners could repent and change, though Arthur Huntingdon represents her modest view of how far that might happen in practice.

Branwell, then, was one topic of conversation on the journey to York. The progress of literary composition is likely to have been another. Anne's poems of that year were bleak and sad, but they were beginning to have some power. Emily's were sublime; the copy-books were filling with gems. The very idea of copying poems suggests that the sisters discussed (either at this time or at others) the possibility of publication. There was also the matter of Anne's work 'Passages in the Life of an Individual', which occurs in her diary paper. Discussion that summer may have covered prose as well as verse.

The firm evidence for this work of Anne's is minute. 'I have begun the third volume of "Passages in the Life of an Individual",' she records in her diary paper. 'I wish I had finished it.' Most biographers assume without discussion that this work is *Agnes Grey*.[18] Certainly the timescale does suggest that Anne would be writing something towards the book at this stage. I feel that the assumption should be examined, since there are complications about accepting it unquestioningly. We cannot avoid linking with this examination the matter of Emily's prose work, also mentioned in her diary paper.[19] Both sisters are writing profusely by the end of July, and since within a year they would have 'prose works' for Charlotte to send round various publishers, it would be helpful to know just what they were writing.

In her paper, Emily writes: 'I am at present writing a work on the First War. Anne has been writing some articles on this, and a book by Henry Sophona.' Anne writes: 'Emily is engaged in writing the Emperor Julius's life. She has read some of it, and I want very much to hear the rest. She is writing some poetry too. I wonder what it is about? I have begun the third volume of "Passages in the Life of an Individual." I wish I had finished it.' It is typical of the confusion surrounding Gondal that the two sisters' accounts of what they are writing diverge completely. One is bound to ask whether Henry Sophona was the 'Individual' about whom Anne was writing passages. Was the Emperor Julius involved in the First War? On the face of the matter, it must seem as though Henry Sophona, not Agnes Grey, is writing an account of his experiences.[20]

This is not quite a satisfactory conclusion for various reasons. The first notice we have of the three Brontë novels comes from a letter of Charlotte's, dated 6 April 1846, in which she says the sisters are 'now preparing for the press' three distinct and unconnected tales.[21] They are not 'writing' the tales, but have evidently done so already, despite a very busy autumn and winter selecting and revising poems. This date puts the actual primary composition of the novels into 1845 at the latest. It thus seems that in mid-year Anne must be writing both Gondal work (Henry Sophona) *and* a first version of *Agnes Grey*. Either may qualify for the title 'passages in the Life of an Individual' for both are biography. The only alternative is to suppose that Henry Sophona is Agnes Grey's pseudonym; this seems impossible in view of the very feminine nature of the novel as we have it.

In *A Life of Emily Brontë* I have developed a suggestion of Mary Visick's that Heathcliff derives from 'the Emperor Julius'.[22] Julius was at the forefront of Emily's mind in 1838 when she was teaching at Law Hill. Some elements of the geography of Halifax appear to be one of the roots of *Wuthering Heights*, so it is possible that at the beginning of her novel Emily cast her mind back six or seven years to the time when she started teaching. *Agnes Grey* is concerned with the same period in the Brontës' lives: its first events correspond roughly with the events of early 1839, when Anne went to Blake Hall. This similarity can hardly be coincidence. It looks as though the two younger sisters had discussed the setting and themes of their novels just as they had discussed Gondal over the years. It may seem fanciful to detect a similarity between *Agnes Grey* and *Wuthering Heights*, but though the two developed into such divergent novels, there does seem to be this seed of common purpose.

The events used by Anne for *Agnes Grey* begin about 1839 and she does not seem to make much use of anything after early 1843, when her teaching load was reduced to one pupil; this is mirrored in the situation in chapter 11 of the novel. The pursuit of Rosalie by Hatfield may be based on the behaviour of Lascelles before his marriage in December 1841; William

Weightman, who makes up one strand in the character of
Edward Weston, died in September 1842, and so on. Weston
is clearly a composite. He is unlike Weightman in many ways
– the fact that his surname begins with the same letter may
have misled earlier commentators. His hair is dark, and not
curly like Weightman's. He is a 'habitual thinker' and Agnes
has not seen him smile by the end of chapter 11, though
Weightman was perpetually joking. Mr Weston is 'thoughtful
and stern', which is not our impression of the flirtatious and
charming lightweight of whose suitability as a clergyman
Charlotte had doubts.[23] But Weston, like Weightman, visits
the poor and is generous. Other clergymen are surely combined in this ideal curate of Anne's: James la Trobe, the calmly
optimistic, future bishop is one, and Anne's enthusiasm for
Scarborough may imply a sensitive minister at St Mary's or
Christ Church.[24] Edward Greenhow was not from a county
family; he too may have contributed to Weston's character.

The section following Mr Weston's description at the end of
chapter 11 takes place in mid-March, but the spirit of the
'primroses' episode is like that of the bluebells of 1840; it
induces 'sad thoughts of early childhood, and yearnings for
departed joys'.[25] It is, doubtless, the consideration of some of
these points that leads Winifred Gerin to place the beginning of
the composition of 'Passages in the Life of an Individual'
(which she equates with *Agnes Grey*) as far back as 1842.[26] But
if the novel had been roughed out before 1845 two markers
from that year support, though not conclusively, a date of
1845 for the systematized version. In chapter 7 there is a
reference to an emigrant, who might 'awake some morning
and find himself in Port Nelson, in New Zealand, with a
world of waters between himself and all that knew him'. It
was in March 1845 that Mary Taylor, one of Charlotte's
closest friends, went out to New Zealand to make a new life.
Discussion of emigration would have been intense in letters
from Haworth during that month.

At the end of chapter 13 comes a passage where Rosalie and
Matilda are teasing Agnes about 'flirting' with Mr Weston.
They reach the Hall and Agnes climbs the stairs to her own
room where she shuts the door and prays to be married to
him, though she strives to say 'Thy will be done'. '*Thou* wilt
not despise,' she ends the prayer, using words that are identical
with words in Anne's poem 'Confidence' of 1 June 1845. 'I

might have been deceiving myself,' Agnes goes on, 'but that idea [that she was praying for another's happiness too] gave me confidence to ask, and power to hope I did not ask in vain.' The identical phrase and the abstract noun together connect the novel to the poem at this point, and make it seem possible that this part of *Agnes Grey* was written in June 1845: this could support the identification of the 'Life of an Individual' with the novel against our previous link with Henry Sophona.

Anne's novel plan then took her back to April. It was a very gloomy day when Agnes listened to the curate at the afternoon service. In describing the experience Anne again writes close to her poetry. Agnes finds that at church 'I might look without fear of scorn or censure upon a form and face more pleasing to me than the most beautiful of god's creations: I might listen without disturbance to a voice more charming than the sweetest music to my ears!'[27] The same characteristics are mentioned in a number of poems to Anne's ideal clergyman, based on Weightman.[28] A tinge of self-satire mocks the idealization in *Agnes Grey*. Mr Weston offers Agnes the use of his umbrella as the rain begins to pour down. 'No thank you, I don't mind the rain!' answers the shy Agnes, in a tone which sounds as if it reflects Anne's own. In her narrator's voice she then adds to the reader, 'I always lacked common sense when taken by surprise.' The defensive reply and the self-mockery are surely Anne writing of herself.

There then follows a thoughtful discussion on the nature of beauty, with two balancing viewpoints as so often in the poems and *Wildfell Hall*. It begins as Agnes is musing about her appearance, which, like 'Olivia Vernon' in 1840, she admits to taking some pains with. She decides, after describing facial characteristics that are similar to Anne's own, that she is not beautiful, and begins to say that it does not matter. Character is more important than prettiness – an Evangelical view which the girls must have heard many times from Aunt Elizabeth. From this point on, however, Anne carefully argues that beauty is a gift from God and not to be despised. A child, she suggests, loves a bird better than a toad. The little girl (Anne herself, of course) will not hurt the toad, but 'she cannot love it like the bird, with its graceful form, soft feathers, and bright, speaking eyes.'

Ranging in her mind over the events of the past five years,

[127]

Anne is able to call on a clear aural memory. The tones and cadences of Mrs Murray's speeches are so distinctive as to be drawn, surely, from life. Left with only Matilda to teach, Agnes fails to stop her interest in the stables, kennels and coach-house. She is reprimanded by Mrs Murray as Anne must have been reprimanded by Mrs Robinson, though I am not sure that Anne's sole pupil, Mary, was the Robinson girl most likely to be found in the stables. In conveying Mrs Murray's speech, Anne uses italics, and we catch a personal rhythm and intonation.

> '*Dear* Miss Grey! it is the strangest thing. I suppose you can't help it, if it's not in your nature – but I *wonder* you can't win the confidence of that girl and make your society at *least* as agreeable to her as that of Robert or Joseph!'[29]

Joseph Dickinson was the name of a servant at Thorp Green who had been born on 16 July 1826; I cannot identify 'Robert'.[30]

Mrs Murray is very prone to sermonizing. She tells Agnes that her pupils will reflect her teaching. 'You will excuse me dropping these hints,' she goes on heavy-handedly: 'You know it is all for your own good. Many ladies would speak to you much more strongly ... I know the advantage of a place like this to a person in your situation; and I have no desire to part with you, as I am sure you would do very well if you will only think of these things and try to exert yourself a *little* more ...' This recipe 'for your own good' sounds very like what we can gather about Mrs Robinson, the daughter of 'pious, canting' Gisborne. In some of these speeches, it seems as though Anne were reporting verbatim. The speech just quoted occurs just before Agnes leaves to attend the deathbed of her father; this is equivalent in Anne's life to the leave she obtained in autumn 1842 for the funeral of Aunt Elizabeth Branwell. After this, Agnes returns to Horton Lodge only for a short while, and holds a final conversation with Mr Weston during which she alludes to the 'honesty' of Matilda and admits that she is not without regret at parting company with her.

The sharp accuracy of the passages in which Mrs Murray and Rosalie speak their minds make us stop to consider whether Anne kept notes, or even a diary, at Thorp Green. If she made sketches of Little Ouseburn with the intention of using them in composite pictures, it may well be that she kept written reminders as well. She calls the poems written by Agnes 'pillars of witness' to experiences along her road and doubtless regarded her own poems in just that light. Prose pillars of witness might well include a diary. Anne was much drawn to the form: there were the four-yearly diary papers written by herself and Emily, and there is the central portion of *Wildfell Hall* where Helen puts her dreadful sufferings on record. We may well imagine that Anne kept a diary between 1840 and 1843 and could draw on it when she came to compose *Agnes Grey*. This diary, however, if it existed, was the material for a novel, not the novel itself.

One day, in the autumn of 1845, I accidentally lighted on a MS volume of verse in my sister Emily's handwriting . . . it took me hours to reconcile her to the discovery I had made, and days to persuade her that such poems merited publication. I knew, however, that a mind like hers could not be without some latent spark of honourable ambition, and refused to be discouraged in my attempts to fan that spark to flame.

Meanwhile, my younger sister quietly produced some of her own compositions, intimating that, since Emily's had given me pleasure, I might like to look at hers. I could not but be a partial judge, yet I thought that these verses, too, had a sweet sincere pathos of their own.[31]

There can be no better known quotation from the Brontë story. But like all Charlotte wrote in her introductions and presentations of her sisters, it is an edited version, with Charlotte's gloss on it. Here the word 'accidentally' conceals the importance of the timing. Anne was finally free of Thorp Green. The plan to set up a school had finally been dropped. Something else must be sought urgently. The three sisters should revert to their intermittently held dreams of authorship. We have suggested that Emily and Anne were ready for such a chance in that both had revised poems to offer and probably embryonic novels stemming from their early days as teachers.

In this scene, Anne seems to side with Charlotte. At least on the surface, Emily was furious at the discovery, and it can hardly have helped to have Anne sidle up to Charlotte with a sheaf of poems to add fuel to her enthusiasm. She is accentuating her slow drift from being an echo of Emily and making a clear indication of her intent to further the publication project. Charlotte's consistent attitude to Anne is also conveyed in her description of the scene. She suggests that sisterly indulgence alone approved the poems, as though she lacks confidence in Anne's power to attract her own audience. Charlotte persists in seeing the child in Anne, though the 'sweet, sincere pathos' she discerns evinces womanly, not childish, feeling.

Meanwhile there was a shock at Thorp Green. Branwell had not succeeded in eloping with Mrs Robinson, but on Monday, 20 October, 'Miss Lydia Robinson made her exit with Henry Roxby, a play-actor . . . They went to Gretna Green and got married that night. She was just a fortnight turned 20 years that day. A bad job.'[32] There can be little doubt that this information was quickly related to Anne. The evidence for the correspondence between her and her ex-pupils is clear, but scanty. It comes from letters of Charlotte which date from eighteen months later than the point we have now reached and will be assessed in detail in due course. Not one of the many, perhaps hundreds of letters Anne received has survived, and the large number she wrote has vanished too. The loss of these letters creates a gaping hole in the midst of our evidence and we have to do the best we can to fill in the gap by deduction and conjecture. We do not even know if the two sisters remaining at Thorp Green wrote jointly or individually. The situation now that Branwell was banned from the house was most delicate, yet this correspondence between Mrs Robinson's daughters and Branwell's sister flourished. We may conclude that she could not control any of the daughters and was indulgent of their faults.

It used to be said that the Robinsons disowned their eldest daughter. Three days after the elopement Mr Robinson sent her £5, entering it in his account book. This must have been his first action on receiving a letter from her, written after her marriage. Less than a month later, Mr Roxby and his new wife paid their first married visit to Thorp Green. The account book shows a new payment to Lydia of £2, and George Whitehead records cheerfully 'Mr & Mrs Roxby came to Thorp Green first time on Tuesday, Nov. 18th, and left on Thursday, Nov. 20th. All right.'[33] Eventually a regular payment was arranged for Lydia, who seems to have lived mostly in Manchester. The way in which her 'exit' was treated is interesting: dyspeptic Mr Robinson does not forbid her his house and village gossip considers things are 'all right'. There is something easy-going in this attitude which illustrates Anne's difficulties in getting the girls to study in a disciplined way. One of her targets in *Wildfell Hall* is the indulgent attitude of Arthur towards his small son: just the way the Robinson parents might have acted towards the young Edmund.

Charlotte's project seems to have caught Anne's interest speedily. At any rate she wrote her last Gondal poem for the moment on 1 October and did not produce any further poetry of any kind until May 1846. Her time was to be devoted to editing the earlier poems, completing *Agnes Grey* and writing to the Robinsons. There must have been many domestic chores, though Emily would take on a large share of them. It would be fair to suppose that the three sisters would work together at their literary tasks during the late evenings, following their teenage pattern. For Anne, the editing process revolved around the removal of Gondal references and a few other small matters of tidying. How far this was a joint process, shared by the three, with all three sisters contributing to alterations in the work of all, is unclear.

The publishing history of *Poems* by the three 'Bells' (as they decided to call themselves) was studied by G. D. Hargreaves as long ago as 1969. He uses specialist bibliographical knowledge, combined with Charlotte's letters, to establish some firm facts about the way in which the poems were given to an extremely unappreciative public. It is a little harder to establish the facts about the prior editing process. The manuscripts of Anne's poems show little sign of the late alterations seen in Emily's A and B copy-books. Nevertheless, stanzas appear in print which are not in the copy-books, and lines are omitted. This selection and editing work went on during the forthcoming winter while Charlotte was trying to find a publisher. By the end of January she had settled on Aylott and Jones of Paternoster Row, London. The trio had now decided to pay for publication themselves, and the completed copy was sent to London on 6 February. A. M. F. Robinson says it was written 'in three different hands'. Certainly the sisters had agreed that their poems would be distinguished by a signature, Currer, Ellis or Acton, appended to each. We do not know where A. M. F. Robinson got her information, and Charlotte's covering letter, emphasizing the signatures as the dis-

[131]

tinguishing mark, may suggest that the handwriting was the same throughout.[34]

Branwell was not fit to take part in any of this venture. In October he was trying to obtain a place on the railway again. A letter of 25 October requests the position of 'Secretary to the Manchester & Hebden Bridge & Keighley & Carlisle Junction Railway'.[35] Two other letters of about the same date, which have been given prominence by Winifred Gerin and Daphne du Maurier, indicate Branwell's aggrieved and petulant, but unchastened mood.[36] We have already quoted the later of the two in discussing, in chapter 7, how Branwell's view of his relations with Mrs Robinson would be seen by Anne. These letters indicate that his current writing was based on his view of Mrs Robinson as an oppressed and neglected woman who must be pining for a white knight to liberate her from her now ailing husband. Anne's poem 'The Penitent' was probably written in September. It refers to the poet's delight in witnessing the mournful sorrow (thought of as repentance) of a sinner. The penitent is not named, but the general assumption that Anne is referring to Branwell seems plausible. Branwell was indeed sorrowing, but not in penitence over his foolishness. He could not believe, to judge by the tone of the letter to Grundy, that Mrs Robinson had rejected him, and hoped for the day when her husband would be dead. She would then marry him and transfer the Thorp Green estates to Brontë hands. The total improbability of such an event involving a family with the landed gentry's deeply dynastic outlook escaped Branwell completely. Anne, if 'The Penitent' has been rightly interpreted, misunderstood the causes of Branwell's grief.

Emily also showed herself to be living in a dream. Anne's attitude to the childish reverie on the York outing, where Emily lived wholly in her imagination at a time when Branwell needed practical help to extricate him from trouble, was of despair. Only Charlotte seemed to be seeking sound answers to economic questions. Anne backed this glimmer of realism, since both sisters failed to understand how poor the market for poetry was. As the saga of the poetry book continued, Anne would note that Charlotte's aims were right, but her judgement faulty. In her later poems and the two novels, she would make a plea for rational judgement, basing action on clear-eyed, dispassionate forethought.

9

Artistic Independence

E arly in 1846 Emily Brontë wrote her last fully revised poem. The high spirits and creativity of 1845 were coming to an end.[1] Many biographers have noted the growing differences between Emily and Anne, the beginnings of which can be traced to Anne's post at Thorp Green, but which did not become invariable until 1845–6.[2] There began to be an artistic gulf between them, though there were points on which they would always agree; for example, they would both cling to Newby as a publisher long after Charlotte had formed good relations with Smith, Elder. But any idea that the 'twins' of Ellen Nussey's early observation continued to be close to each other will not survive careful scrutiny. Readers who are interested to see the development of this process from Emily's side should refer to *A Life of Emily Brontë*.[3]

By May 1846 cross-currents at the parsonage were legion. Anne puts the point in 'Domestic Peace', as Charlotte would later call it. Written on 11 May 1846, in its original version the poem laments the discord in the Brontë household on the eve of correcting the poetry proof sheets:

> *Why should such gloomy silence reign;*
> *And why is all the house so drear,*
> *When neither danger, sickness, pain,*
> *Nor death, nor want have entered here?*
>
> *Each feels the bliss of all destroyed*
> *And mourns the change – but each apart.*

Anne is not writing only about Branwell's despair. If she had been, all the three sisters would have been together, unhappy

[133]

about Branwell, but united. Anne says they mourn the change, *each apart*. In the final stanza, this is underlined: writing of 'Domestic Peace', Anne says,

> *Sweet child of Heaven, and joy of earth!*
> *O, when will Man thy value learn?*
> *We rudely drove thee from our hearth,*
> *And vainly sigh for thy return.*

It is all the family, 'We', who have caused peace to depart. It has not returned, as is emphasized by the word 'vainly'. Peace, in the sense of concordance of views, would not return to the three sisters.

This poem constitutes first-hand evidence that not all had gone smoothly as the poems were being edited. It may also suggest that the first drafts of the three novels, *The Professor, Wuthering Heights* and *Agnes Grey*, were causing dissension too. We need to be wary of a complacent view of relations between the three, emanating from the pious anecdotes told by Charlotte to her friend Mrs Gaskell and supported by Ellen Nussey. Resistance to Charlotte's managing spirit is shown in Emily and Anne's decision to continue with Newby as publisher, and objection to Emily's quietistic despair in the face of misunderstanding is shown by the expedition by Charlotte and Anne to London, which will be dealt with later. The three sisters did not act in harmony during this period of their lives. Anne's artistic and moral challenge to the content of her sisters' novels comes in *Wildfell Hall*. Until this is recognized, readers may see the book as a pale version of *Wuthering Heights*, when it is in some aspects a critique of it.

'Domestic Peace' was Anne's first poem for six months. She had been completing *Agnes Grey* and editing her own poems for the collection. According to Hargreaves, three plain copies without permanent binding had been sent to Haworth on about 7 May, and A. M. F. Robinson records a copy of Emily's own with the date 7 May in it.[4] Within four days the tension in the house had led to the composition of 'Domestic Peace'. We may feel that the sight of her poems in print had renewed Emily's qualms; we must recall too that all the sisters could now read the poems of the others at leisure, studying them carefully. The differences so observed might well lead to heated dispute.

In this state of turbulence, what was happening to the three novels? In *A Life of Emily Brontë* I pointed to two anomalies in the record as it is usually accepted.[5] In her 'Biographical Notice' Charlotte claims that the writing of the novels was a response to the rejection by the public of the poems: 'Ill-success failed to crush us: the mere effort to succeed had given a wonderful zest to existence; it must be pursued. We each set to work on a prose tale.'[6] Unfortunately, this is not a true account. The rejection of the poems dates from July 1846, when the reviews began to come out, or later, when no copies were sold. But in the letter of 6 April 1846 she says that the three are 'now preparing for the press a work of fiction'. Charlotte's chronology is often hazy, either by accident or by design. The three novels must have been far advanced by April 1846; the manuscript of *The Professor* is dated 27 June.

A second anomaly arises from consideration of what precisely it was that Charlotte first forwarded to Henry Colburn on 4 July. She writes that it is '3 tales each occupying a volume'. The 'tales' can hardly be other than *The Professor* (finished about a week previously), *Wuthering Heights* and *Agnes Grey*. But there is great difficulty in supposing these are the novels as we know them. *Wuthering Heights* is almost twice as long as *Agnes Gray* and in 1847 Newby finally printed it in two volumes, leaving one for *Agnes Grey*. Following a suggestion of Tom Winnifrith, who analyses the lengths of the novels in more detail, I consider it likely that *Wuthering Heights* was rewritten before Newby printed it. If accepted, this suggestion helps us to understand the conception and production of *Wildfell Hall*.[7]

One argument against this view is provided by Charlotte's allegation that the *three* novels were 'perseveringly obtruded upon various publishers for the space of a year and a half'.[8] Her story, which tells us more about Charlotte than the novels, has led commentators to invent a letter from Newby, which Winifred Gerin says dates from 'the midsummer of 1847' in which he rejects *The Professor* but accepts *Agnes Grey* and *Wuthering Heights*.[9] No such letter has ever been discovered. We do know that *The Professor* reached Smith, Elder in a paper parcel with the names of other publishers crossed out, 'simply scored through' as Mrs Gaskell puts it.[10] In *The Cornhill* (1900), Mr Smith says that the parcel bore 'the scored out addresses of 3 or 4 other publishing houses'. Clement

Shorter says 'It was offered to six publishers in succession', and Winifred Gerin thinks Newby was the fifth of these.

As we have seen, Charlotte's memory for the details of how the novels came to be published was weak or evasive. Her skill as a creative writer did not desert her even when recalling factual matters. *The Professor* went the rounds of publishers for a year, from July 1846 to July 1847, not for eighteen months. This need not imply anything about *Agnes Grey* or Emily's book. It was following the apparent success of the poems, in appearing in print, that the three novels were first sent off. They were returned, either by Colburn, or by a second publisher, seven weeks later, in late August. We shall return to them.

In her 'Biographical Notice of Ellis and Acton Bell' Charlotte links the writing of *Wildfell Hall* directly with the behaviour of Branwell. Since his romantic débâcle coincides chronologically with the beginnings of the novel, and since the whole passage presents us with Charlotte's edited view of Anne, it will be valuable to quote the passage in full:

The Tenant of Wildfell Hall, by Acton Bell, had . . . an unfavourable reception. At this I cannot wonder. The choice of subject was an entire mistake. Nothing less congruous with the writer's nature could be conceived. The motives which dictated this choice were pure, but, I think, slightly morbid. She had, in the course of her life, been called on to contemplate, near at hand, and for a long time, the terrible effects of talents misused and faculties abused: hers was naturally a sensitive, reserved, and dejected nature; what she saw sank very deeply into her mind; it did her harm. She brooded over it till she believed it to be a duty to reproduce every detail (of course with fictitious characters, incidents and situations,) as a warning to others. She hated her work, but would pursue it. When reasoned with on the subject, she regarded such reasonings as a temptation to self-indulgence. She must be honest; she must not varnish, soften, nor conceal. This well-meant resolution brought on her misconstruction, and some abuse, which she bore, as it was her custom to bear whatever was unpleasant, with mild, steady patience. She was a very sincere and practical Christian, but the tinge of religious melancholy communicated a sad shade to her brief, blameless life.

This passage from the 'Biographical Notice', on which I have already drawn extensively, shows how Charlotte viewed Anne, and especially explains what she thought was the origin of *Wildfell Hall*. As we have seen, Anne was concerned with the social and educational problems brought to her attention in her years of tuition at Thorp Green just as much as she was by the contemplation of Branwell's abuse of his talents, although Charlotte, who was to misunderstand the friendship between Anne and the Robinsons, cannot be blamed for failing to realize this. At the moment when Anne began to work out the themes for her new novel, the two concerns, Branwell and the Thorp Green family, once again met in a common focus, the death of Edmund Robinson.

I have tried to balance Charlotte's one-sided view of Anne's motivation, just quoted, which has provided the basis for much comment on *Wildfell Hall*, by using external evidence about Thorp Green and the Robinsons to help us towards an understanding of the situation there, as it would have been at various times known to Anne through the letters of the girls. We have some evidence on the effect of the death of Mr Robinson both on the Brontës, through Branwell, and on the family and community at Thorp Green. The implication in Branwell's letter of October 1845 – that Mr Robinson was erratic and choleric – is supported by his treatment of servants as shown in his account book. In early 1846 he fired a gardener, hired a new one, then fired him too.[11] His illness is shown by the fact that he was being attended by a Dr Simpson as well as Branwell's friend Dr Crosby at this time. In one entry in the account book he calls his wife 'Mrs R' instead of his usual 'Lydia', but his writing does not deteriorate until 18 May. The entries for that date are the last he wrote in the book, and he died on 26 May 1846. There is something quite pathetic about the final entry, his subscription to the 'Oddfellows' whose meetings he would never attend again. Sixty of them followed after the family (which did not include the Roxbys) at the funeral, when he was buried on 5 June.[12]

We may be sure that the situation at Thorp Green was of acute interest to both Branwell and Anne. The announcement was made in several northern newspapers and, significantly, in the *Derby Mercury*. Though Branwell was waiting for some signal from Mrs Robinson, her signals were intended to be read by the county families in the north Midlands rather than by him. She was plainly very upset by the loss of her husband, giving £5 each to the poor of Great and Little Ouseburn 'for Edmund's precious sake' and paying Mr Lascelles' £5 fee for 'Edmund's sad funeral', as well as describing him on the blotting paper as 'My Angel'. But she knew herself to be an incompetent manager. She had now lost two of her chief male props, for her husband's death had been preceded on 28 March by the death of her father. Her signals to the widowers of Derbyshire (but not to Branwell) were economic as much as romantic, as Anne Brontë would not fail to notice.

Meanwhile there are clues to suggest that the emotional outlook of the erstwhile 'twins' had been reversed. In 1845 Emily had been cheerful and Anne despondent. But 'Mirth and Mourning', written at this time, suggests that Anne was trying to rally Emily's spirits, which were low, in part because of Branwell's despair. Mrs Robinson's chief adviser was William Evans, a rich manufacturer of Derby, and her brother-in-law. Interestingly, her own brothers, apart from Matthew, kept away. There now began the hiatus in the correspondence between Anne and the Robinson daughters. It is a fair guess that this resulted from an edict given at Derby by their Uncle William. Since she genuinely needed to know how her ex-pupils were faring, Anne must have watched Branwell carefully, trying to make sense of the garbled stories he told her. In course of time, there came a visit from Mrs Robinson's coachman, reported by some biographers to be called Mr George Gooch. According to Branwell, he told him that Mrs Robinson had been forbidden to communicate with the former tutor, and rightly reported that Mrs Robinson was distraught at her husband's loss.[13] Mrs Robinson's coachman was not called George Gooch, still less 'Mr' Gooch, and there was no one of that name in the Thorp Green district. If it really was the coachman who came to see Branwell it must have been William Allison, who later went to live at Great Barr with Mrs Robinson's new entourage.[14] 'George Gooch' may be a misreading introduced by Francis Grundy, Branwell's friend.[15]

At Thorp Green Mrs Robinson showed signs of financial distress and began to pay off her labourers, dismissing John Abbey, Thomas Briggs, Richard Bowser Jr and George Kaye; she also let the land to tenant farmers. That year the Robinsons went to Redcar instead of Scarborough, perhaps fearing to meet Branwell or even Anne, or to discuss affairs with mutual acquaintances.[16] At Haworth, things were enlivened by a visit from James Brunty, Patrick's brother from Ballynaskeagh, though we are not quite sure in which month this took place. It seems likely that his visit was connected with a tour of harvest labouring, and it may have been prompted partly by recent poor crops in Ireland which had caused the family at home to seek out their relatively prosperous relation in York-shire. It is recorded that Anne said she would have liked to go 'home' with James, and her interest in Irish matters is under-lined by her choice of the unYorkshire name Fergus for a character in *Wildfell Hall*.[17]

By now the lack of success of the edition of poetry was becoming clear. Uncle James had to spend some of his time rescuing Branwell from the Black Bull, where he tried to drown his sorrows whenever he could get the money. Mr Brontë's sight was declining badly, and Charlotte took Emily to Manchester to see whether they could engage a surgeon to clear a cataract from his eye. Emily wrote nothing, unless she was engaged in some Gondal prose. The weather began to be hot, and life stagnated. The novels did not find a publisher.

As we look for chronological landmarks in the later summer of 1846, we stumble upon a vital clue in Mrs Gaskell's biogra-phy of Charlotte.[18] Here, with no axe to grind and nothing to conceal, Charlotte is on record as recalling that *The Professor* 'came back upon her hands . . . on the very day' of Mr Brontë's eye operation, that is 25 August 1846. As both Emily and Anne were at Haworth, and only Charlotte in Manchester with her father, it seems as though they must have unwrapped the parcel of rejected books, extracted *The Professor* to send to Manchester, and kept the two others at Haworth. Mrs Gas-kell's implication on the same page is that Charlotte's book was henceforth sent off separately.

At this point we need to study Mrs Gaskell very carefully. Three paragraphs after the rejection of *The Professor* is men-tioned she tells how the sisters reverted to an old practice of theirs, when once or twice a week each read to the others what she had written during late evening 'workshop' sessions in the sitting room. It was on one of these sessions that Charlotte determined to make her heroine 'plain, small and unattractive'. Unless Charlotte's memory is again at fault, we are in at the birth of *Jane Eyre*, whose life story, says Mrs Gaskell, was begun in 'this time of care and depressing inquietude'.[19] What

[139]

books, then, were Emily and Anne working on during the sessions when Charlotte planned *Jane Eyre*? *Agnes Grey* was complete. We have no second novel from Emily, who perhaps did begin one, but it was not very far advanced by early 1848 and certainly could not have been discussed in late 1846. It seems that Anne must have begun *Wildfell Hall* as her contribution to the symposium, and that Emily was rewriting *Wuthering Heights*.

However, it took Emily and Anne some time to respond in this way. Their first impulse was to return to Gondal. Emily began her long narrative which would never be satisfactorily finished. Anne also wrote a narrative poem on 14 September, in which she seems to refer to Branwell's cheerful boyhood. Once again she shows her ability, beyond the powers of Charlotte, to create male characters who have a life of their own. The poem is a first person narrative. Unfortunately, the name of the narrator has proved impossible to read. It has been roughly erased from the manuscript and only the initial letter Z is clearly legible. 'Z' is a 'bold and careless youth' much like Branwell as a boy and we may assume that Branwell's character is the model for him, possibly with additional material observed recently by Anne in the personality of William Greenhow at Ouseburn. He and a 'younger boy' explore the mountain glens. The younger boy shares the pastimes of the elder as Edmund Robinson had followed William.

There were times when both Branwell and Emily could have said that they 'loved free air and open sky/ Better than books and tutors grim.' Typically, the two boys instead of exchanging endearments as girls might have done, enjoy a fight:

> *I bore him struggling to the earth*
> *And grappling, strength for strength we strove –*
> *He half in wrath, – I all for love;*
> *But I gave o'er the strife at length,*
> *Ashamed of my superior strength . . .*

Z puts all this reminiscence into a dream, compounded from Anne's recollections of Branwell and such friends as Hartley Merrall, with more boyish and recent brawls from Thorp Green. All this observation of young male inconsequence helps Anne when she comes to create Gilbert and his teasing brother Fergus.

Both the topic and the treatment of this poem show Anne's objectivity when contrasted with Emily's obsessive need to work and rework the problems of her own psyche. In the poem she began at the same time she is concerned with rebellion, treachery, guilt and loneliness of soul. The Gondal context of Anne's poem seems to be an attempt to rescue Emily from some of her loneliness. Anne's own lack of enthusiasm for Gondal had reached its lowest point when she wrote in the 1845 diary paper, 'I for my part cannot well be *flatter* or older in mind than I am now.' Her current temporary revival of interest represents both disappointment with the non-Gondal fiction which had been tried in *Agnes Grey* and an attempt to commune with Emily. With *The Professor* withdrawn from the joint publishing enterprise there must have been discussion about the future of the two remaining books. It must have been about this time that Anne began seriously to think about *Wildfell Hall*.

In due course she was to write a 'Preface' to her second novel which gives a reasoned account of her aims in publishing it. We shall eventually look at this formulation of her ideas and try to evaluate them. But it would be rash to suppose as Anne started to think about a book to parallel *Jane Eyre* and *Wuthering Heights* that she could have made her motives totally explicit at that point. No doubt these aims developed as she discussed her work with her sisters; many of the poems grow and change in just this way. *Wildfell Hall* plainly begins, in autumn 1846, with *Jane Eyre* and both a current and retrospective look at *Wuthering Heights,* but it develops so that its intentions, almost its genre, become very different from them.

Presumably it was late September or October when Charlotte announced to the others that she had decided to make her new heroine 'plain, small and unattractive in defiance of the accepted canon'.[20] In doing so she was taking a leaf out of Anne's book, since *Agnes Grey* represented a heroine with a sprightly spirit but no great personal advantages. Charlotte was intending to make Jane a reflection of her own self-image. This was not Emily's intention in *Wuthering Heights;* Catherine had developed from a Gondal heroine, and in Gondal everyone was larger than life. But even Charlotte balked at doing the same to her hero as she had to her heroine; the hero was to remain Byronic, a suitably grandiose personage, who would condescend to Jane. The strictly logical Anne needed to follow

[141]

out her principle with male as well as female protagonist. The mysterious stranger at the old deserted hall would be de-romanticized and Gilbert, the impetuous and sometimes peevish young farmer who falls in love with her, would be as unByronic as possible.

Anne begins with the man, the mystery and a location. Wildfell Hall is an old mansion which mocks Wuthering Heights, even in its initials. It is an historical, desolate, run-down place like its prototype. But Anne knew nothing of High Sunderland near Halifax, the basis of Wuthering Heights, and was unconcerned to start a legend about Top Withens on the moors outside Haworth. She had travelled the roads to the north of Scarborough and the location of her deserted Hall becomes clear when her characters go in a party to the sea coast one day. The cliffs, 'five miles' from Wildfell Hall, are between Scarborough and Whitby, while the Hall itself clings to the North Yorkshire moors.

Charlotte recalls shuddering under the grinding influence of natures 'so relentless and implacable' as she heard the draft of *Wuthering Heights* read aloud.[21] She had a long history of remonstrating uselessly with Emily, dating back to Emily's childhood tempers. She objected, but in her heart she feared Emily, as well as fearing *for* her. Anne was able to argue more determinedly because she knew her sister better and had had a great deal of practice down the years, as she records in 'Self-communion'. The present situation called for artistic rather than personal argument. As *Wildfell Hall* developed from common ground with Emily, Anne used her story to show how very different was her 'moral' view from Emily's 'poetic' one.[22] This argument, involving matters of realism, morality and indeed differing world views, began to pervade the new book. It does, finally, become Anne's considered 'answer' to *Wuthering Heights*.

It also comments on *Jane Eyre*. Rochester is a hugely warm-hearted, larger-than-life Byronic hero. Anne splits him in two, giving his intensity in love to Gilbert (though realistically damping down his selfless ardour) and his thoughtlessness, arrogance and riches to Arthur Huntingdon. Gilbert would walk through the book with a host of male faults. He would be petty, self-centred, impulsive, short-sighted and insensitive. Through him Anne intended to portray the male of the species as she had really found him: very unheroic. In choosing to make her hero so uncouth, but without Heathcliff's attractive excess, Anne imperilled the book. She borrowed aspects of Lockwood, Edgar, Weightman, Edmund Robinson, Branwell and other men, fictional and actual, to create a character whom she, the author, could hardly love. Unfortunately, the reader may begin to doubt whether Helen can. Only when she came to write the Preface in 1848 did Anne put into words the reason for her style of characterization.[23]

It may be worth pausing to consider the change in Anne Brontë's attitude to the major male role in her new novel since the writing of *Agnes Grey*. Edward Weston is at least an honest male, who shares a few characteristics with William Weightman, whom, to judge by her poetry, Anne had seen in a rose-tinted glow. As a girl she had been touched by his good qualities, but despite her desire to romanticize him, she had also experienced his vacillation and unreliability. Branwell was even more obviously unreliable, though essentially good-hearted. Between the writing of *Agnes Grey* and that of *Wildfell Hall* Anne had seen a further decline in Branwell's grasp on reality. She had had time to reflect on Weightman's inconsistencies, and was hearing of the faults of the young men to whom the Robinson girls were being attached. The urgent and high-spirited foolishness of Henry Roxby would also be in her mind. The stronger characters in *Wildfell Hall* are all women, reflecting Anne's experience in a life where the only man to combine power with rationality had been her father. Otherwise there had been weak irrational men like Branwell, or violent, irrational men like Joshua Ingham, or ineffective and dyspeptic men like Edmund Robinson. These men, in various combinations, make up the male cast of *Wildfell Hall*.

The narrative method of *Wildfell Hall* comes partly from *Wuthering Heights*: a story within a story. This method allowed Anne to write a diary, something she had practised from the age of fourteen in the periodic 'diary papers' even if she had not (as I have suggested she may have) kept a chronological record of events at Blake Hall and Thorp Green. It seems that she may not have given her heroine a name at the start, since it is not until chapter 12 that she is called Helen, by which time Charlotte had perhaps chosen that name for her philosopher girl in *Jane Eyre,* Helen Burns. Helen Graham and Helen Burns almost share their name with Ellen Dean, and I have speculated as to whether it was the late invention of Ellen which allowed Emily to rewrite her novel so successfully (though this hypothesis should be approached with caution). Helen as a young girl (then Helen Lawrence, though we are given only slight clues to her surname) shares Anne's own enthusiastic and romantic character and paints symbolic pictures in oils. We see her fall in love with Arthur as charmingly as Alexander and Zenobia did in the 1837 poem, or the 'Ellen' of 'Maiden, thou wert thoughtless' (whose name had originally been Olivia).

Even at the start, Helen Lawrence may take some characteristics from Mary or Bessy Robinson, whose letters Anne was reading from July 1845 to May 1846. We see Helen first through Gilbert's mystified eyes, but even at that stage Anne must have been working out partial answers to the mystery of Helen's origin. Perhaps renewed signs of friendship between Anne and the Robinsons being to appear about chapter 16, when Anne becomes interested in the process of husband-catching as practised in high society.

The differences of opinion with Emily over the tone of *Wuthering Heights* ran deep. The two factual sources for these differences, 'Domestic Peace' of May 1846 and 'Self-communion', yet to be written, admit that Anne loved Emily deeply and accept her share in the disruption of trust. Yet she is brave to face up to the pathos of the quarrel:

> And as my love the warmer glowed
> The deeper would that anguish sink,
> That this dark stream between us flowed
> Though both stood bending o'er its brink.
> Until, at last, I learned to bear
> A colder heart within my breast;
> To share such thoughts as I could share,
> And calmly keep the rest.

The 'dark stream' is the stream of evil, Emily's acceptance of conflict and her delineation of drama. Anne too bends over it, but sees it differently, as an influence to be fought and conquered. *Wuthering Heights,* in Anne's view, exhibited elements she later stigmatized as 'soft nonsense' in the 1848 preface. She clearly regards Emily's romantic attachment to scenes of torment and wild passion as 'soft', using the word to indicate intellectual error. As usual it is logic that is driving Anne.

'Ellis Bell', however, would 'wonder what was meant' by the objections of her sisters when they heard *Wuthering Heights* read aloud. In her second novel Anne gives her answer, explaining to Emily what she meant by her objections. She parodied Emily's scenes of violence in episodes she found so hard to write that Charlotte wrote 'she hated her work, but would pursue it'.[24]

There is a well-known passage in *Wuthering Heights* (in chapter 24), where ideals of happiness are discussed. Linton Heathcliff, the weakling, is allowed to represent the point of view of 'calm'. He prefers to spend a hot July day lying quietly on a bank of heather, while Catherine prefers the west wind and 'the whole world awake and live with joy'. She summarizes the matter: 'He wanted all to lie in an ecstasy of peace; I wanted all to sparkle, and dance in the glorious jubilee.' The poetic nature of Linton's vision is unlike him, and Emily is less interested in characterization than expressing her own point of view against another's. Anne, so frequently called 'calm', is here allied with peevish Linton. She needed to make it clear to Emily and others that her ideals of peace were not spineless.

Here we may bear in mind Anne's attachment to the archetypal elements of the sea, as revealed years before in her 'Sunrise at Sea' picture. Helen and Gilbert first experience sympathy as they reach the sea in a location based on the cliffs north of Scarborough 'five miles' from Wildfell Hall. We meet a lyrical passage when

> the blue sea burst upon our sight! – deep violet blue –
> not deadly calm, but covered with glinting breakers –
> diminutive white specks twinkling on its bosom, and
> scarcely to be distinguished by the keenest vision, from
> the little sea-mews that sported above, their white wings
> glittering in the sunshine: only one or two vessels were
> visible; and those were far away.[25]

Like the sea, Anne's eyes, windows of her soul, were 'violet blue', according to Ellen Nussey. But (she says symbolically in this passage) they did not reflect a spirit that was '*deadly* calm'. Behind the blue eyes is a lively scene such as Catherine Linton would have liked. Appearances are deceptive, and none more so than the outward appearance of Anne Brontë who, like Agnes Grey, could be a 'resolute dissembler'. Anne's dream of

[145]

the sparkling sea was resolutely pursued, and at last, two and a half years later, she was fittingly to be buried beside it.

A constant factor in Anne's mind, too, was her vocation, that of teacher. In this respect she took after her father, whose character is often thought to be so different from hers. In the 1790s at Glascar he had been an almost inspired teacher, using exciting methods to illustrate his lessons, pursuing pupils to their farmhouses when they underachieved, and sought after by different classes of people.[26] In *Agnes Grey* Anne had shown her excitement, through her heroine, at the very idea of guiding youngsters, and in exile at Thorp Green she had made headway in counselling the Robinsons. At last those weary years were bearing fruit; the girls voluntarily turned to Anne this winter when their mother began to try to persuade them against their natures to attract men whom they did not like.

Anne no longer had children to teach day by day, but she would educate the young in her books. As she thought through the implications of her poem 'Dreams', she gave education very careful consideration. If she ever did have a child it would not stay a baby for ever; it would grow to be rational, and would have to be brought up according to principle. As in 'Z's dream' she enjoyed picturing the young, cheerful, vital life of boys, and put her heart into the creation of Helen's young Arthur. In these scenes she identifies with Helen, and proposes a scheme by which Branwell could have been cured very early of his propensity to alcohol.[27] It was beginning to seem unlikely that she would ever have her own child, and the delineation of young Arthur was all the more heart-easing. The difficulties of educating boys were not to be glossed over; as Mrs Markham says of the local clergyman, 'I wish to goodness he had a son himself! . . . He'd see what it is to have a couple of boys to keep in order.'[28]

There were some appealing elements in *Wuthering Heights* for Anne to adopt. It was tied tightly by an exact timescale. This helped Emily very much when she came to refer back and forth to events remote from the present. The effect could be a little disjointed, but Anne must have seen the value of being able to allude to remote events accurately. She also adopted a rigid calendar expressed through the diary but carried on after it finishes into 1827. If she wrote the first pages of the novel first, she must have returned once the diary had been completed, to tighten the chronology so that such phrases as

[146]

'On the following Tuesday' and 'one bright February morning' can be assigned to certain dates, (30 October 1827 and February 1828 respectively). The third part of the book, in which Helen and Gilbert lose touch but finally meet again and marry, abandons this scheme to some extent, possibly because Anne's almanac ran out.[29]

On 16 November 1846, while *Wildfell Hall* was in composition, the Robinsons left Thorp Green. Mrs Robinson had found running the estate beyond her capability, and may well have been in the state of mental collapse of which Branwell had heard.[30] She needed to seek other male props, and at this first decent opportunity left for Allestree where William Evans and Mary could offer firm support. According to Charlotte, correspondence between the girls and Anne was renewed about Christmas time.[31] By this date Mrs Robinson had moved on to Great Barr, the home of Sir Edward Dolman Scott, who had married her cousin, Catherine Juliana Bateman. The Batemans had ancestry in Derby and Sutton Coldfield, and Lydia undoubtedly felt that society in the counties of Stafford and Derby would be open to her if she lived in that area. Even now she was presumably seeking a new husband, and was certainly prospecting for the girls too. In their letters to Anne, Bessy and Mary would give details of the kind of alliances she was trying to make.

On her journey south Lydia Robinson called at her old home, Yoxall Lodge near Barton-under-Needwood. The old house was to be occupied by her brother, but she brought some furniture from it first, including a table, chair and inkstand.[32] It looks as if she spent Christmas at Great Barr, perhaps with her daughters. Another visit was to Darley Abbey, near Derby, the home of William Evans' brother. Over the next two years most of her time and that of her daughters was to be spent at Great Barr or Allestree. Just at the point where Anne needed to write about Helen Huntingdon's earlier life far from Yorkshire she was fortunately provided with a supply of information about such a life among the gentry in far away Derbyshire.

It has been pointed out that the other locations of the novel, apart from the North Yorkshire moors, are very vaguely described.[33] However, Anne seems to conceive of Grassdale (the name is perhaps in part from early reading of *Eugene Aram*) as being in the Midlands. It is 'a hundred miles' from

London. Derby was 126 miles in those days by road from London, and Great Barr about 115, but Anne is not interested in precision. She gives a rather generalized description of Grassdale in chapter 25, in which the manor seems more like Allestree than Thorp Green. Helen says she wanders 'in the ancient woods'. Allestree was surrounded by old woodland, and indeed its name has been supposed to mean this, though perhaps wrongly. Thorp Green had some old trees but much new plantation. However, Helen does have a view of the sun setting behind 'woody hills', which suggests Thorp Green.

The lake at Grassdale is described as 'the little lake'. Kirby Hall had quite a considerable lake, the result of damming the Ouse. Thorp Green had no lake as such, only a round fish pond in the garden. Yoxall had a small lake formed from a brook, while Allestree's lake was larger and shaped like a fish. Helen's pleasant description of the grounds of Grassdale in July would seem to be an amalgam of Allestree and Kirby, with perhaps a dash of the view near Little Ouseburn church, where the swallows skimmed the little lake while feeding their young, hatched in the barns of Moat Hall just beyond the church.[34]

Like the characters in *Wildfell Hall* Sir Edward Dolman Scott had his London residence, as had William Evans. Both had reputations as good landlords and benefactors of their local communities and it seems hard to associate with them the kind of scandalous behaviour that obtains in Huntingdon's circle, though there was an illegitimate brother in the Evans family.[35] It seems likely, though, that Anne was using the Robinsons' reports about the marriage market when she came to write about Helen's early skirmishes with such men as Boarham. The liaison between Huntingdon and Annabella may have deeper roots. Here we reach an important point about the themes of Brontë novels, built on the themes of the juvenilia.

Ever since she had been a young girl Anne had been used to hearing of the affairs of married men and women with other married men and women. Adultery was the stock in trade of the Brontës' childhood and adolescent writing. This obsession did not come from the life patterns of the Brontë elders; it must be entirely from literary roots.

Both Charlotte's and Emily's current novels highlighted the topic. Branwell had been finally hoist with his own petard in this direction; he had written so much verse and prose on the topic that he began to believe his own imaginings and thought Mrs Robinson was in love with him. It would have seemed to Anne that all her three siblings were fascinated with adulterous love.

But Anne considered she knew more about human nature than the others. She had lived more in the world, and when it came to writing about immorality in high society she doubtless thought she could tackle the question with more realism. During her five years at Thorp Green she had seen many of the gentry, though usually at a distance, and occasionally some of the aristocracy. On holiday at Scarborough she had lived in lodgings with them. Social calls were made and there were meetings at the spa and along the shopping streets. Bessy and Mary gossiped. The younger Lydia, Anne's own pupil, eloped with an actor she must have been meeting in Anne's presence at Scarborough, and the runaway had been tolerated. In drawing Rosalie for *Agnes Grey,* Anne found herself understanding the actions of a self-centred flirt. Now she came to write of a worse seductress, and she amazingly gave the woman her own name: *Anna*bella. Lady Lowborough's character represents the punishable, irresponsible facets of Anne, against which her hymns at Thorp Green are a plea.

In *Wuthering Heights* the narrative dealt with a host of attractive villains whose names begin with H: Heathcliff, Hindley, Hareton. Anne replied with a list of unattractive villains whose names also begin with H: Hattersley, Hargrave, Huntingdon. This element surely must be a parody of Emily's novel. Meanwhile one of the most sinister, Hargrave, produces arguments suggesting that Helen should go to live with him that seem to satirize Rochester's pleas to Jane Eyre.[36] In Anne's eyes, the very attractiveness of Rochester and Heathcliff adds a pernicious element to the novels in which they appear. Her own anti-heroes would be made to seem unattractive, and thus leave the reader unmoved by vice.

Drink had ruined Branwell: it too should be attacked by Anne in *Wildfell Hall*. Possibly Edmund Robinson was also a drinker. Thus Anne produces Helen's method of making drink unattractive to Arthur as a child and hopes the reader will take the hint.[37] In *Wuthering Heights* Hindley is frequently drunk, but the ill-consequences of this are hardly felt. Anne is deter-

[149]

mined that her readers will feel the degradation of drunkenness. Chapter 31 is typical of those where she laboured hard
against her inclination: the gentlemen swear, brawl, make
maudlin speeches, boast, throw chairs, blaspheme, threaten
murder, hurl books about the room, are sick and burn each
other with a candle. It was scenes like this, no doubt, that
caused Charlotte to think Anne had made a mistake in her
choice of subject. She was to answer neatly in her Preface.
Such large-scale 'stirs' as the Kirby Hall wedding must have
produced some parallel scenes, taxing to watch and bad in
their effects on such frail humans as Branwell. There is no
doubt of the cost to Anne in realistically portraying these
scenes, but – as Charlotte said – she must persist to provide a
graphic deterrent.

As she composed Helen's diary, Anne could contemplate
how she herself might react if her judgement led her to marry
unwisely. She must have wondered if a marriage with William
Weightman could have been successful, though Weightman is
no more likely to be a model for Huntingdon than for Mr
Weston. As a counter to *Wildfell Hall* she wrote a sad retrospective poem in March 1847, 'Severed and gone', meditat-
ing on Weightman's life, death and burial in a damp corner of
St Michael's church, in which she wonders how he would
look now if she could see a vision of him in heaven. Not much
like Arthur Huntingdon, clearly. Yet Weightman's evasiveness
is not totally different from Huntingdon's.

Writing this 'truthful' novel was taxing Anne's physical
strength. In December 1846 she had a severe bout of asthma,
though she bore her affliction 'without one complaint', as
Charlotte wrote.[38] The winter was a cold one, and the dissension between the sisters not improving. *Wuthering Heights* was
still in the forefront of Anne's attention as a view of human life
to be countered. It must have been about this time that she
came to write an incident for chapter 14 in *Wildfell Hall,*
entitled 'The assault' in earlier editions. By this time Gilbert
Markham is suspicious of Lawrence's relations with Helen; he
has no idea that the two are brother and sister and has begun
to feel very jealous of Lawrence. He feels a 'dammed up fury'
foaming within him. One morning he is travelling along the
same road as his 'rival' and looks for a pretext to use his whip
on him. Lawrence gives him no real opportunity, but nevertheless, 'impelled by some fiend at my elbow' he seizes the

whip by the small end and brings it down violently on Lawrence's head.

> It was not without a feeling of savage satisfaction that I
> beheld the instant, deadly pallor that overspread his face,
> and the few red drops that trickled down his forehead,
> while he reeled a moment in the saddle, and then fell
> backward to the ground...Had I killed him? – an
> icy hand seemed to grip my heart...as I bent over
> him, gazing with breathless intensity upon the ghastly,
> upturned face.[39]

It is illuminating to compare this with the passage in *Wuthering Heights* (chapter 17) where Isabella tells Nelly how Heathcliff, with his 'sharp, cannibal teeth', forced his way into the
house and attacked Hindley. When Hindley's knife closes on
its owner's wrist Heathcliff pulls it away, 'slitting up the flesh
as it passed on'. He then puts the knife, dripping blood, in his
pocket. Blood gushes from 'an artery, or a large vein'. Heathcliff then tramples on Hindley and dashes his head repeatedly
on the flagstones. He finally stops when out of breath. There is
so much blood on the floor that Joseph is told to mop it up
with a towel. Surprisingly, Hindley lives and is said to be
'sitting, deadly sick' next morning. At no point in this sadistic
recital does Emily let us feel Hindley's dreadful pain, though it
is said to be 'excessive': such a colourless adjective is calculated
to diminish the real feeling of the passage. Of the blood,
Heathcliff says to Joseph, 'Wash that stuff away.'

On the other hand, in a long paragraph, Anne describes
Lawrence reeling in the saddle, falling off the horse, then
moving his eyelids and uttering a slight groan. As so often,
she is weighing each word to reduce romanticism ('soft nonsense') and present a 'truthful' view of violence. On returning
from his visit to town, Markham finds Lawrence still seated in
the road, looking white and sickly and holding a handkerchief
to his brow. The violence and its aftermath is meant to be felt;
the flow of blood described is to be consistent with an attack
which was not to kill its victim. In reality Hindley must have
died from the severing of his artery, even if he had not been
trampled, kicked and had his head banged against limestone
repeatedly. Lawrence is ill for a long time though he landed on

'grass, sodden with rain'. Thus Anne takes her sister's balladic episode and demythologizes it.

In view of Newby's bad record for slipshod work and delays, it seems that Emily and Anne sent *Wuthering Heights* and *Agnes Grey* to him in spring 1847; they were published in the autumn. They must have been delighted with his letter accepting their work but it has not survived and we do not know when it was sent or received. However, *Wildfell Hall* must have been reaching its conclusion if Halford's dating of 10 June 1847 is really a concluding date. Branwell's descent continued. In a passage in chapter 30 of *Wildfell Hall* Anne discusses Helen's complicity with her husband, who demands to be allowed to drink six bottles of wine at once. He speaks in a bombastic manner comparable with Branwell's tone in his letters: 'I've lived more in these four months, Helen,' he says, 'than you have in the whole course of your existence.' As in Branwell's case the 'living' in question has consisted mainly of dissipation. In return, Helen is accused of 'keen feelings' and 'interesting force of character', accusations which must have been brought against Anne as she argued with her brother.

So in the book she makes Helen argue with Arthur, but to no avail. And Helen herself feels tainted by Arthur's behaviour. She is 'gradually losing that instinctive horror and repulsion which were given me by nature, or instilled into me by the precepts and example of my aunt'.[40] For once, Elizabeth Branwell is cast in precisely the role of one of the Brontë novel aunts. Helen continues with a piece of internal dialogue comparable to Anne's dialogues in the poems. She considers she may be implicated in Arthur's downfall, and wonders how she can remain genuinely sympathetic, as a wife should be, as Arthur deteriorates into ruin. These are Anne's thoughts, surely, about a sister's proper response to a brother's collapse.

By now letters from Bessy and Mary Robinson were reaching Anne frequently, perhaps several times a week.[41] It is in chapter 32 that Esther Hargrave becomes prominent, as Anne begins to wrestle with a now recurrent problem: how to warn young people about the pitfalls of life without robbing them of their spontaneity. Replying to the Robinsons she would have had to force herself to suppress their ebullience at times. Their letters were 'crammed with warm protestations of endless esteem and gratitude'.[42] In reply, Anne was giving kindly advice, and from this exchange Esther Hargrave grew. She is a little younger than the Robinsons, not yet out of the schoolroom, and Anne is looking back a year or two. 'It seems as if I should feel her disappointment even more deeply than my own,' writes Helen. Anne cannot avoid sympathy with youth even while preaching. Helen admits that 'in my judgment what the world stigmatizes as romantic, is often more nearly allied to the truth than is commonly supposed; for, if the generous ideas of youth are too often overclouded by the sordid views of after-life, that scarcely proves them to be false'.[43] The point being made is that, in paradisal humanity, generosity and 'romanticism' are human attributes, but they have been sadly overlaid by the 'sordid' (and sinful) habits into which other people grow.

A passage written about this time reflects the poem 'In memory of a happy day in February' of 1842. In chapter 33 Helen discovers Huntingdon with Annabella in the woods at Grassdale. She finally knows that what she has feared so long is true; Arthur is unfaithful. She struggles to pour out her heart's agony to God but cannot. It is Nature which comes to her rescue when

> a gust of wind swept over me, which, while it scattered the dead leaves, like blighted hopes, around, cooled my forehead, and seemed a little to revive my sinking frame ... I breathed more freely; my vision cleared; I saw distinctly the pure moon shining on, and the light clouds skimming the clear, dark sky; and then, I saw the eternal stars twinkling down upon me; I knew their God was mine, and He was strong to save and swift to hear ... Refreshed, invigorated if not composed, I rose and returned to the house.[44]

This passage is curiously sympathetic to Emily's view of 'Nature' as inspiration and eternal sustainer.

With *Wildfell Hall* completed in June, Anne's mind turned in the summer of 1847 to new ways of expressing her moral message. Ideas for an allegorical poem were forming in her head, based on a searching poem from the 1846 collection in which Emily had written of triple influences on life through the eyes of a 'seer'; entitled 'The Philosopher' it has defied attempts to interpret it to this day. Anne also saw things in triads. Her poem would be about three 'guides', of which the worst possible was Pride, the downfall of Branwell, Emily and Mrs Robinson. 'Spirit of Pride' in Anne's new poem, 'The Three Guides', would have a resemblance to Emily's worse side. Anne's own preference went to 'Spirit of Faith', but the third contender was 'Spirit of Earth', a strange and enigmatic choice. In the next chapter I shall refer to several poems of Emily's in which she sees 'Earth' as a 'mother' of all humans, pantheistically sacred. In Anne's new poem 'Spirit of Earth' is very different. It represents the spirit of (masculine) rationality, far from Emily's mysterious 'Mother'.

The spirit Anne now attacks is the very one she has used in some degree herself. The thrust of *Wildfell Hall* is all in the direction of demystifying the lonely figure of an exiled woman who intrigues the locals at Linden Carr. Helen's story of deluded romance is a warning, and she herself, like Anne in her poems, is always arguing rationally. But throughout Anne's work there have been reminders that the belief in reason alone is insufficient. A good example is in 'Views of Life' and Helen's understanding of Esther's romantic hope is another. Anne is warning herself and her readers against too rigid an application of the rationalist calculus.[45] Eventually the new poem was sent to *Fraser's Magazine*.

As 1848 dawned Anne continued to hear regularly from the Robinsons. Their mother was ever more concerned to find husbands for them, and had set her own sights on becoming part of the Dolman Scott household at Great Barr. (Having achieved this, in the 1851 census she records herself as 'Baronet's wife'.) Even Charlotte was moved to sympathize with the girls who, she says in a letter of 28 January 1848, 'still continue to complain of their mother's proceedings'. The contact between Anne and the two Robinsons was destined to become even closer, and their liaison puzzled Charlotte. Though we must suppose that *Wildfell Hall* was now complete, and had been offered to Newby following the success of *Jane Eyre,* Anne may still have made modifications in the light of these recent letters.

The story of Newby's attempt to confuse the public has been well documented. He was quite determined to cash in on *Jane Eyre*'s success, by conflating all the 'Bells' together as one author. In February he wrote to Emily, enclosing his letter in a letter to Anne.[46] It is likely that she had tried to impress on him that the three Bells were three separate authors, a theme she returns to in the 'Preface' to *Wildfell Hall*. It may be supposed that Anne had begun to think about another novel, but her actual composition was poetic, 'Self-communion'. This long poem was not published in Anne's life-time, nor by Charlotte in 1850. It stirred too many difficult issues. In it she made a bold attempt to discuss the main trends of her thought and feeling during her life's course. It has no parallel in the work of Charlotte, Branwell or Emily. Though she conceals events and names, she reviews the main developments and conflicts of her life with a clear eye, writing within a tradition that she had always upheld, that poetry was a personal record. As Emily might have done, she begins with a consideration of 'Time' which will not 'rest or stay'. Anne was now twenty-eight, and her novels had eased but not satisfied her. To be published and well reviewed certainly increased Anne Brontë's literary confidence, but her personal life still held a void. Once again she stresses the value of 'Memory's store' as she had done several times. To rethink one's life was almost a duty, and certainly an easing of pain. But, after childhood's happy, frightened time was over, she could only discern that

> ... *time and toil and truth*
> *An inward hardness can impart, –*
> *Can freeze the generous blood of youth,*
> *And steel full fast the generous heart.*

The conflict of 'The Three Guides' was still very close. 'Reason, with conscience by her side ... will prove a surer guide/ Than those sweet instincts of our youth'. And, she adds,

> *Thou that hast felt what cankering care*
> *A loving heart is doomed to bear,*
> > *Say, how canst thou regret*
> *That fires unfed must fall away,*
> *Long droughts can dry the softest clay,*
> > *And cold will cold beget?*

At twenty-eight Anne was not reconciled to the cold isolation that, as a lone young woman, parted both from her hopes of

Weightman and her pleasure in Emily, she must now bear. To have emerged from the shadow of Charlotte and Emily in order to write a different kind of book was a taxing procedure and it seems that Anne must have received a good deal from Bessy and Mary Robinson, though she writes,

> 'Tis sweet the helpless to befriend,
> To watch the young unfolding mind,
> To guide, to shelter, and defend;
> To lavish tender toil and care,
> And ask for nothing back again,
> But that our smiles a blessing bear,
> And all our toil be not in vain.

As for Weightman, after a passage extolling the joys of 'happy love', in which she writes perhaps more warmly than anything she produced in the Helen–Gilbert relationship, she typically lets herself and the reader down to earth with:

> Such speechless raptures I have known,
> But only in my dreams.

This is a clear admission that the idealized clergyman buried in the old church, whose sunny smile is now stilled, did not live up to Anne's expectation in life. Her final answer, of course, is obedience to God's decrees, a hard test she will have to undergo personally within the next year. 'However wide this rolling sea', she suggests, using a metaphor of which she has been fond, she will eventually reach heaven and meet 'those that I have loved and lost', including the clergyman from Appleby.

The final stanza of the poem is a most moving declaration of her determination to reach the other side of the wild sea and walk 'on that sunny shore'. In this and other poems Anne's challenge is to herself, to 'toil' and not shun hard tasks. This may be seen as a contrast with both Branwell and Emily. By this time Branwell's nerve had totally failed. He accuses himself in a letter of 24 January 1847 of 'querulous egotism' and maintains that even if he were to step into York Minster at once, he could not be happy. If he had shared his complaint with Anne, she could have had little sympathy with his undervaluation of the inspirational building she held in such high esteem. Meanwhile Emily too had lapsed into a dream. An examination of the draft manuscript of her final poem, with its false starts and heavily blotted substitutions, shows her frustration and disorientation, a state from which she never recovered. Meanwhile, Anne had toiled, against her inclination if we are to believe Charlotte's comment in the 'Biographical Notice' ('She hated her work, but would pursue it'), until she had been able to complete her powerful and 'truthful' novel.

10

To See the Shuffling Scamp

O ver the years Anne must have written letters to various correspondents as well as to her former pupils. Only five remain, though surely there must be more undiscovered among family collections and archives. P. J. M. Scott calls 'each a marvel of tact – self-effacement which is not . . . self-regarding.'[1] There are three to Ellen Nussey, two of which complain mildly of the east wind. The second of these, written in January 1848, laments that Anne can give no news 'for we have been nowhere, seen no one, and done nothing (to *speak* of) since you were here.'[2] This is strictly truthful, since Anne and the others apparently agreed that they would not reveal their novel-writing to acquaintances or friends. This attitude seems to have been taken mostly in deference to Emily, but Anne admits to being secretive by nature on several occasions: 'you must know that there is a lamentable deficiency in my organ of language, which makes me almost as bad a hand at writing as talking unless I have something particular to say'.[3]

Wildfell Hall had been something particular. But Anne was not pleased when Newby, her 'scamp' of a publisher, tried to cash in on the new popularity of *Jane Eyre* to sell Anne's book. It was being advertised in the third week of June, and was apparently published very late in June or early in July. Newby printed 'Press Opinions' opposite the title page. They were actually comments on *Wuthering Heights* and *Jane Eyre*. Harper Bros, the American publisher, added insult to injury by claiming that 'Acton Bell' had written *Wuthering Heights*. Despite the problems over her 'organ of language', Anne had something quite particular to say about that. But Charlotte too had become involved when, on Friday, 7 July, a letter came from Smith, Elder, which seemed to question the honour of the Bells. Newby had dragged all three into his mire of deceit.

Fiercely honourable, Charlotte knew she must take a firm, direct line to counter this. Mrs Gaskell relates that a discussion took place between the sisters about what should be done.[4] Perhaps Charlotte and Anne suggested abandoning the 'Bell' pseudonyms, but Emily would not agree. Charlotte then proposed going to London to show Smith, Elder that she was their author, and presumably asked Emily and Anne to go with her. Emily flatly refused, but Anne gave her whole-hearted support to the proposal. Not since she was a girl had Anne gone anywhere with Charlotte. The last journey together had been in 1837 when she finally left Roe Head. Since then Charlotte and Emily had been to Belgium, and for a short time to Manchester. Emily and Anne had been to York, when Emily was lively and Anne 'flat'. Anne had accompanied Branwell to Thorp Green and twice to Scarborough. Now, she must have doubted how she would get on with her mildly disapproving sister. In actual fact she was to stand up to the physical and emotional tensions better than Charlotte.

After presenting their plan to Patrick, the pair packed a small trunk and discovered a boy who was going down to Keighley. We have two principal sources for the journey that ensued: a letter Charlotte later sent to Mary Taylor and Charlotte's small cash book covering expenses. To this we may add external sources such as contemporary timetables and guide books, which fill out the detail from wholly objective documents. For example, Charlotte says little in her letter about the long overnight train journey, though the cash book laconically provides some firm data. But the high adventure provided for Anne by this expedition should not escape us. The experience of long-distance travel and the impact of London were quite fresh to her, and we should be failing to do justice to her experience if we did not attempt to fill out the meagre personal record with verifiable information from contemporary sources.

From the cash book we learn that the sisters paid the boy one shilling and sixpence to take their trunk on the cart with him and deliver it to the railway station at the far end of Keighley.[5] The weather threatened as they ate their tea. They had no alternative to a four-mile walk to Keighley and soon the heavens opened in a thunderstorm.[6] The pair must have been thoroughly soaked, and there was nowhere to dry themselves. The change of clothes sent on by cart would be very necessary, but could not be effected soon. We must find the entry into Keighley that evening of two bedraggled women – two of the outstanding novelists of the nineteenth century – very moving. The manner of their arrival exemplifies their tenacity of purpose, their lack of convention and their poverty.

It is important to note that the Brontës had great sympathy for trains as a mode of transport. Branwell had worked on the railway and Emily had learned to understand railway finance.[7] Anne would have used the line from Keighley to York as part of her journey to Thorp Green in later years. The mid-decade development of railways in Yorkshire and throughout England, partly by George Hudson, a local entrepreneur, was not a development that left the Brontës neutral or uninterested. Despite a tendency to retrospection shown in all the three novels which were the immediate cause of this journey, they were far from turning their backs on this particular development of industrialization. Charlotte's words to Ellen Nussey of 29 September 1840 are often taken to be ironic when she says: 'Patrick Boanerges [Branwell] has set off to seek his fortune in the wild, wandering, adventurous, romantic, knight-errant-like capacity of clerk on the Leeds and Manchester Railroad.'[8] Though there is doubtless an element of exaggeration here, such a positive attitude to railways is a part of the Brontës' acceptance of their world which is not often noticed.

However, we should not forget the feeling of novelty and adventure associated with trains in those early days. It was possible in 1848 for the two sisters to reach London from Yorkshire overnight, something that would have been inconceivable in their childhood. Trains ran to a carefully prepared timetable, which was already being reliably attained as frequently as that of the coaches, which were rapidly being replaced. This was being done without employing the whips on animals against which Anne protested, for example during her last days at Scarborough. In all ways, we may believe, Anne would see the railway an improvement to coach travel, though some manifestations of it might be alarming and the speed of travel tiring.

The cash book emphasizes what we can learn from *Bradshaw*, that through-booking was limited, so that Charlotte and Anne began by taking tickets for Leeds. Their train would have been the 6.24 p.m. from Keighley, the track following in part the same route as the present line. Thus they passed Kirkstall Abbey in the waning evening light. It is unlikely that Charlotte, with her lively interest in Gothic ruins, would have failed to comment on this, the place about which their father had written a poem, and where he had proposed to their mother.[9] However, we need also to recall the degree of discomfort they would both have been feeling sitting in their slow-drying clothes and the determination this betokens on the part of both sisters to face hazards in pursuit of enforcing a truthful stance upon Anne's publisher.

From the cash book we learn that a porter was employed to carry their trunk from the Keighley trains to the London express. Meanwhile the pressing need still was for warmth, and they were apparently able to find a pot of tea for four shillings to settle and comfort themselves. Judging by Charlotte's letter, they were both too excited to sleep on the main line train, but they made the best arrangements they could by taking first class tickets, which would have ensure them comfortable upholstery.[10]

Bradshaw shows that the train by which they left Leeds was the 7.55 p.m., travelling by the tall viaduct, which still stands, very slowly because of the sharp curve. We may recall that Anne and Emily had intended to make a series of expeditions together, the first of which was the one to York in 1845. The expectation had not been fulfilled – another casualty of the differences of opinion and temperament between Emily and Anne. Now, unexpectedly, Anne was journeying with Charlotte, the elder, disapproving sister, with whom she had not felt at ease since childhood. Altogether the train took more than eight hours to reach London, first passing through the coalfields and by-passing Sheffield, then, in the darkest part of the night, reaching the area of which Anne had recently written under the name of Grassdale. By sunrise, they had arrived at Euston, which must be visualized without the booking hall and saloon, but already furnished with the famous Doric arch, an architectural feature which would quite certainly have attracted the sisters.[11] Both *Bradshaw* and Charlotte's letter show that they were allowed to stay in the railway carriage

[161]

until about 7 o'clock, before setting out to find accommodation from which they could visit both publishers. Before long Charlotte was to complain of a headache.[12] She does not record that Anne complained of anything.

Emerging from the station they took a cab direct to Paternoster Row, where Charlotte had decided they would stay at the Chapter Coffee House. (As she later wrote to Mary Taylor, 'We did not well know where else to go'.)[13] This had been one of Mr Brontë's haunts in the past and Charlotte and Emily had stayed there on their way to Belgium. It was situated among bookshops and stationers, and was not far from Cornhill, where the sisters were going. Paternoster Row runs along the north side of St Paul's churchyard, and they would have been able to see the dome of St Paul's as the cab neared the end of the journey. Soon they were alighting at the Coffee House, situated on the corner of Paul's Alley, a bookshop and map-seller on one side and another bookseller on the other.[14]

Mrs Gaskell visited the Chapter House before writing her *Life of Charlotte Brontë,* by which time it had become vacant. She was able to inspect the old building and left a graphic description:

> Paternoster Row ... is a flagged street, lying under the shadow of St Paul's; at each end there are posts placed, so as to prevent the passage of carriages, and thus preserve a solemn silence ... The dull warehouses on each side are mostly occupied at present by wholesale stationers; if they be publishers' shops they show no attractive front to the dark and narrow street. [The Coffee House] had the appearance of a dwelling-house, two hundred years old or so, such as one sometimes sees in ancient country towns; the ceilings of the small rooms were low, and had heavy beams running across them; the walls were wainscotted breast high; the staircase was shallow, broad and dark, taking up much space in the centre of the house ...[15]

Here the two sisters arrived at about eight o'clock that morning and in Mrs Gaskell's words 'touched the heart of the old waiter', who found them a long, low, dingy upstairs room and brought them breakfast.[16]

An hour or so later, having washed and perhaps changed

into the clothes they had put into the trunk before starting out, they walked out into the Row, turning right on their way to Cornhill. Strangely, they lost their way, but never thought of taking a cab. It took them an hour to find Smith, Elder's shop. Nothing of their route is recorded, and it is tempting to speculate that part of the hour was spent in turning aside for a closer view of St Paul's.

At first their reception at Smith, Elder's shop was hardly rapturous. Charlotte took the lead, as was only right since this was her publisher. An assistant went to see whether Mr Smith was busy, and on this hectic Saturday morning he was. It was a little time before the strange provincial pair were ushered upstairs to his room. When they appeared he must have been puzzled to know who they were and why they had come. Charlotte put his own letter into his hands, but he still had no idea who she was. George Smith was quite incredulous as he began to realize that the small woman facing him was Currer Bell, and beside her was Acton. Explanations were 'rapidly gone into' and blame for the confusions over authorship laid on Newby. Then Smith, Elder's reader Mr Williams was called the room and there was a 'long, nervous shaking of hands'.[17]

Many years later Mr Smith wrote in the *Cornhill Magazine* his impressions of Anne, formed that morning and on the next few days. He described her as

> a gentle, quiet, rather subdued person, by no means pretty, yet of a pleasing appearance. Her manner was curiously expressive of a wish for protection and encouragement, a kind of constant appeal which invited sympathy.[18]

Perhaps one of the things negotiated at that meeting was the transfer of the *Poems* to Smith's publishing house, and there he would find Anne's poem to William Weightman, entitled 'Appeal', on page 140. Nevertheless, Anne's appearance did not tell the whole story. One should also recall the remark of Agnes Grey, who speaks for her creator in saying, 'I was a resolute dissembler.' Beneath the 'constant appeal' for sympathy was determination to do without it if necessary.

It is worth making another point. By now, Charlotte had a headache, which would last the rest of the day. This was

[163]

hardly surprising in view of the hurry and turmoil they had experienced; but nothing at all is said of Anne's health. Did Charlotte take it for granted that Anne could stand up better than she could to long train journeys? Or was Anne's head as bad as Charlotte's? We may feel that if Anne's manner was an appeal for encouragement, she would not get it from Charlotte, at any rate not as an adult, though she had done so as a child. We must remember that Charlotte was deeply offended at Anne's latest book. She saw it as a botched and ungainly work, which was now being confused in the minds of her readers with her own, dear, *Jane Eyre*. Later she would fight to have the book forgotten. [19] Though we have Anne's word for it that she never wasted speech, the presence of Charlotte must have been inhibiting throughout the weekend.

The most puzzling thing – but in view of these last points not too surprising – about the sisters' stay in London is the absence of evidence about their call on Thomas Newby. It seems almost certain to have taken place on Monday, 10 July, but there are gaps in the timetable we cannot fill before that. It seems that they left Cornhill about lunchtime on Saturday having agreed to go to Covent Garden in the evening, and to be entertained by Mr Smith and Mr Williams while they were in London. So far as business was concerned, they now had only Mr Newby to see. If they could have met him on Saturday afternoon they would presumably have done so, returning to Yorkshire as soon as possible. Space must therefore be found in tracing their movements for a visit to Newby on Monday. Now, they walked back to the Coffee House and spent part of the afternoon resting.

Mrs Gaskell quotes George Smith as saying that he found the pair sitting on a window seat later that day when he came to collect them for the opera. Charlotte was by this time feeling very ill with a 'thundering headache and harassing sickness'. [20] George Smith arrived dressed for the opera, with his sisters. There was no possibility of Charlotte and Anne looking fashionable. They were dressed simply in the 'plain high made country garments' they had brought with them. They followed the party to the carriage and set out for Covent Garden. Charlotte wrote to Mary Taylor of her pleasant excitement in spite of the persistent headache. Anne meanwhile was 'Calm and gentle, which she always is'. The performance of Rossini's *Barber of Seville* lasted until after midnight, and the two were taken back to the Coffee House later than one o'clock. We have no record of Anne's view of the opera, though Charlotte thought there were things she would have liked better. The talk turned to church sevices, and Anne declared she would like to hear Dr Croly, an evangelical preacher. Accordingly Mr Williams came to call for the sisters at about ten o'clock next morning to take them to St Stephen Wallbrook, but Croly was not preaching.

They seem to have had a quiet lunch that Sunday at the Coffee House, but in the afternoon Mr Smith and his mother came to collect them and take them to Westbourne Place. It seems that at first the Smiths had thought of Charlotte coming in a cab, since she wrote down directions for Westbourne Place in her account book; but the plan was changed, perhaps because Mr Smith had realized how very little money they had, and they all drove to Bayswater together. Throughout, Smith and Williams showed immense tact and friendliness in dealing with these two unexpected guests.

The Brontës enjoyed a 'fine dinner' with Mrs Smith, the two sisters they had met earlier, a small brother and an even smaller sister, and were then brought back to the Coffee House, so far as one can base deductions on the account book. Charlotte's letter to Mary Taylor is wearing thin by this point, and Monday receives a good deal less coverage than the previous three days. Hence one has to try to make deductions from the payments for cab hire from the account book. It does not help that Charlotte perhaps scribbled her entries into it, not singly as they occurred, but possibly at night or in the Coffee House. After the train tickets purchased at Leeds she records the cab hire on arrival at Euston, then the purchase of two pairs of gloves and two parasols (the weather was unpredictable and later in the month very stormy). The next three entries at the foot of the page are:

Cab hire ———— 0 – 4 – 0
Cab hire ———— 0 – 1 – 0
Do   ———— 0 – 4 – 0

and there is a record, at the top of the next page for

Exhibition ———— 0 – 2 – 0

[165]

The 'Exhibition' was at the National Gallery and Royal Academy, as Charlotte's letter to Mary Taylor tells us.

The Brontës had needed no cabs on Sunday, when they were conveyed by the Smiths. The three cab fares therefore refer to Monday morning, when Mr Smith was at work; they represent a long journey, a short journey and another long journey. It seems likely that the first is from the Coffee House to Mortimer Street, not far from Oxford Circus, where Newby's office was situated. The second is from there to Burlington House, and the third to Westbourne Place, which Charlotte now knew well enough to be able to direct a cab driver. Since Charlotte suppresses every detail of the Newby visit, we have only this cab fare to show it took place. Anne left no comment at all. However, the poem edition was transferred from Aylott and Jones, and Anne planned to transfer her next book to Smith, Elder.[21] This shows not only the respect with which the sisters were received at 65 Cornhill, but also indicates that Newby still appeared less attractive. Anne, in effect, transferred her loyalty from Emily's choice to Charlotte's. It is hard to know what to understand by Charlotte's omission of details of the meeting from her letter to Mary; presumably if Anne and she had been in complete agreement, they would have laughed together at Newby, and this would have been relayed gleefully to Mary. Possibly Anne agreed with Charlotte only reluctantly.

There is no account book entry for lunch this Monday, so it seems that the two economized with their scanty funds. Both Mr Smith and Mr Williams were to entertain them later in the day, and they had by now become accustomed to expect quantities of food from them which were too large. They must have been tired and hungry by the time they arrived at Westbourne Place sometime in the afternoon. It seems to have been after tea there that they visited Kensington Gardens. Mr Williams had collected them and was taking them home for the evening. The relationship between Charlotte and W. S. Williams was to result in many letters, and even Anne wrote to him on Charlotte's behalf in September of that year. The evening was quiet and pleasant; the house party included 'a daughter of Leigh Hunt's', who sang Tuscan airs to the company.

It is not clear quite when Charlotte and Anne had time to visit a bookshop to buy a book for Emily. Possibly this was also on Monday, but if the order of items in the account book has any meaning, it may have been on Tuesday, 11 July. On the other hand, the most likely train for them to have caught is the 10.30 a.m. mail train, which would have left little time for shopping. This time they took second class tickets, perhaps realizing that they would do better to spend any remaining money on a hotel in Leeds on Tuesday night. The mail train stopped at Derby from 3.40 to 4.00 p.m., and shortly afterwards passed through Allestree. The Hall can be seen from the railway, and surely Anne would have cast a glance at the place from which she had received so many letters, and where her former pupils were probably staying at that very moment. Ten minutes later they were at the spa town of Belper, and then crossing some green hills to Chesterfield, where the crooked spire is clearly visible from the station.

Leeds was reached at 6.30 p.m., though of course we do not know whether the train was on time. A night's stay in a hotel cost the Brontës 4–6d each, plus 1–2d for the boots service. They then caught a train to Keighley, probably the 9.30 a.m. arriving there for 10.22 a.m. and enabling them to walk comfortably back to Haworth by lunchtime. The journey cost half a crown each. It was Wednesday, 12 July, and Anne's horizons had been immeasurably extended in six days. Charlotte records Emily's interest as she narrated 'again and again' all that they had seen and done on the visit. Presumably she included full comment on the meeting with Newby, an event we should much like to know about.

One thing was quite clear to Anne as she reconsidered this extraordinary week: she must explain *Wildfell Hall* to its readers with total clarity. It took nine days to marshal her thoughts into the 'Preface' which would accompany a so-called second edition, thought by G. D. Hargreaves to consist of unexhausted sheets of the first (London) edition.[22] The Preface is thus dated 22 July 1848; it turned out to be the last time that Anne would address a reading public direct. It must have cost much labour and recasting, for Anne was quite determined to be entirely honest and to shirk no difficulty in explaining. She takes a high moral tone, dry as the letters she wrote to Ellen Nussey and W. S. Williams. If we had her letters to Bessy and Mary Robinson, the tone might not appear much more cordial despite Anne's great desire for the romantic warmth of youth. Dry, but not unimpassioned if we can detect the earnest power in every sentence. We shall examine the work paragraph by paragraph.

She begins by noting the success of her work, though perhaps this amounted to the sale of about 250 copies.[23] Then she goes on to explain her purpose:

> My object in writing the following pages [the novel] was not simply to amuse the Reader, neither was it to gratify my own taste ... I wished to tell the truth, for truth always conveys its own moral to those who are able to receive it ...

It is an aim to be found in Swift. Plainly, Anne did enjoy her work in general, though Charlotte says she 'hated' it, but would pursue it. It was the necessity for detailing violent and drunken scenes she hated. However, if she is to show moral cause and effect, she must illustrate defective morality. In this way she will exhibit truth unvarnished, though it 'hides at the bottom of a well' and we need courage to dive for it. We might ask why this image was chosen, and may recall that the parsonage well proved very dirty when cleaned out by 'pump sinker and two men' in September 1847.[24]

She next defends herself against 'a morbid love of the coarse, if not of the brutal'. It is easy to see how this charge could be made, as she tries to give a realistic picture of the kind of scene Emily passes over with poetic selectivity. Among such scenes are that where Gilbert beats Lawrence with his stick, and the drunken brawl in which Helen keeps her temper with Huntingdon's guests under great provocation.[25] The mythic violence of Heathcliff is stripped of its glamour and shown as sordid. 'When we have to do with vice and vicious characters,' Anne writes, 'it is better to depict them as they really are than as they would wish to appear.' Heathcliff can be taken for the hero of *Wuthering Heights* because Emily depicts him sympathetically; though Anne does not abandon Huntingdon, and will not allow Helen to do so, his faults are not excused. As we can see now the novels are poles apart in feeling and intention, but to Anne, 'if I can gain the public ear, I would rather whisper a few wholesome truths therein than much soft nonsense'; this is almost an accusation against Emily.

There is a strong eighteenth-century flavour to Anne's determination not to cover the 'snares and pitfalls of life' with 'branches and flowers'. Hypocrisy, the fault with which Victorians are so often charged, played no part in Anne's fiction. She demands that there should be 'less of this delicate concealment of facts'. The attack on delicacy is interesting; here she is in total agreement with Emily's attitude towards ordinary language, going far beyond Wordsworth. The 'facts' she wishes to confront are not the 'facts' pilloried in *Hard Times;* Anne is referring to the facts of human nature, some of which she has discovered by the Evangelical method of introspection and some by close observation of others. It is this last point that has ensured the vital life of such characters as Fergus, Rose and Mrs Markham. Anne turns out to be an observant reporter, whose next novel might have turned out rather like those of George Eliot.

It was the discrepancy between *Agnes Grey* and *Wildfell Hall* that shocked Charlotte. Yet the two books have a great deal in common. In the fourth paragraph of her Preface Anne sets forth the aim of building on the tradition she is establishing; if she has left a disagreeable impression in *Wildfell Hall* she will try to do better next time, 'for I love to give innocent pleasure.' But she must add a moral dimension, even if it means speaking 'an unpalatable truth'. *Merely* to amuse would be to misapply her talents. Nor does she wish to produce 'a perfect work of art'. In essence, Anne is placing herself, as she does in her poems, in the line of Bunyan and Milton. The world is a battlefield, and she is taking part in the battle, adding her weight to the side of 'truth'. It is not a utilitarian view of truth that she propounds, but the understanding of morality which goes back through Aquinas to Plato, and sees the definition of the *arete* of mankind as linked with both rational counsel and emotional fulfilment.

In her final paragraph she again addresses the confusion induced by Newby and Harpers between the three Bells. This is not a mere bid to be treated as an individual: Anne has a totally different 'message' to deliver, especially from that of Emily. It is ironic that her plea is still disregarded, and she can be seen as a competitor of Emily rather than a critic. She ends with a discussion of sexual equality:

> if a book is a good one, it is so whatever the sex of the author may be. All novels are *or should be* [my italics]

[169]

written for both men and women to read, and I am at a loss to conceive how a man should permit himself to write anything that would be really disgraceful to a woman, or why a woman should be censured for writing anything that could be proper and becoming for a man.

The fruit of Patrick Brontë's equal treatment of boys and girls at his Glascar school in the 1790s is here.

At this point Anne Brontë's life suddenly became submerged in turmoil, both at home and at a distance. Branwell, whose health had been bad for a long while, died on 24 September. No one had any premonition that his death was imminent. He had been in Haworth village on Friday, but stayed in bed on Saturday, 23 September. On Sunday morning he died, reconciled to his family and quieter in mind.

The funeral was held on the following Thursday. Either this date or the Sunday after, when the memorial service was held, was the last time that Emily left the parsonage. She too now gave evidence of being seriously ill. In these circumstances, Anne began to incline towards Charlotte, with whom she had shared the long journey to London. Meanwhile, in Derbyshire, events were moving towards other conclusions. Writing on 28 July to Ellen, Charlotte says:

> Anne continues to hear constantly, almost daily, from her old pupils, the Robinsons. They are both now engaged to different gentlemen and if they do not change their minds, which they have done two or three times, will probably be married in a few months. Not one spark of love does either of them profess for her future husband, one of them declares that interest alone guides her, the other, poor thing! is acting according to her mother's wish, and is utterly indifferent to the man chosen for her. The lighter headed of the two sisters takes pleasure in the spectacle of her fine wedding dresses and costly wedding presents; the more thoughtful can derive no gratification from these things and is much depressed at the contemplation of her future lot. Anne does her best to cheer and counsel her, and she seems to cling to her former governess as her only true friend. Of the mother I have not patience to speak.[26]

This is an important source for our knowledge of Anne's relations with the Robinsons, and shows that, with her novel safely relaunched with its new Preface, Anne was free to spend a great deal of time in pursuing the friendship. It is quite possible, of course, that the death of Branwell freed the Robinsons for this new intimacy, which could have been embarrassing while he was alive, for they intended to visit Haworth, and soon fulfilled their intention. The two were engaged respectively to a Mr Milner, who appears in the Robinson papers, and to Henry Clapham, a Keighley squire. It is unfortunately impossible to say which of the two was the 'lighter headed' and which the 'more thoughtful'. In view of Anne's greater influence over Mary, one might have suspected she was the latter, but it was Bessy who broke off her engagement, presumably due at least in part to Anne's intervention.[27]

It is not clear what Anne reported to Charlotte 'of the mother'. She seems to have been at Great Barr during this time, and since the death of the wife of her cousin, Sir Edward Dolman Scott, had drawn closer to him. Charlotte's view of her since the crisis of 1846 had been that she was a scheming seductress, and this view must have been confirmed to some extent in the letters Anne was now receiving. It should be mentioned, however, that her alliance with Dolman Scott was not as bizzare as it has been represented; he was not twenty years older than her, as some biographers claim, but about six. The whole thrust of *Wildfell Hall* had related to the need to show the young the miseries of ill-considered marriage, so we can assume that Anne wrote in similar vein to the Robinsons now, but it is unlikely that she admitted to being the author of a new novel on these topics.

That Bessy did break off her engagement is authenticated fact. Three years later she married the industrialist and engineer William Jessop of Butterley, with whom she seems to have been happy.[28] Thus Anne Brontë had a quite remarkable personal effect on the life of her friend and the friend's subsequent family. Mary continued her engagement to Henry Clapham, whom she married at Allestree, on 19 October. The 'almost daily' letters would have carried news of the wedding, and perhaps of political events in Derby, where the MPs had been unseated by petition concerning the probity of the election machine. Matthew Gisborne had been approached to stand as a Whig candidate, but had turned down the offer. The Evanses and Gisbornes were distancing themselves from the Radicals in an industrial town at a crucial time.[29] Judging by the tone of her recent Preface Anne Brontë had not intended to conclude her messages to the public, and all such material would have been added to her store of information to be used in future works. Though Emily's health was by now giving great cause for alarm, it is impossible to think that Anne would have spent no time considering what her next literary venture might be.

Fraser's magazine for August 1848 contained Anne's poem 'The Three Guides'. This poem bears the date 11 August 1847 in the copy manuscript, and so there was apparently twelve months between final revision and publication. There are several mysteries connected with it, to none of which unequivocal answers can be given. First, there is the strange report in Mrs Gaskell recalling a memory of Ellen Nussey's. She claimed to have seen Anne one day with a copy of *Chambers' Journal*:

> and a gentle smile of pleasure stealing over her face as she read. 'What is the matter?' asked the friend [Ellen]. 'Why do you smile?' 'Only because I see they have inserted one of my poems,' was the quiet reply; and not a word more was said on the subject.[30]

A search of *Chambers'* has failed to produce any poem likely to have been by Anne Brontë, and one must assume that it is the present poem that Ellen refers to. But she was not at Haworth in or around August 1848, in fact not until just after Christmas, when circumstances were harshly different. 'I see they have inserted one of my poems' would by that time hardly have been a reasonable response to such a question, though perhaps weight should once again be given to Agnes Grey's remark about resolute dissembling. Ellen appears to be recalling this incident to show Anne's modesty, but it may also show an Emily-like disinclination to discuss her views where they might be misunderstood.

There is also considerable difficulty in coming to a certain conclusion about the meaning of the poem. It deals with three would-be spiritual guides, given the names 'Spirit of Pride', 'Spirit of Earth' and 'Spirit of Faith'. The similarity between the first of these and the character of Heathcliff has often been noted, initially by Muriel Spark.[31] One is not surprised to find the poet choosing 'Spirit of Faith' as her guide, but only after an examination of the first spirit and the second, 'Spirit of Earth'. Attempts have been made to equate 'Pride' with Emily and 'Earth' with Charlotte. Though at first sight this may seem a difficult identification, Elizabeth Langland points out that 'The Three Guides' dates from about the time when *Jane Eyre* was being completed, and the penultimate sections of the book are much concerned with St John Rivers.[32] She quotes the phrase in which Charlotte describes Rivers as 'a master spirit . . . redeemed from the earth'. Though finally Charlotte allows Jane to marry the humbled Rochester, this turn may not have been clear to Emily or Anne as the chapters were read aloud during the evening 'workshop' sessions. St John's rationalistic and duty-bound approach and his utter rejection of romance may well be the source of Anne's revulsion, though it is not so easy to see Rivers' character as the epitome of Charlotte's art as it is to see Heathcliff as the keynote of Emily's. However, Elizabeth Langland's suggestion deserves very careful consideration.

Alternatively, perhaps both 'Pride' and 'Earth' are facets of Emily's work. 'Earth' to Emily was embued with mystical life: 'How beautiful the earth is still . . . !', 'In the earth – the earth – thou shalt be laid . . .' 'Shall Earth no more inspire thee . . . ?' Emily's pantheism saw the earth in near-pagan terms as a generating and embracing mother. Anne's 'Spirit of Earth' is nothing like this, but a dull, unenterprising spirit. It is possible that she is once again fulfilling her plan of deromanticizing Emily's best-loved concepts. As a possible indication that Emily did indeed see 'The Three Guides' as relevant to her art, as a kind of challenge, we might refer to the small poem 'Often rebuked', the only one of Emily's poems which has no manuscript, perhaps because it was composed on a small piece of paper instead of direct into the B manuscript, currently being used for the last long fictional poem. In 'Often rebuked', the poet declares, 'It vexes me to choose another guide', possibly in answer to persuasion by her sister that she should choose the 'Spirit of Faith'.

However, this final autumn, Emily was rapidly declining, in a process I have charted elsewhere.

As her end approached Charlotte made frequent appeals to

her to adopt some kind of cure, but in vain. Meanwhile the Robinsons, Bessy now with her engagement broken off and Mary married to Henry Clapham, decided to come to visit Anne at Haworth. Charlotte's gloss on their proposed visit, as she writes to Ellen, must have been far from Anne's viewpoint:

> The new Mrs Clapham is said to be cutting a prodigious dash. She infuriates the Keighley gentry with her pride and assumption of superiority. . . . It is our wish to have as little to do with them as possible, and sorry we are that they have brought their grandeur and weakness so near.[33]

The letter's opinions are all Charlotte; it is highly unlikely that Anne would have continued her friendship with the pair if she had felt like this about them. It seems unlikely that Charlotte ever saw the Robinsons' letters to Anne in which they gave evidence of their affection for her. Charlotte's own forays into governess life had brought her no such enduring love; as so often we get a hint of jealousy in Charlotte's relations with Anne. It was surely a sign of genuine affection that the Robinson sisters were willing to make a determined effort to reach Haworth, to visit someone whose status could not compare with the affronted Keighley gentry.

The visit was finally reported to Ellen on 10 December, having taken place about a week previously. The Robinsons were shown into the sitting room where Anne greeted them, and they 'were clinging round her like two children' when Charlotte entered. (Emily was very ill indeed, and must have been out of sight in the kitchen.) Anne's response to the fulsome greeting was to look 'perfectly quiet and passive'; perhaps she had to do so, as her breath may have been short. Charlotte was amazed to note that the Robinsons were 'stylish and attractive-looking girls'.[34] There is a change in tone in Charlotte's letter, which suggests that seeing the Robinsons in real life, she ceased to blame them for Branwell's downfall, and began to accord Anne more respect at her success with them. The present reunion was certainly intended as a mark of favour and gratitude to Anne, and would have been so accepted.

Christmas was gloomy beyond measure. Emily died on 19 December; the quartet of Brontës had been reduced to two.

Hardly noticed by Charlotte, Anne had been declining too, with shortness of breath and tiredness indicating consumption as well as asthma. Steps could now be taken to seek a cure, since Emily was no longer living to be affronted by the very idea, in her words, of 'poisoning' doctors. Meanwhile, Anne became involved in religious controversy. The tone of *Wildfell Hall*, like that of some poems including 'A Word to the Elect' had been Universalist, that is, it had suggested that in the final issue, all humans would be 'saved' by God. Dr David Thom, a Liverpool minister, had written to 'Acton Bell' through Smith, Elder, having seen her anti-Calvinist poem in the reissued *Poems*. Thom had studied on the Continent and had obtained a doctorate at Heidelberg. He had been the minister at several Liverpool chapels; by 1825 he was at the Scotch Church in Rodney Street, but by the time of his correspondence with Anne he was minister of Bold Street chapel. He had a variety of interests, shown by his recognition of the Lancashire and Cheshire Historical Society, to which he presented a group of his publications in 1849.

His own letter to Anne is lost, and we have only her reply, written on 30 December and returned to Dr Thom through W. S. Williams. She is notably more cautious in writing to a theologian than in the novel, to which she introduces Dr Thom. Helen's arguments from passages in the Bible are toned down as '*mere* suggestions' and she comes quite near to saying that even though the doctrine of eternal punishment is not true, God might wish to use 'doubtful language' so as to employ the dread of future punishment to produce right minds and good behaviour in the people. For a proponent of truth, this sounds oddly equivocal. However, it is perhaps typical of Anne to present both sides of the argument and to be willing to hold firm decision in abeyance. These were not abstract philosophical arguments with her, but related to the destinies of Branwell, the Robinsons and especially Emily. 'Only let our zeal be tempered with discretion', she suggests, 'and while we labour let us look humbly to God who is able to bring his great work to perfection in his own good time and manner.'[35] This dependence on God is typical of Anne, and the struggle to maintain it is the drama to which we must now turn.

11

Sunset over the Sea

———◦◦●◦◦———

Throughout Charlotte's many letters to Ellen Nussey, her sister Anne played almost no part. We have seen many examples of short, half-sentence references to her, but there are virtually no detailed discussion of her activities or her personality. She has been seen as the quiet, well-controlled other sister, shadily lurking beyond Emily's vitality. She had been 'omitted' from the school plan, dismissed as a possible attraction for William Weightman, misunderstood when she returned to her duty at Thorp Green but more often just forgotten, until Charlotte was forced to take her to London to show her publishers that there was more than one Bell. But once Branwell and Emily were dead, Charlotte turned to Anne, and her letters to Ellen were full of her. Yet even at this point, as Anne's last six months on earth opened, Charlotte would try hard to deny her jurisdiction over her own life. As Anne realized how near she was to death's door, and felt her only hope lay in travelling to Scarborough, Charlotte obstructed her wishes and would not help. Since, as has been made clear, Charlotte's view of Anne did much to set the tone for subsequent biographical and literary comment, we shall try hard to understand the motivation of each sister in these final months.

It must be emphasized that Charlotte was in some ways a sympathetic, almost doting mother figure. She had no idea consciously that she had slighted Anne throughout her life and would continue to thwart her. She genuinely saw her young sister as dependent, physically weak, 'nun-like'. But she did fail to recognize Anne's mature personality and well-organized intellect. We need to remember Charlotte's own deep inferiority complex over her size and looks; Anne threathened her supremacy with a physical presence which George Smith had called 'pleasing' and with the disconcerting capacity to get her poems published, as witness the August number of *Fraser*. During these final months, Charlotte persisted in seeing Anne as a child, to be protected and guided, not a mature and independent young woman. Though Anne in life and her works after her death partly eluded this destiny, the tone of some of Charlotte's remaining letters show why they have not quite done so.

The final six months of Anne Brontë's life present the biographer with a problem. There is so much material in Charlotte's letters and the reminiscences of Ellen Nussey that it would be easy to dwell unduly on these times and present a picture of Anne as predominantly ill, whereas in this respect the last six months are untypical. On the other hand, because Anne's attitudes are now given a prominence in the letters that they have never previously achieved, important evidence about her surfaces now in a way that never happened before. I do not wish to distort the story of Anne Brontë's life by undue emphasis on this period, despite the abundance of evidence, and my use of quotations will therefore be relatively sparing. One point concerning the relation between her personal (non-Gondal) poetry and her real opinions is clarified in this final period.

I have referred to the passage in *Agnes Grey* where the heroine gives as a reason for writing poetry that a poem becomes a 'pillar of witness', that is, it puts on record the feelings and thoughts occasioned by a specific experience.[1] It is this attitude to personal poetry which has allowed us to use some of the poems written by Agnes Grey's creator as evidence of her own thoughts and feelings. Additional proof that this is a valid procedure comes in the tone and content of Anne's only poem written in 1849 and her letter to Ellen Nussey, dated 5 April 1849. Not only is the clear, deliberate sentence structure similar, but the thoughts expressed in each piece of writing echo each other. Both, as we shall see, are arguing, self-persuasive pieces of work, setting out rational points of view without denying the emotional life beneath. Both are communicating, clear and seeking sympathetic response.

During the autumn Charlotte had been asked to visit Ellen

[177]

Nussey, but had sadly declined because of Emily's ill-health. After Emily's death, she invited Ellen to Haworth. Thus we have Ellen's report of the visit to Anne of the Leeds doctor, Mr Teale. She wrote to W. S. Williams:

> While consultations were going on in Mr Brontë's study, Anne was very lively in conversation, walking round the room supported by me. Mr Brontë joined us after Mr Teale's departure, and, seating himself on the couch, he draw Anne towards him and said, 'My *dear* little Anne'. That was all – but it was understood.

At some stage Mr Brontë wrote a note in his *Modern Domestic Medicine*, 'Mr Teale, Surgeon, Leeds, said that change of place and climate, could prove beneficial only in the early stages of consumption.' This suggests that even now consideration was being given to sending Anne away to the sea or another health resort. We note that Anne, if she wished, could be 'very lively in conversation', and as this is the first and only time since childhood when she is seen to be vivacious, we need this picture as a counterbalance to the silent Anne who has appeared so many times in Charlotte's letters. Ellen also reports in the same letter that Anne looked 'sweetly pretty' and 'in capital spirits for an invalid'. However, despite the show of cheer, the situation was serious enough for Ellen to cut short her visit.

The manuscript of Anne's last poem, called by Charlotte 'Last Lines', is at Haworth. It is written in Brontë small script and provides useful evidence of her composition methods. With hindsight, we know it was to be her last poem, but she of course could not know this, and thus the way in which she writes will be normal for one of these 'pillar of witness' poems. Taking a half-sheet from an unlined notebook she begins, without leaving any wasteful margin, 'Jan 7th', using pencil and adding alternative words which would later be edited out. The use of pencil is rare with Anne, but we have very little in the way of drafts from her, and cannot be certain how untypical this was. However, when she comes to complete the poem three weeks later, she uses ink, and both the tone of the poem and the firmness of the writing are enhanced. It seems probable, therefore, that the pencil of 7 January was a temporary and unusual expedient, and may indicate that the

[178]

poem was begun away from her portable writing desk, where ink would be available.

It is clear that in writing this poem, Anne uses the paper, as Agnes does in the novel, as a friend with whom she can communicate her dilemmas. With Dr Teale's visit, a death sentence has been pronounced. The worst moments of Anne's taxing life were approaching, and the first nine stanzas of the poem were written under this appalling cloud. The 'dreadful darkness' that closed on her 'bewildered mind' in early January was fear, both spiritual and physical. She was now called to harsh and persistent suffering, but this was not the worst of her difficulties; she feared that suffering would bring 'sin': the sin of unbelief and perhaps also of cowardice. As always, Anne is demanding perfection of herself, as Maria had taught her long ago.

Her laments fall profusely from her pen:

> *I hoped amid the brave and strong*
> *My portioned task might lie,*
> *To toil amid the labouring throng*
> *With purpose pure and high.*

This has been the attitude we have seen in *Wildfell Hall*. Life is an adventure in which 'toil' is expected and acceptable. In this poem Anne is trying to recover from the shattering recognition that she may not be given the strength to toil again as she did over *Wildfell Hall*.

For now, in the person of Dr Teale, God has 'taken my delight/ And hope of life away'. There is no revolt at this point, however; Anne is not to repeat the behaviour of Branwell and Emily in questioning God's purpose, even His existence. Long ago, as she has already told us, she has grown 'wiser than her teachers' and accepted the message of Christian tradition, with the added unorthodoxy of Universalism, even though this must be expressed guardedly. The stark honesty of this poem seems unexampled anywhere. After 34 lines, which include some verbal alternatives, Anne turns the page. She can manage two lines further on 7 January and then gives up her task for the moment.

However, the death blow did not fall. Amazingly, Anne felt no worse by the end of the month, and though she was very troubled by pain at night, she did not seem to be declining.[2]

[179]

There was to be a period of several weeks when she seemed to be rallying. The second part of the poem reflects this new balance. In it she no longer accepts death as inevitable:

> If Thou shouldst bring me back to life
> More humbled I should be;
> More wise, more strengthened for the strife,
> More apt to lean on Thee.

It might be asked how Anne Brontë could possibly be more humbled or more apt to lean on God, since her story had rarely included any sign of revolt or pride. It is little wonder that Charlotte considered her personality to be hidden under 'a sort of nun-like veil'.[3] But we have also seen how great energy and spirit had to be tamed to serve Anne's God and that humility and acceptance has called for a great struggle.

'Last Lines' (to return to Charlotte's title for it) is an argumentative poem. It is written as a communication between Anne and her soul. With calm logic she discusses the possibilities for the rest of her short life. The poem is typical of a great deal of Anne's work in taking fierce, strong emotions and reasoning with them. There is no sense in which one can call Anne Brontë a cool writer, though she is often a rational and a balanced one. Charlotte and others frequently commented on Anne's serenity; but this was achieved at the cost of rational persuasion and firm will. 'Last Lines' exhibits not a naturally weak young woman welcoming death as a release, but a very strong and independent person determining to control her response to the most painful circumstances possible, for which she could be excused for being very angry.

As January turned to February, Charlotte's letters to Ellen and to W. S. Williams give details of the remedies Anne was trying. She took cod-liver oil, although she found it 'nauseous', and bought a respirator for 30 shillings through Ellen Nussey. Dr Forbes, editor of the Medical Review, added the weight of his opinion to that of Dr Teale, and said that any change of residence should not be thought of for the moment. The idea of such a change is mentioned so many times in the letters of this period that it seems Anne herself must have been suggesting it persistently, and it seems certain that the change she desired was to go to Scarborough. By early February

Charlotte was half-inclined to think that her sister might recover:

> Consumption . . . is a flattering malady, but certainly
> Anne's illness has of late assumed a less alarming charac-
> ter than it had in the beginning: the hectic is allayed; the
> cough gives a more frequent reprieve.[4]

In mid-January Anne 'cannot study now, she can scarcely
read', but by February she is 'engaged with one of Frederika
Bremer's tales'.[5] She expressed a wish to see the reviews of the
poems, now reissued, according to the agreement apparently
negotiated during the visit to London the previous July by
Smith, Elder. During this time, the only really trying kind of
weather was frost, when Anne's sense of languor increased and
her cough became worse. But in general, changes of tempera-
ture of any sort proved an affliction. Ellen, genuinely a friend
of Anne just as of Charlotte, invited her to Brookroyd, but
Anne felt it best to refuse.[6] However, it was at this point that
the plan first emerged that when, if at all, Anne might be well
enough to take a holiday either at 'the seaside or some inland
watering place' (perhaps Harrogate was thought of), Ellen
might go with her as companion.[7] Though Charlotte felt this
would be an undue burden on Ellen, Anne received a letter
from her agreeing to go if her friends would let her.

It was in answer to this letter that Anne wrote the one
previously mentioned, whose tone is similar to that of 'Last
Lines'.[8] It is too long to quote in full, but is characterised by a
firm, delicate, tactful and determined tone, as well as giving
evidence of Anne's continuing moral purpose. The manuscript, at Haworth, is in clear and regular, very legible writing. Dated 5 April, the letter begins by thanking Ellen for
agreeing to come with her friend, 'as a companion, not as a
nurse'. She cannot think of coming to Brookroyd, where she
would be a 'silent invalid stranger'. What Anne is seeking is a
holiday free of social obligations, and she is surely, despite the
previous mention of an inland spa, thinking of the Scarborough breezes. She next debates the best time for the holiday.
Ellen is unable to come before the end of May, and 'we are
almost certain of some fine warm days in the latter half, when
the laburnums and lilacs are in bloom'. In this sentence we see

Anne putting the sight of lilacs and laburnums before herself as a goal to be reached. For her, they symbolize the warmth and brightness of a May day at Scarborough.

In the final section of the letter, Anne discusses death much as she has already done in the January poem. 'I have no horror of death; if I thought it inevitable, I think I could quietly resign myself to the prospect....But I wish it would please God to spare me not only for papa's and Charlotte's sakes; but because I long to do some good in the world before I leave it. I have many schemes in my head for future practice, humble and limited indeed, but still I should not like them all to come to nothing, and myself to have lived to so little purpose.' In writing to Ellen, who still knew nothing about the Brontës' publications, Anne is playing down her literary ambitions. Nevertheless, we may consider what these 'many schemes' might have been. We recall that as the illness struck, Anne was corresponding with the Universalist, Dr Thom. Her first literary act on discovering the seriousness of her condition was to write a poem; it is a fair deduction that her 'many schemes' would have included another novel along the lines discussed with the Liverpool minister, and more poetry. The latter would have included some poems like 'The Three Guides', which if our supposition was correct, Anne must have been reading to herself during Ellen's visit in January.[9]

There is no record of any letters from the Robinsons that year, but when we recall the enthusiastic meeting between Anne and her former pupils in December 1848, we can hardly suppose the friendship had died. Anne was by now aware that she had done 'some good in the world' by counselling Bessy to reject an ill-fated marriage. In addition to her plans for more poetry, then, we can be fairly certain that among the 'many schemes' would be a novel based on the further experiences of the Robinsons. In a letter written by Charlotte to W. S. Williams on the same day as Anne's to Ellen, it is made clear that Anne is frequently well enough to read, though nothing is said about writing. Yet we have the clearly written letter to Ellen, with little sign of weakness, to show that Anne was still sitting by her desk at least at such a favoured moment. We shall never know whether or not any of her 'schemes' reached paper, in the form of a plot outline or character detail, but it is not beyond possibility that something was pencilled out at this time. Despite the pressures Charlotte continued to write

Shirley.[10] It does not seem likely that Anne would make no move whatever to put her plans on paper in sketch form, and we may also guess that if she did so, Charlotte would have held such plans in little favour, having regard to her lack of understanding of Anne's artistic and moral success in *Wildfell Hall*. After her death, plans for prose work, unlike the tiny manuscript of 'Last Lines', would have been destroyed.

By the beginning of May it looked very much as if the plans for a holiday at Scarborough could be implemented. Finance was not difficult, since the death of Fanny Outhwaite in February had resulted in a legacy of £200 for Anne.[11] Warm, dry weather was now trying to her lungs, but the colder spell in early May brought relief. Many of Charlotte's letters indicate that although Anne was reluctant to admit any decline, and could sometimes seem lively, she was becoming thinner: 'emaciated' is Charlotte's word for it in a letter to Ellen of 1 May.[12] Though Anne was going out each day, she was very short of breath. 'We creep, rather than walk,' says Charlotte. Nevertheless, the plans for a visit to Scarborough were advancing, and it was settled that they would stay at 2, Cliff, where the elder Mrs Robinson sometimes stayed. These lodgings had a sea view and would have been out of the financial range of the Brontës in earlier days. Ellen would be able to come too, and Anne still had hopes of a cure in the sea air.

The last days of Anne Brontë are recorded for us in letters from Charlotte and a long narrative written by Ellen and quoted verbatim in Mrs Gaskell's biography.[13] This is supported by the primary evidence of yet another account book of Charlotte's which, like the previous one, contains abbreviated and scribbled notes.[14] It had been intended to start for Scarborough on 23 May, and Ellen was to have met the two sisters at Leeds. It appears that Anne was too ill to travel, and Ellen waited at Leeds fruitlessly.[15] On the next day Ellen went to Haworth and arrived in time to help carry Anne into a chaise which had been hired to take them to Keighley. The chaise does not occur in Charlotte's account book, and could have been paid for by Mr Brontë. Charlotte insisted on paying first class rail fare from Keighley to Leeds, though there appears to be some confusion about the times of trains. Judging by the evidence of the contemporary *Bradshaw* they would have caught the 3.05 p.m. train from Leeds arriving in York at 4.40 p.m.[16]

[183]

Ellen records that on arrival at York 'the dear invalid was so revived, so cheerful, and so happy' that she and Charlotte began to feel a temporary improvement could be gained from this holiday which they had been so fearful of. The highlight of the visit was the Minster:

> By her request we went to the Minster, and to her it was an overpowering pleasure; not for its own imposing and impressive grandeur only, but because it brought to her susceptible nature a vital and overwhelming sense of omnipotence. She said, while gazing at the structure, 'If finite power can do this, what is the . . . ?' and here emotion stayed her speech, and she was hastened to a less exciting scene.[17]

In these words Ellen gives us a poignant picture of Anne's awe-filled reaction to the sight of a building which had been her favourite for nine years. In an expanded account Ellen Nussey mentioned the George Hotel as the place where the party stayed, and in her biography of Anne Brontë Winifred Gerin argues that this was the George in Coney Street, which would have been known to Anne from the fact that the York–Scarborough coaches had started there before the building of the railway, so that Anne would have travelled from the George on several occasions with the Robinsons.[18]

Ellen's original account now celebrates Anne's happiness on this visit:

> Her weakness of body was great, but her gratitude for every mercy was greater. After such an exertion as walking to her bed-room, she would clasp her hands and raise her eyes in silent thanks, and she did this not to the exclusion of wonted prayer, for that too was performed on bended knee, ere she accepted the rest of her couch.[19]

Charlotte again insisted on paying first class rail fares to Scarborough. On arrival, probably at two o'clock on Friday, 25 May, they drank dandelion coffee and bought two tickets for the bridge over Mill Beck, where Anne had walked with the Robinsons on many occasions.

Anne's breath did not become much easier, but she was determined to treat the visit as a holiday, introducing Ellen and Charlotte to the delights of her favourite place. On Saturday she hired a donkey cart and drove the donkey herself, so that the driver should not overtax the animal. 'When joined by her friend,' says Ellen, 'she was charging the boy-master of the donkey to treat the poor animal well. She was ever fond of dumb things, and would give up her own comfort for them.' Recalling Anne's interest in young people, and in the upbringing and character-formation of boys, we may suppose she was also concerned for the donkey boy himself. On the next day, Sunday, she wanted to go to church, but Ellen and Charlotte thought she was too weak and dissuaded her. She walked along the beach a little in the afternoon and then sat on a bench near the sea while the others walked further.

It seems fitting to use extracts from Ellen's account to Mrs Gaskell to describe her final hours:

The evening closed in with the most glorious sunset ever witnessed. The castle on the cliff stood in proud glory, gilded by the rays of the declining sun. . . . The view was grand beyond description. Anne was drawn in her easy chair to the window, to enjoy the scene with us. Her face became illumined almost as much as the glorious scene she gazed upon. . . . She again thought of public worship, and wished us to leave her, and join those who were assembled at the house of God. We declined. . . . On returning to her place near the fire she conversed with her sister upon the propriety of returning to their home. . . . She was fearing others might suffer more if her decease occurred where she was. [Next day, after a good night] nothing occurred to incite alarm until about 11 a.m. . . . She believed she had not long to live. . . . The doctor admitted that the angel of death had already arrived and that life was ebbing fast. She thanked him for his truthfulness . . . and reverently invoked a blessing from on high, first on her sister, then upon her friend, to who she said, 'be a sister in my stead. Give Charlotte as much of your company as you can.'

She was borne to the sofa. . . . Shortly after this, seeing that her sister could hardly restrain her grief, she said, 'Take courage, Charlotte; take courage'. . . . The doctor came and went two or three times. . . . So little was the house disturbed by the presence of the dying . . . that din-

[185]

ner was announced as ready, through the half-opened door, as the living sister was closing the eyes of the dead one.

It was Whit Monday, 28 May 1849.

To Mr Williams Charlotte wrote, 'I have buried her here at Scarbro' to save Papa the anguish of the return and a third funeral. . . . He and the servants knew that when they parted from Anne they would see her no more. All tried to be resigned. I knew it likewise, and I wanted her to die where she would be happiest. She loved Scarbro'. A peaceful sun gilded her evening.'[20]

Commenting on this final scene Ada Harrison says, 'Anne is almost awesomely in command. She rises supremely to her last occasion, and as long as she is conscious, she directs it.'[21] There are so many ways in which her death and burial at Scarborough are symbolic that it would be tedious to underline them. The burial record at Christ Church underscores one of the main points. Here Anne is recorded as of 'Scarboro, from near York'. This is a clear reference to her Thorp Green connections, and shows that the clergyman knew Anne well enough on her own account not to be influenced by any details Charlotte could give to her. Anne, the youngest sister, had in her final hours escaped from the kindly dominion of the Brontë family, as she had throughout her artistic life laid claim to judgement not as a minor Brontë, but as a major literary figure in her own right.

Notes

Abbreviations used in the notes

AB = Anne Brontë   BB = Branwell Brontë   BL = British Library   BPM = Brontë Parsonage   *BST* = Brontë Society Transactions   CB = Charlotte Brontë   EB = Emily Jane Brontë   EN = Ellen Nussey   PB = Patrick Brontë   WG = Winifred Gerin   WSW = W. S. Williams. There is no secure edition of CB's letters, but texts of many of them may be found in the Shakespeare Head Press Brontë, *Lives and Letters*. A selection is to be found in M. Spark, *The Brontë Letters*.

Notes to Introduction

1 See T. J. Winnifrith, *The Brontës and their Background, Romance and Reality*, especially chapter 2.
2 G. D. Hargreaves, 'Incomplete texts of "The Tenant of Wildfell Hall"', *BST* (82), pp. 113ff; and 'Further omissions in "The Tenant of Wildfell Hall"', *BST* (87), pp. 115ff.
3 They consist of letters to EN, dated 4 October 1847, 26 January 1848, and 5 April 1849, at BPM; one letter to W. S. Williams, dated 29 September 1848, at BL, and one letter to Reverend David Thom, dated 30 December 1848 and printed on 21 June 1923 in the *Times Literary Supplement*, of which the manuscript is not currently available.
4 The manuscripts of Anne's diary papers were apparently among the Law collection of Brontë manuscripts, the whereabouts of which is still uncertain.
5 See E. Chitham, *A Life of Emily Brontë*, chapter 9 and notes.
6 E. Chitham and T. J. Winnifrith, *Brontë Facts and Brontë Problems*, chapter 4.

7 An example is the letter to EN of 4 January 1838 (*Shakespeare Head Brontë* no. 44), in which Charlotte clearly thinks of herself *in loco parentis*.

8 E. Chitham, *The Poems of Anne Brontë*, pp. 28ff, and table p. 208.

9 See below, chapter 11.

10 Even the Gondal poems of both Emily and Anne appear to reflect their current moods in a fictional context at times. All the non-Gondal poems do so, whether they may be classified, in the case of Anne, as 'religious', 'philosophical', 'dialogue' poems, or in other ways. See *The Poems of Anne Brontë*, Introduction.

11 For the circumstances of its composition, see chapter 10 below.

12 In 'Believe not those who say/ The upward path is smooth', dated 24 April 1848, she advises the pilgrim to 'trample down rebellious lust/ Or it will hold thee back.'

Notes to Chapter 1

1 Preface to so-called second edition of *The Tenant of Wildfell Hall* (hereafter *Wildfell Hall*).

2 See E. Chitham and T. J. Winnifrith, *Brontë Facts and Brontë Problems*, chapter 9.

3 I have not repeated the Thornton period here. It is covered in *The Life of Emily Brontë*, chapter 1. The story of Anne's angel appears in E. Chadwick, *In the Footsteps of the Brontës*, p. 172.

4 I have examined the evidence concerning Patrick's 'weird Irish stories' in *The Brontës' Irish Background*, chapter 10.

5 Some examples, contained in Lock and Dixon, *A Man of Sorrow*, include letters concerning relief from the cholera (p. 320), opening a prison at Haworth (p. 321), cremation (pp. 365–6), horizontally firing shells (p. 414).

6 See PB's 'The Harper of Erin', from *The Rural Minstrel*.

7 I have explored the character of Maria in *A Life of Emily Brontë*, chapter 4 and elsewhere.

8 The view of Maria found in WGBB and elsewhere is based on Mrs Gaskell's report of Charlotte's memories, recollections of the servants reported by Mrs Chadwick and particularly an interpretation of BB's poems, especially the 'Caroline' poems. In my view, fair inferences are made, though I suggest in *A Life of Emily Brontë* that the six-year-old girl who read her father's proofs was Emily, not Maria (*A Life of Emily Brontë*, pp. 31–2).

9 I have examined the evidence for the different character of Elizabeth in *A Life of Emily Brontë*, chapters 2–4.

10 In particular, Elizabeth's practicality seems to be established, while Maria was loving but impractical.

11 Charlotte's short-sightedness was a partial cause of this staring. My adjective 'little' has been bestowed advisedly; her wedding dress, preserved at Haworth, shows this aspect of her physique. For the staring, see my *The Brontës' Irish Background* for some non-traditional evidence.

12 For Emily as a girl, see *A Life of Emily Brontë*, chapters 2–5; for Emily's 'Royalism', which enthused her when acting the part of King Charles, see Stevie Davies, *Emily Brontë*, pp. 7–8.

13 A sound evaluation of Branwell's development is to be found in Daphne du Maurier, *The Infernal World of Branwell Brontë*.

14 Mrs Gaskell mentions one attempt by the Brontës to socialize in *The Life of Charlotte Brontë*, chapter 3; Mrs Chadwick mentions another in *In the Footsteps of the Brontës*, p. 87.

15 Chitham, *The Poems of Anne Brontë*, pp. 151ff. WG also uses the poem to illuminate Anne's thoughts and retrospective feelings.

16 See *A Life of Emily Brontë*, chapter 6.

17 EN in 'Reminiscences of Charlotte Brontë', *Scribner's Monthly* II, May 1871. Her words are, 'She still pursued her studies, and especially her sewing, under the surveillance of her aunt.'

18 See Chitham, *The Poems of Anne Brontë*, pp. 151ff, lines 57–64.

19 cf. also the early drawings from Bewick's *British Birds*.

20 See *A Life of Emily Brontë*, p. 38.

21 A range of hymns sung at Haworth church may be found in the specially printed hymn sheets and orders of service at BPM.

22 I refer later to the drawing 'What you please' (1840), but there are also drawings of trees done at Roe Head (27 October and 13 November 1835) and at Thorp Green (19 October 1843), probably at Thorp Green (16 December 1843) and several without dates. Some of these may have been copied from copy books now lost. Emily also drew a symbolic tree and gave it to her friend Louise Bassompiere in Belgium (*A Life of Emily Brontë*, pp. 151–2). The fir tree episode in *Wuthering Heights* and the chestnut tree episode in *Jane Eyre* are well known.

23 See *The Brontës' Irish Background*, chapter 8.

24 W. G. Briggs, 'Richmal Mangnall and her school at Crofton Old Hall'.

25 This seems a fair deduction from *Agnes Grey*, chapter 24.

26 Briggs, 'Richmal Mangnall', p. 29, gives the basic cost at 33 guineas per annum. This seems to be more than twice as much as Cowan Bridge.

27 The identification of the school began with the publication of PB's letter to Mrs Gaskell of 20 June 1855, in *BST* 1933, p. 89. I have included this section on Crofton Hall though it is not

strictly related to Anne, since Maria and Elizabeth are not likely
to attain a full biography.

28 The matter of the precise accent spoken by the Brontës, and that
spoken by their Yorkshire contemporaries, is vexed. Charlotte
shows in *Shirley* that manufacturers spoke provincially without
shame. Mary Taylor, who came from one of these families,
noted 'a strong Irish accent' in Charlotte when she first met her
at school (Letter from Mary Taylor to Mrs Gaskell, 28 January
1856).

29 Mrs Chadwick mentions the whooping cough (and measles) (*In
the Footsteps of the Brontës*, p. 70). Her informant will have been
one of the Garrs sisters, who seems to be explaining the eventual
death of Maria and Elizabeth by reference to a previous illness.

30 CB, 'History of the year 1829', BPM.

31 See WGBB, chapter 3.

32 The evidence for Anne's asthma is vague and appears principally
in a letter of CB to EN dated 15 December 1846, together with
EN's remark in her 'Reminiscences' that Anne's voice was
'weak, but very sweet in tone'. Anne's delight in the clear air of
Scarborough, as transmuted to *Agnes Grey*, chapter 24, supports
the view that she was asthmatic.

33 C. Alexander, *Early Writings of CB*, p. 20.

34 CB, 'History of the year 1829' BPM.

35 See below, chapter 3.

36 See *The Brontës' Irish Background*, chapter 8.

37 CB–EN, 'Shakespeare Head', *Lives and Letters*, vol. I, p. 147, of
doubtful date. 'Aunt's' has been supplied for the gap.

38 See T. J. Winnifrith, *The Brontës and their Background: Romance
and Reality*, pp. 19–20.

39 T. Shaw, *A History of Cornish Methodism*, p. 32.

40 See Anne's poem, 'To Cowper', in *The Poems of Anne Brontë*,
p. 84.

41 The 1834 dairy paper, almost entirely written by Emily, is well
reproduced in B. Wilks, *The Brontës*, p. 73, and N. Brysson
Morrison, *Haworth Harvest*, following p. 136.

42 Fragment at Haworth. This is the only fragment of Anne's early
writing we have. It suggests an absence of precocity when
compared with Emily's reputation at Cowan Bridge. If Anne
was a slower learner than Charlotte and Emily, and seemed
more comparable with Elizabeth than Maria, this helps us to
understand Charlotte's failure to take her seriously.

43 Pictures at BPM. Reproduction of the church in e.g. P. Bentley,
The Brontës and their World, p. 29.

Notes to Chapter 2

1 See E. Chitham, *A Life of Emily Brontë*, p. 58.
2 Ellen uses the word in her 'Reminiscences', already quoted, and again in a letter quoted by C. K. Shorter in *Charlotte Brontë and her Circle*, pp. 178–80.
3 e.g. by T. J. Winnifrith in *Brontë Facts and Brontë Problems*, chapter 7.
4 R. Wilson, *All Alone*, pp. 27ff.
5 See *A Life of Emily Brontë*, chapter 6.
6 There are no poem manuscripts before 1836, and no Gondal prose sagas have survived. Exactly when the two sisters destroyed their juvenilia is uncertain. Much of Charlotte's and Branwell's survives.
7 1837 diary paper, BPM. A very clear enlarged reproduction may be found in B. Wilks, *The Brontës*, p. 55.
8 See *A Life of Emily Brontë*, chapter 5.
9 The final words are very indistinct, and it is not quite clear what the sisters' decision was. What is important is that the two are shown to be engaged in a joint writing venture which sometimes needs walking in the open air as a catalyst.
10 See *A Life of Emily Brontë*, pp. 92, 93, 201.
11 The influence of Shelley on Emily and Anne Brontë has been impossible to define precisely. I have discussed it at many points, typically in *A Life of Emily Brontë*, pp. 72–3, where I argue for almost a personal commitment to him from Emily. In *Emily Brontë*, pp. 34 and 100, Stevie Davies touches on the same points, mentioning 'Epipsychidion'.
12 1834 diary paper, BPM. Well reproduced at the places mentioned in chapter 1, note 40.
13 See chapter 7 below.
14 *BST* vol. 20, (1990), pp. 7ff.
15 'Biographical Notice of Ellis and Acton Bell', 19 September 1850.
16 *BST* (1985), p. 347.
17 *loc. cit.*, pp. 3–11.
18 Greenwood's tracings are at BPM. There is an attempted reconstruction in *BST* (1959), following p. 352.
19 It is reproduced as the second plate following p. 24 in *BST* (1951). A letter dated 1 July 1974 from the then archivist, Amy Foster, states that it was 'from Miss Brown of Ramsgill in 1950'. Ms Foster tried to discover the circumstances of its acquisition for me, but was unable to do so. It is not clear from the list of 'Recent Gifts and Other Additions to the Museum and Library' in BST (1951), pp. 54–5, which if any of the items

referred to is this one. I have given the reference number in the text, but on a visit of 12 August 1974 to BPM, I was unable to discover any more from the stockbook about the provenance of this picture.
20 See below, chapter 4 and note 13.
21 EN, 'Reminiscences', in *Scribner's Magazine* II, May 1871.
22 'Self-communion', lines 75ff.

Notes to Chapter 3

1 See WGBB, chapter 9.
2 PB–Mrs Franks (formerly Elizabeth Firth), 6 July 1835.
3 CB in 'Introduction' to 'Selections from the Literary Remains of Ellis and Acton Bell'.
4 EB, 'No coward soul is mine', C. W. Hatfield (ed.), *The Complete Poems of Emily Jane Brontë*, no. 191, p. 243.
5 Charlotte's 'Roe Head Journal' at BPM mentions Anne infrequently and is very rude about the other pupils. Samples of it may be found in WGCB, pp. 103–7.
6 Charlotte apparently went through a period of religious doubt, as is shown by several of her (dubiously dated) letters from Roe Head. WG considers Charlotte's religious crisis in WGCB, chapter 7 and says on p. 102: 'Anne . . . like Charlotte, experienced a severe religious crisis during her school-days at Roe Head.' Apart from the visit of Reverend la Trobe, summoned, apparently, to give spiritual aid in a physical illness, there is no clear evidence for this.
7 See *The Brontës' Irish Background*, pp. 105–6. This incident should not be dismissed as an inflated or idle story.
8 A picture of Roe Head is dated 27 October 1835 in WGAB. However, there is a drawing by CB very similar and one could be an adaptation of the other, not drawn from life. 'Anne's' drawing is labelled 'Roe Head, Mirfield', but not in her writing. CB's drawing (if it is indeed by CB) is attributed to Anne in P. Bentley, *The Brontës and their World*, p. 35. In both these sketches the bays seem understated, but they are clearly there.
9 WGCB has a description of Roe Head on pp. 57–9.
10 It rather looks as though she and other commentators have been misled by the present or recent state of Roe Head, which has been extended several times.
11 WGCB, chapter 7 collects, from the Roe Head journal and letters to EN: A. Cook, Ellen Cook, E. Lister, Miss Marriott, as pupils of CB. Anne brings the number to five; there is also Ann

Notes

Carter, the Woolers' niece. Margaret Wooler must have taught a group of about the same size as CB. WGCB (p. 57) says there were ten boarders when CB first went there. Unfortunately, by the date of the 1841 census the school had moved, and this way of checking on the numbers at Roe Head is ruled out.

12   Advertisement for the sale, by Jno. Smith of Birstall, in local papers, 5 October 1876. Article, 'Sylvan Beauty of Roe Head's surroundings' in *Yorkshire Weekly Post*, (?) 20 May 1911.

13   Undated advertisement at BPM.

14   1838 valuation of Mirfield, MS book at Huddersfield Central Library.

15   1876 advertisement, see note 13.

16   See chapter 1, note 22. In addition to examples in her novels, Anne uses trees as a metaphor for herself and Emily in 'Self-communion', lines 205ff.

17   Quoted WGCB, p. 103.

18   WGCB, p. 65.

19   CB–Mrs Franks, 2 June 1836.

20   G. Redmonds, *Old Huddersfield*, pp. 4ff.

21   Reported in a letter from EN to Wemyss-Reid, and discussed in *Brontë Facts and Brontë Problems*, pp. 128–9. The date is certainly 1833, not 1838.

22   P. Ahier, *The Parish Churches of St. Peter the Apostle, Huddersfield*, p. 125.

23   e.g. in Belgium, on visits to the Jenkins family, reported in WGCB, p. 200.

24   CB–EN undated, but about 8 July 1836, manuscript in Huntington Library. 'Shakespeare Head', *Lives and Letters*, vol. I, pp. 145–6.

25   Weather records, Cliffe Castle, Keighley, and *Philosophical Transactions of the Royal Academy*. Details of the church and its rebuilding are from P. Ahier, *The Parish Churches*.

26   See chapter 1, note 31.

27   See note 24 above. For factual details of Lascelles Hall incorporated here, see K. Brickhill, *The Halls at Lascelles Hall*, (typescript at Huddersfield Central Library).

28   CB's snobbery has been explored in T. J. Winnifrith's *The Brontës and their Background: Romance and Reality*.

29   1841 census, microfilm at Huddersfield Central Library.

30   See chapter 10 below.

31   See *Brontë Facts and Brontë Problems*, chapter 3.

32   ibid. p. 32.

33   CB–EN, 'Shakespeare Head', *Lives and Letters*, vol. I, p. 163.

34   W. Scruton, *BST* (1898), p. 27. While this book was in the production stage, further evidence to show that Anne suffered

only one illness, and that this was at Roe Head, was discovered by the Brontë scholar, Margaret Smith. I am extremely grateful for her information. She points out that CB's letter of 4 January 1838 is endorsed by Ellen Nussey: 'After A's (B's) [i.e. Anne Brontë's] illness at Roe Head Jan 38.' This appears to be firm evidence that the illness which la Trobe recalled at Roe Head and the illness which CB wrote of in January 1838 are one and the same.

35 *Halifax Guardian*, 1 May 1838.
36 *Philsophical Magazine*, January–June 1837. See *Brontë Facts and Brontë Problems*, p. 30.
37 It was Watt's *On the Improvement of the Mind*. Gérin suggests this choice shows that Miss Wooler saw Anne as a serious-minded girl (WGAB, p. 86). It was probably a conventional enough choice for the time.
38 *The Poems of Anne Brontë*, pp. 60–1, and note on p. 167, though at this time I believed the traditional chronology and therefore assumed that it had been composed as Dewsbury Moor.
39 See note 35 above.
40 See, e.g., CB–EN, 15 April 1839, where Charlotte is discussing Anne's reception at Blake Hall. 'I hope she'll do, you would be astonished to see what a sensible, clever letter she writes – it is only the talking part I fear – but I do seriously apprehend that Mrs Ingham will sometimes consider that she has a natural impediment of speech.'
41 The drawings are at BPM.
42 CB–EN, 4 January 1838.

Notes to Chapter 4

1 CB–EN, 12 March 1839 accurately dated though with some minor textual faults in 'Shakespeare Head', *Lives and Letters*, vol. I, pp. 173–4.
2 EB, 'From our evening fireside now', 17 April 1839.
3 Articles by J. Nussey in *Old West Riding* (1982) and *The York-shire Archaeological Journal*, vol. 55 (1983), pp. 119ff. S. Brooke in *BST* (1958); Mirfield Rate Book for 1848–9 (MS) and 'An assessment for the relief of the poor, 7 February 1840' (MS) at Huddersfield Central Library.
4 Brooke, *BST* (1958).
5 CB–EN, 15 April 1839.
6 *Agnes Grey*, chapter 2.
7 Mirfield Rate Book, 1848–9.

8 Brooke, *BST* (1958).
9 J. Nussey, in *The Yorkshire Archaeological Journal*, p. 139.
10 H. Pobjoy, *A History of Mirfield*, pp. 38, 57.
11 *Agnes Grey*, chapter 4. However, Elizabeth Crowther evidently did not 'lose her place', so the identification may be incorrect.
12 CB–EN, 15 April 1839.
13 CB–EN, 20 January 1842.
14 *The Poems of Anne Brontë*, pp. 87–8.
15 Ibid., pp. 71–2.
16 The word 'allegorical' is used in the Brontë Parsonage catalogue, apparently compiled by Dr Mildred Christian, for the similar picture 'What you please' of mid-1840, which will be discussed later.
17 *Wildfell Hall*, chapter 18.
18 I am indebted to Mrs Joanna Hutton for suggestions about the Brontës' observation of pictures and subsequent use of them.
19 The way in which art relates to a symbolized self-image is discussed by the educationalist David Holbrook in *The Exploring Word* (Cambridge, 1967) especially chapter 9.
20 cf. W. B. Yeats, 'To a child dancing in the wind'.
21 Almost all the material about Weightman's background was researched for me by C. Roy Hudleston at Kendal Record Office. For more precise detail, see *The Poems of Anne Brontë*, notes 71 and 72.
22 Information from Mr A. D. Burnett, Durham Univeristy Library. See *The Poems of Anne Brontë*, pp. 17 and 44.
24 CB–EN, 17 March 1840.
25 It is sometimes said that Emily's nickname 'the major' was given her because of her firm chaperoning. If CB was also trying to guard Anne from Weightman, some of the seeds of Helen's resentment against her aunt in *Wildfell Hall* may have been sown here.

Notes to Chapter 5

1 The arguments for this date are complex but seem to me convincing. They are given in *The Poems of Anne Brontë*, p. 10. For sources of weather knowledge, see chapter 3, note 25.
2 The revised date modifies slightly the account in *The Poems of Anne Brontë*.
3 Plans of Thorp Green Hall occur on the estate plan of 1863 in the Robinson deeds at BPM, the 1st edition OS 6" map, and the 25" sheet 156.5, a copy of which is at BL. The last mentioned

shows late alterations and appears to date from not long before the fire in which the hall was burnt down.

4   North Yorks Record Office PR OUL 5/1–2.
5   AB's sketch of Little Ouseburn church, BPM.
6   George Whitehead's diary.
7   As sources for material on the early life of Lydia Gisborne: Staffs Record Office: Registers of Barton-under-Needwood. Catalogue numbers 820/3, 820/4 and 820/8 throw some light on Gisborne and the enclosure of Needwood Forest.
8   Little Ouseburn parish registers, copy at North Yorks Record Office.
9   Robinson deeds, BPM.
10   Chapter 28 is mainly, and chapter 29 partly located in the nursery. In chapter 29 Helen says she 'flew' to the nursery, but its character is not described.
11   Robinson deeds, 93/7 BPM.
12   'The Bluebell', 22 August 1840; 'O! I am very weary', 28 August 1840; 'Oh, they have robbed me of the hope' (ND).
13   *Agnes Grey*, chapter 17; *The Poems of Anne Brontë*, pp. 28–32.
14   The most likely species of flower in the poem is *campanula rotundifolia*.
15   The title is a minor argument against the traditional date for Anne's arrival at Thorp Green, March 1841.
16   CB–EN, 14 July 1840.
17   Ripon Diocesan Records, Leeds Public Library.
18   CB–EN, June 1840,
19   EB, 'A little while, a little while'.
20   *The Poems of Anne Brontë*, p. 77. The words 'may I' in the text should be reversed and are correctly given now.

Notes to Chapter 6

1   CB–EN, 2 April 1841.
2   Little Ouseburn parish registers.
3   See, 1841 diary paper, printed e.g. in A. Harrison and D. Stanford, *Anne Brontë*, pp. 73–4. See also note 6 below.
4   See *A Life of Emily Brontë*, pp. 178–9.
5   The nickname stresses the supposed masculine character of Emily, but it also represents an allusion to the military inclinations of the family shown by their toy soldiers in infancy and Mr Brontë's propensity to shoot at targets. There is little trace of this interest in Anne's novels or poetry.
6   *Agnes Grey*, chapter 24, where Anne puts on to Agnes's pen the

feelings occasioned by Scarborough, though not incidents that happened there. Her choice of site for Agnes' school shows that she had thought carefully about where a school should best be situated. The diary paper first appears in C. K. Shorter, *Charlotte Brontë and her Circle*, p. 148–9.

7   *Agnes Grey*, chapter 21.
8   *The Poems of Anne Brontë*, pp. 80–1. The third word in line 11 should read *fell*.
9   See chapter 4, above, note 13.
10 AB's 1845 diary paper, like the 1841 paper, was in the Law collection. Its first transcribed publication is in C. K. Shorter, *Charlotte Brontë and her Circle*, pp. 152–3.
11 Little Ouseburn parish registers, North Yorks Record Office. Birth certificate of William Kettlewell.
12 1845 diary paper, see note 10 above.
13 Robinson deeds, BPM. 1841 census.
14 *BST* (1951) records the purchase on pp. 24, 55. This is not to be confused with C 60 SB 1564–3, to which I have referred in chapter 2 above.
15 *The Poems of Anne Brontë*, p. 24. I was unduly influenced by the note in *BST* (1951) at the time.
16 Slater's *Directory of Yorkshire*, 1848.
17 It appears to have no stock-book or accession number, but the photograph number is NKH 32494/ L 11.
18 *Scarborough Herald*, 21 July 1842 and following edns.
19 CB–EN, 29 September 1840.
20 The poem was first printed by Harrison and Stanford in *Anne Brontë* (1959). See *The Poems of Anne Brontë*, p. 87.
21 See *A Life of Emily Brontë*, pp. 178–9.
22 In the letter referred to above, 29 September 1840, Charlotte says he poured out his 'whole, warm, fickle soul' in praise of Agnes Walton. There is a chance, since Agnes's higher status may have prevented an engagement, that 'Agnes' is a code name for Anne. The evidence already presented shows that Weightman was a leg-puller. Is it pure coincidence that Anne Brontë chose 'Agnes' for her *persona* in the novel?
23 *Agnes Grey*, chapter 18.

Notes to Chapter 7

1   The date is calculated from Mr Robinson's 1845 account book.
2   The standard biography of Branwell is still WGBB, supplemented by Daphne du Maurier, *The Infernal World of Branwell Brontë*.

3   *Agnes Grey*, chapter 11.

4   See also 'Further thoughts on Branwell Brontë's story', a symposium with Dame Myra Curtis, Dr Phyllis Bentley, Dr Mildred Christian and others, *BST* (1962).

5   E. Gaskell, *The Life of Charlotte Brontë*, chapter 13.

6   Correspondence to and from the Robinsons of Newby Hall is indexed in the National Register of Archives, but no letter to or from the Thorp Green Robinsons appears in the catalogue.

7   WGBB pp. 304–5.

8   Various entries in the account book and two sale documents (Robinson papers, BPM) mention stables, horses, dogs, a stud groom, etc.

9   George Whitehead's Register.

10   Information from external sources on the Gisborne background comes from Staffs County Record Office, *The Dictionary of National Biography* and the British Library *Catalogue of Printed Books*.

11   Miniatures of the Gisborne family are at Derby Art Gallery and Museum. The background to Lichfield in the early years of the nineteenth century is in H. Clayton, *Coaching City*, especially chapter 6.

12   A typical example of Mrs Murray's moralistic speeches comes in chapter 18, where she urges Agnes to devote herself to her calling 'body and soul', as a '*judicious* governess' should. 'You will excuse my dropping these little hints,' she says, 'you know it is for your own good.' The emphases, shown by italics in the printed version, depict the speech rhythm and strongly suggest that Anne is writing from life.

13   Robinson deeds: inventory of house contents.

14   E. Gaskell, *Letters* ed. Chapple and Pollard, no. 328 (29 December 1856).

15   CB–BB, 1 May 1843.

16   George Whitehead's Register.

17   Anne's Music Manuscript book, BPM; facsimile edition, ed. R. Rastall, Boethius Press, 1980.

18   Sketches by AB, BPM.

19   George Whitehead.

20   George Whitehead. Little Ouseburn parish register.

21   Memories of Mrs Knox and Dowager Lady Meysey-Thompson, per Helier Hibbs, Little Ouseburn.

22   George Whitehead.

23   See WGBB for an attempt to disentangle Branwell's story, and the parts played by Ann Marshall, Dr Crosby and other employees or servants of the Robinsons at Thorp Green (chapter 16).

24   A copy of another German purchase, Noehden's *A Grammar of the German Language*, came to light in January 1991.

Notes

25 George Whitehead, register.
26 'When sinks my heart in hopeless gloom' (June 1845), later called 'Views of Life'; *Wildfell Hall*, chapter 32, passages dealing with Esther Hargrave.
27 See *A Life of Emily Brontë*, p. 175ff.
28 *Agnes Grey*, chapter 9.
29 CB–EN, 23 January 1844.
30 'Views of Life', referred to above, note 25; 'Home' has no manuscript, see *The Poems of Anne Brontë*, pp. 99–100.
31 ibid.
32 B. Berryman, *Scarborough as it was* (the book is unpaginated).
33 *Scarborough Herald*. She was at 27, Cliff. This was not one of Mr Wood's lodging houses.
34 WGBB, p. 233.
35 *Scarborough Herald, Scarborough Record*. Summer numbers 1844.
36 *Agnes Grey*, chapter 25. Anne's funeral in 1849 took place at Christ Church, Vernon Road, and she was entered in the register as 'from near York' (see chapter 11, below). This suggests that she was known to the Christ Church clergy, since Charlotte certainly would not have given this address.
37 Letter (undated) from BB–Francis Grundy, in *Pictures from the Past* and many times quoted since, e.g. du Maurier, *The Infernal World of Branwell Brontë*, p. 173.
38 CB–EN, 13 January 1845.
39 George Whitehead, register.
40 A. M. F. Robinson, *Emily Brontë*, pp. 116–7.
41 Robinson deeds, BPM; George Whitehead, register; Little Ouseburn parish register; Greenhow appears in the 1841 census for Great Ouseburn, but moved to Green Hammerton in September 1846. Details of his family are from the 1841 census. Details of William Greenhow and his travelling with the Robinsons as a friend for Edmund are from the 1845–6 Robinson account books.
42 Anne could either walk along the same lanes as took her to Little Ouseburn or cut through Kirby Hall estate. No biographer seems to have tried to contact the Greenhow descendants, so far as I am aware.
43 *The Poems of Anne Brontë*, p. 113.

Notes to Chapter 8

1 EB, 1845 diary paper.
2 For example, in 1842 the Robinsons were at Scarborough by 7 July, so Anne must have been at Haworth, if she was to have a month's holiday, by about 9 or 10 June. In 1844, both Anne and Branwell were at home by 23 June.

3   Robinson account book, BPM.

4   As far back as their time at Cowan Bridge, the Brontës (Maria, Charlotte and Emily) were destined for governesses, according to the entries in the school register. It is plain that an assumption was made, and it was not until later in 1845 that they examined this assumption and found it wanting. Anne would therefore have returned in June 1845 expecting to go back to another post as a governess later.

5   CB–EN, 18 June 1845.

6   *WGB*, p. 239.

7   There have been many explorations of this episode, which is of some significance in the Brontë story; see WGCB, chapter 15, and D. du Maurier, *The Infernal World of Branwell Brontë*, pp. 160–5. I have tried to use the Robinson account book to check all the possibilities, and regard the present outline as carrying on the discussion somewhat.

8   There is no evidence to show whether the Brontës went all the way back to Thorp Green each year, or whether they met the Robinsons at York. The latter seems more likely.

9   Anne must have suspected Branwell's story, told to Charlotte. Yet she did not contradict it, or Charlotte would not have acted as she did. Anne was therefore an accessory to his lies.

10 CB–EN, 31 July 1845.

11 George Whitehead, register; Robinson account book.

12 du Maurier, *The Infernal World of Branwell Brontë*, p. 162. The *Scarborough Record* for July gives simply Reverend E. Robinson, Mrs and Misses Robinson as arrivals at Scarborough, but Edmund is not mentioned by name in the newspapers in previous years.

13 EB–EN, 11 July 1845.

14 It seems possible, if we contrast Charlotte's letters to EN with what Anne surely must have known and Emily, if I am right here, must have been told by Anne, that the two sisters were not clearly honest with Charlotte at this point. Though later Charlotte and Anne would join forces to go to London, and exclude Emily, at this stage the old alliance between Emily and Anne seems the more powerful.

15 EB's account book fragment, transcribed in *A Life of Emily Brontë*, pp. 270–2.

16 EB's 1845 diary paper in C. K. Shorter, *Charlotte Brontë and her Circle*, pp. 150–1.

17 EB's account book and diary paper.

18 WGAB, pp. 176, 225. Harrison and Stanford, p. 96.

19 I have given a discussion of this point in *A Life of Emily Brontë*, pp. 180ff.

20 It needs to be emphasized that the Gondal story has never been

elucidated despite many attempts, and that there is far too little evidence for a confident reconstruction to be made. See E. Chitham and T. J. Winnifrith, *Brontë Facts and Brontë Problems*, chapter 5.

21 CB–Aylott and Jones, 6 April 1846, BPM.
22 M. Visick, *The Genesis of Wuthering Heights*.
23 'He ought not to have been a parson. Certainly he ought not.' CB–EN 20 August 1840.
24 See chapter 7, note 35 below.
25 *Agnes Grey*, chapter 16.
26 WGAB, p. 176. It seems to me that either Miss Gerin is right, and the novel was begun while Anne was still at Thorp Green (whether or not it is to be equated with 'Passages in the Life of an Individual') or else Anne must have kept a diary in which she recorded the speeches of Mrs Robinson.
27 *Agnes Grey*, chapter 16.
28 See *The Poems of Anne Brontë*, pp. 15–16, for discussion of the constant characteristics of the idealized clergyman in Anne's poems.
29 *Agnes Grey*, chapter 18. This quotation substantiates my suggestion above and at the end of chapter 6 that Anne noted down Mrs Robinson's talk, unless she simply called on a long memory.
30 George Whitehead, register; 1841 census.
31 CB, 'Biographical Notice'.
32 George Whitehead, register.
33 WGBB, p. 252; George Whitehead, register; Robinson account book.
34 A. M. F. Robinson, *Emily Brontë*, p. 139. See G. D. Hargreaves, 'The Publishing of "Poems by Currer, Ellis and Acton Bell"' in *BST* (1969), pp. 294ff.
35 BB–Hebden Bridge Railway Co., BPM.
36 See du Maurier, *The Infernal World of Branwell Brontë*, p. 173.

Notes to Chapter 9

1 I have tried to trace this process in *A Life of Emily Brontë*, chapter 14.
2 The first published work to point this out, so far as I am aware, was M. Spark and D. Stanford, *Emily Brontë*. See also E. Chitham and T. J. Winnifrith, *Brontë Facts and Brontë Problems*, chapter 9.
3 See above and in *BST* (1975).
4 A. M. F. Robinson, *Emily Brontë*, p. 141. There has been a good

deal of speculation about this copy, which is not now to be located.

5 Biographers should be exceedingly wary of taking Charlotte's accounts at their face value. She is generally trying to direct the reader, sometimes away from problem areas in her sisters' lives.

6 'Biographical Notice'.

7 Some reviewers of *A Life of Emily Brontë* took this point as an invention of my own. It is, however, first raised by Tom Winnifrith in *Brontë Facts and Brontë Problems*, chapter 8. The matter of how *Wuthering Heights* could first be one of three novels to fill a three-volume set and later one of only two to fill a similar set does need some careful consideration. Readers have liked to suppose that the novel was spontaneous, and therefore unlikely to have been revised. The opposite is true of the poems, where the revisions in the manuscripts show how Emily returned, sometimes on a number of occasions, to the same piece of work.

8 'Biographical Notice'. But the three volume set was sent to Colburn in July 1846 and there is no record after September 1846 of these three books going the rounds of the publishers together.

9 WGAB, p. 226; WGEB, p. 207. We must make allowances for CB's need to reassure herself that her books would not be rejected *more* than those of her sisters.

10 Gaskell, *The Life of Charlotte Brontë*, chapter 16.

11 George Whitehead, register.

12 Ibid.

13 The original story comes from Branwell's (undated) letter in Grundy, *Pictures of the Past*.

14 George Whitehead, register. William Allison is called 'stud groom' in du Maurier, *The Infernal World of Branwell Brontë*, p. 161, referring to a legacy he received in Edmund Robinson Jr's will. He had moved from Great Barr by the time of the 1851 census.

15 My hypothesis for the cause of the misunderstanding is that Grundy may have misread an abbreviation in Branwell's letter of coachman ('coachmn' or 'Coachmn'?) as a proper name and assumed that it was 'Gooch'.

16 George Whitehead, register.

17 For James Brunty's visit, see *The Brontes' Irish Background*, pp. 107–8. Anne's choice of Christian name poses a real problem. There are no such plainly Irish names in the current (Slater's) directory of Scarborough and district. Though after the Chartist years some children were called by the names of Chartist leaders I have never seen a non-Irish child with such a name in any parish register or census between 1841 and 1851.

The situation is made more curious when we consider that the action of *Wildfell Hall* takes place in the 1820s.

18 Gaskell, *The Life of Charlotte Brontë*, chapter 15.
19 Ibid.
20 Ibid.
21 CB, Editor's Preface to *Wuthering Heights*.
22 See I. Ewbank, *Their Proper Sphere*, where the differing aims of the three novelists are well explored.
23 E. Langland, in *Anne Brontë: the Other One*, especially chapter 2, has much to say about the differing views of CB in *Jane Eyre*, and AB.
24 'Biographical Notice'.
25 *Wildfell Hall*, chapter 7.
26 See *The Brontes' Irish Background*, chapter 8.
27 *Wildfell Hall*, chapter 3.
28 Ibid.
29 See Introduction to *Wuthering Heights* ed. H. Marsden and I. Jack, Oxford, Clarendon.
30 Robinsons' account book.
31 CB–EN, 1 March 1847.
32 Robinsons' account book.
33 E.g. in H. Sambrook, *Notes on the Tenant of Wildfell Hall*, p. 45. She interestingly observes, 'Writing at a time when set descriptive pieces were almost compulsory in a novel, Anne Brontë seems to pay very little attention to this convention.'
34 OS 6" map; M. Boyes, *Allestree Hall*; memories of Mrs Knox and Dowager Lady Mesysey-Thompson.
35 Boyes, ibid.
36 *Jane Eyre*, chapter 27.
37 *Wildfell Hall*, chapter 3.
38 CB–EN, 15 December 1846.
39 *Wildfell Hall*, chapter 14.
40 Ibid., chapter 30.
41 *The Poems of Anne Brontë*, p. 30.
42 CB–EN, 1 March 1847.
43 *Wildfell Hall*, chapter 32. The portrait of Esther is very lively and strong. It is usually thought, and it seems to me reasonable, that Mary Robinson was the model (cf. WGAB, p. 157). However, I should not regard the parallel between Mrs Robinson and Mrs Hargrave as established (WGAB, pp. 244–5).
44 *The Poems of Anne Brontë*, p. 82. *Wildfell Hall*, chapter 33.
45 E. Langland in *Anne Brontë: The Other One*, pp. 20 and 43ff. discusses this topic, and compares 'Spirit of Earth' with the character of St John Rivers in *Jane Eyre*. Her comments are interesting and indicate a possible solution.
46 See discussion in *A Life of Emily Brontë*, pp. 226–8.

Notes to Chapter 10

1 P. J. M. Scott, *Anne Brontë*, p. 132.
2 AB–EN, 28 January 1848. Manuscript at BPM.
3 Ibid. There is, of course, an ironic touch.
4 E. C. Gaskell, *The Life of Charlotte Brontë*, chapter 16.
5 CB's cash book, BPM.
6 CB–Mary Taylor, 4 September 1848. Some biographers have recorded a snowstorm, apparently due to a misreading of the manuscript.
7 See *A Life of Emily Brontë*, pp. 270–2.
8 Most of the letter is printed in Harrison and Stanford, *Anne. Brontë*, pp. 118ff.
9 E. C. Gaskell, *The Life of Charlotte Brontë*, chapter 16.
10 CB–Mary Taylor, 4 September 1848.
11 Contemporary painting and other illustrations, National Railway Museum. See plan of 1838 reproduced in D. Jenkinson, *The London and Birmingham, A Railway of Consequence* (Harrow, 1988), p. 29.
12 CB–Mary Taylor, *loc. cit.*
13 ibid.
14 London Post Office Directory, 1848.
15 Gaskell, *The Life of Charlotte Brontë*, chapter 16.
16 ibid.
17 CB–Mary Taylor 4 September 1848.
18 *Cornhill*, December 1900.
19 CB–WSW, 15 September 1850: '*Wildfell Hall* it hardly seems to me desirable to preserve. The choice of subject in that work is a mistake . . .'
20 CB–Mary Taylor, 4 September 1848.
21 CB–WSW, 14 August 1848: 'should she ever write another work, Mr Smith will certainly have the first offer of the copyright.'
22 G. D. Hargreaves, 'Further Omissions in "The Tenant of Wildfell Hall"', *BST* (1977).
23 Hargreaves (ed), *Wildfell Hall*, p. 120.
24 J. Kellett, *Haworth Parsonage*, p. 64.
25 *Wildfell Hall*, chapter 32, the purported entry for 30 September 1824.
26 CB–EN, 28 July 1848.
27 For some detail about the subsequent history of the Robinson girls, see *The Poems of Anne Brontë*, p. 14. I remain actively interested in tracing their progress and descendants and would be pleased to hear from anyone with information to add.
28 There are occasional traces of the family in the columns of the

Notes

Derby Mercury. Elizabeth died in the Isle of Wight on 16 January 1882, according to a memorial in Pentrich church.

29 The question how far the Brontës understood and sympathized with either the Chartists at home or the victims of famine who took a revolutionary stance in Ireland is vexed and little studied. A number of Marxist critics have seen a class-based strand in Heathcliff's actions. Emily's poem 'Why ask to know the date?', begun in 1846, seems to be about a revolution and its consequences. In *A Life of Emily Brontë*, p. 220, I have pointed to Uncle James as a direct source of information and opinion on the deprivations of Irish tenants, but the letters Anne received from Derby may also have discussed the related question of Chartism and Radicalism.

30 E. C. Gaskell, *The Life of Charlotte Brontë*, chapter 14.

31 M. Spark and D. Stanford, *Emily Brontë*, pp. 88ff.

32 E. Langland, *Anne Brontë: The Other One*, pp. 43ff.

33 The letter, dated 23 November 1848, was purchased by the Brontë Society and transcribed in *BST* (1980), pp. 360–1.

34 CB-EN, 10 December 1848, quoted at the end of the above.

35 Material *re* David Thom is from Liverpool Public Library, where his presentation books are still to be seen. The AB–Dr Thom letter is not in the 'Shakespeare Head' *Lives and Letters*, but is reprinted in full in WGAB (second edition), p. 361.

Notes to Chapter 11

1 See Introduction, above.

2 Extracts from the letters of CB–EN are quoted in Harrison and Stanford, and there are texts of the letters in the 'Shakespeare Head' Brontë, *Lives and Letters*.

3 CB 'Biographical Notice'.

4 CB–WSW, 1 February 1849.

5 Ibid.

6 Through CB, in a letter in which she first mentions Anne's desire to take a holiday.

7 Ibid.

8 AB–EN, 5 April 1849, MS and BPM. The whole letter is written firmly and evenly.

9 The publication of 'The Three Guides' showed that such poems could find a publisher independently of CB. It seems likely that Anne's mind would run on the possibility of producing similar work, also without reference to her sister.

10 WGCB, p. 389.

11 See A. Harrison and D. Stanford, *Anne Brontë*, p. 153.
12 CB–EN, 1 May 1849, quoted e.g. Harrison and Stanford, p. 151.
13 E. C. Gaskell, *The Life of Charlotte Brontë*, chapter 17.
14 CB's account book, BPM.
15 Gaskell, *The Life of Charlotte Brontë*, *loc. cit.*
16 CB's account book. Bradshaw's *Railway Guide* 2nd edition, 1849.
17 EN, quoted *loc. cit.*
18 WGAB, p. 350, offers what appears to be conclusive evidence that 'The George' and not 'The Old George' was their hotel.
19 Gaskell, *Life of Charlotte Brontë*.
20 CB–WSW, 13 June 1849. Ellen Nussey's account of this occasion was apparently written first in her diary, at BPM. It was written up for T. Wemyss-Reid *Charlotte Brontë, a Monograph* (London, 1877).
21 Harrison and Stanford, *Anne Brontë*, p. 160.

Selected Bibliography

The Poems of Anne Brontë contains a fairly detailed bibliography of material relating directly to Anne Brontë on pp. 209–11. E. Langland, Anne Brontë, The Other One (Macmillan, London, 1989) includes a list of books and articles dealing with Anne Brontë in her context as a Victorian woman writer. I am therefore including here works principally used in the present book, to which reference is made in the notes.

The Brontës, including Anne

Alexander, C., The Early Writings of Charlotte Brontë (Oxford, 1983).

Allott, M. (ed.), The Brontës, the Critical Heritage (London, 1974).

Bentley, P., The Brontës and their World (London, 1969).

Butterfield, M. and Duckett, R. J., Brother in the Shadow (Bradford, 1988).

Chadwick, E. A., In the Footsteps of the Brontës (London, 1913).

Chitham, E., A Life of Emily Brontë (Oxford, 1987).

Chitham, E., The Brontës' Irish Background (London, 1986).

Chitham, E., The Poems of Anne Brontë (London, 1979).

Chitham, E. and Winnifrith, T. J., Brontë Facts and Brontë Problems (London, 1983).

Davies, S., Emily Brontë (Key Women Writers) (Hemel Hempstead, 1988).

de Maurier, D., The Infernal World of Branwell Brontë (London, 1972).

Ewbank, I. S., Their Proper Sphere (London, 1966).

Gaskell, E. C., *The Life of Charlotte Brontë* (London, 1857).
Gerin, W., *Anne Brontë* (2nd edition) (London, 1974).
Gerin, W.. *Branwell Brontë* (London, 1961).
Gerin, W., *Charlotte Brontë* (London, 1967).
Gerin, W., *Emily Brontë* (London, 1971).
Grundy, F., *Pictures of the Past* (London, 1879).
Hargreaves, G. D. (ed.), *The Tenant of Wildfell Hall, by Anne Brontë* (London, 1980).
Harrison, A. and Stanford, D., *Anne Brontë* (London, 1959).
Hatfield, C. W. (ed.), *The Complete Poems of Emily Jane Brontë* (Columbia, 1941).
Hewish, J., *Emily Brontë* (London, 1971).
Kellett, J., *Haworth Parsonage* (Keighley, 1977).
Langland, E., *Anne Brontë, The Other One* (Women Writers) (London, 1989).
Lock, J. and Dixon, W. T., *Man of Sorrow* (London, 1965).
Morrison, N. Brysson, *Haworth Harvest* (London, 1969).
Rastall, J. R. (ed.), *Anne Brontë's Song Book* (Clifden, Ireland, 1980).
Reid, T. Wemyss, *Charlotte Brontë: A Monograph* (London, 1877).
Robinson, A. M. F., *Emily Brontë* (London, 1883).
Sambrook, H., *Notes on The Tenant of Wildfell Hall* (Harlow, 1984).
Scott, P. J. M., *Anne Brontë, a New Critical Assessment* (London, 1983).
Scruton, W., *Thornton and the Brontës* (Bradford, 1898).
'The Shakespeare Head Press Brontë': *The Brontës, Their Lives, Friendships and Correspondence*, 4 vols (Oxford, 1932, reissued 1980).
Shorter, C. K., *Charlotte Brontë and her Circle* (London, 1896).
Spark, M. and Stanford, D., *Emily Brontë, her Life and Work* (London, n.d.).
Turner, J. Horsfall, *Haworth Past and Present* (Brighouse, 1879).
Visick, M., *The Genesis of Wuthering Heights* (Hong Kong, 1958).
Wilks, B., *The Brontës* (London, 1975).
Wilks, B., *The Illustrated Brontës of Haworth* (London, 1986).
Wilson, R., *All Alone, The Life and Private History of Emily Brontë* (London, 1928).

Selected bibliography

Winnifrith, T. J., *The Brontës and their Background: Romance and Reality* (2nd edition) (London, 1988).
Brontë Society Transactions, vols 18–20 (Keighley 1980–90).

Topography

Ahier, P., *The Parish Churches of St Peter the Apostle* (Huddersfield, n.d.).
Berryman, B., *Scarborough as it Was* (Nelson, 1972).
Boyes, M., *Allestree Hall* (Derby, 1982).
Brickhill, K., *The Halls at Lascelles Hall* (typescript, Huddersfield Central Library, n.d.).
Clayton, H., *Coaching City* (Lichfield, n.d.).
Pobjoy, H., *A History of Mirfield* (Driffield, 1969).
Redmonds, G., *Old Huddersfield* (Huddersfield, 1981).
Shaw, T., *A History of Cornish Methodism* (Truro, 1967).
Slater's *Directory of Yorkshire* (1848).

Articles from magazines, etc.

Bradshaw's Railway Guide (2nd edition, 1849), timetables relating to Leeds–London and Keighley–Leeds.
Briggs, W. G., 'Richmal Mangnall and her school at Crofton Old Hall' (Wakefield City Library).
Cope, C., *Crofton Hall, Yorkshire* (engraving based on contemporary drawing).
Nussey, J., 'Blake Hall, in Mirfield, and its Occupants during the 18th and 19th Centuries', in *The Yorkshire Archaeological Journal*, vol. 55, 1983 pp. 119ff. (See also J. Nussey, in *Old West Riding* (1982), with different illustrations.)
(unsigned) *The Yorkshire Post*, 20 May 1911.
(unsigned) 'In Search of Vanished Houses' [including Kirby Hall], in *Country Life*, 17 February 1972.
The Bradford Observer (1840ff); *The Scarborough Messenger* (1840ff); *The Scarborough Record* (1840ff); (relevant issues at The British Library, Colindale).

Manuscripts (supplementary to those referred to in
The Poems of Anne Brontë)

George Whitehead: 'Register of Sundries', [Personal] Registers of Births, Marriages and Deaths at Little Ouseburn; [Diaries]. [These are now available in Hibbs, H. (ed.), *Victorian Ouseburn* (Ouseburn, 1990).]

1841 and 1851 census returns for Little Ouseburn and district, Mirfield and district; 1851 census for Great Barr (microfilm at Wakefield and Birmingham Libraries of HO papers at Public Record Office).

Little Ouseburn parish registers (microfilm at North Yorks Record Office, Northallerton.)

Brontë Parsonage: Robinson deeds, especially:
  93/2   Mr (later Mrs) Robinson's account book 1845–6.
  93/3   Cheque books with stubs remaining, 1847ff.
  93/4   Mrs Robinson's account book from 23 June 1848.
  93/7   inventory of Thorp Green Hall, Taken 'by Mr Seaton, Mar. 1848'.

Deeds relating to the Gisborne family at Staffs County Record Office.

Mirfield rate books, etc. (at Kirklees archives, Huddersfield). 'An assessment for the relief of the poor', 7 February 1840. Town Rate book, 1848–9

Mirfield 'valuation', 1838. (ref. U/Mi).

Roe Head sale plan, 1876.

Index

[211]